EDUGORILLA
PUBLICATION

RBI Grade B Officer

Phase 2 (Mains) Exam

Latest Edition
Practice Kit

16 Tests
16 Mock Test

Based On Real Exam Pattern

✓ Thoroughly Revised and Updated

✓ Detailed Analysis of all MCQs

<table>
<tr><td>Title</td><td>: RBI Grade B Officer Phase 2 (Mains) Exam</td></tr>
<tr><td>Author Name</td><td>: Mr. Rohit Manglik</td></tr>
<tr><td>Published By</td><td>: EduGorilla Community Pvt. Ltd.</td></tr>
<tr><td>Publishers Address</td><td>: 12/651, First Floor Opp. Arvindo Park, Near Jama Masjid,
Indira Nagar, Lucknow, Uttar Pradesh-226016, India</td></tr>
</table>

Copyright EduGorilla

ISBN : 978-81-94630-46-3

Second Edition

No part of this book may be reproduced, distributed, or transmitted in any form by any means, without the prior written permission of the publisher.

All Right Reserved

© by EduGorilla Community Pvt. Ltd

Disclaimer EduGorilla

Although the author and publisher have made every effort to ensure the accuracy of information in this book, we do not assume any responsibility to errors and hereby disclaim any liability to any party for any loss, damage, or disruption caused by errors or omissions, whether such errors or omissions result from negligence, accident, or any other cause.

Compiled and created by EduGorilla Community Pvt. Ltd

Printed By EduGorilla Community Pvt. Ltd.

ROHIT MANGLIK
CEO, EduGorilla

Dear Applicants,

People say *"Success comes to those who work hard."* But I've seen people working hard for their exams day in and day out for marginal success. While others succeed in their examinations by putting in just half the work. So are they God Gifted? No! I believe that it's because they work *smart* and not just *hard*. Similarly, for your exams, you should strategize your preparation so as to increase the likelihood of success. Well with EduGorilla get ready to increase your *chances of selection* in your exam by *16x*.

EduGorilla helps you in not only working *hard* but also working in a *smart and strategic* manner. With EduGorilla's preparation package, you get a chance to make your exam preparation easy, and a fun learning path towards selection. Finding the right path to your preparations can be difficult if you don't know in which direction to head. Don't worry, we have you covered! EduGorilla will be your guide to success in your journey. With our Preparation Package, you can prepare strategically and beat the exam in just one attempt.

EduGorilla's Preparation Package includes-

- **Test Series**
- **Books**

Our preparation package is handcrafted as per the latest changes, expert opinions, and students' discretion. Thus, enabling you to get through each stage of the selection process for your exam.

Our Books are designed by the teachers and experts of the respective exam with a combined 150+ years of experience; to provide you with easy, efficient, and effective learning. Our books are smart, in the sense that not only do they give you the answers to the questions but also provide similar questions for practice.

EduGorilla's competent Test Series gives you real-time experience and confidence through which you can clear your offline or online exam in just one attempt. We currently host 83,000+ mock tests for 1,440+ competitive and academic exams.

Thus, EduGorilla misses no chance to assist you in your preparation and covers all stages of the exam, so that you don't have to look anywhere else.

We provide complete preparation packages for defense, banking, teaching, and other National & State-Level exams. Hence, it doesn't matter which exam you aspire to because you will reach your success.

ALL THE BEST !

Let EduGorilla be your Guide to Success.

Rohit Manglik,
Founder and CEO, EduGorilla

INTRODUCTION

EduGorilla focuses on guiding students to succeed in their examinations. With that in mind, our book, titled "RBI Grade B Officer : Phase 2 (Mains) Exam", has been drafted through the collective efforts of our distinguished experts with 150+ years of combined experience. This book consists of questions that are created following the latest changes in the syllabus and exam pattern. We compiled the book on the basis of questions that are most likely to appear in the RBI Grade B Officer. Through EduGorilla's "RBI Grade B Officer : Phase 2 (Mains) Exam" your chances of success will increase 16x.

EduGorilla does this through our Complete Preparation Package. This package consists of well-conceptualized and structured content in the form of questions that are tailor-made according to your needs and will help you practice for exams in a smart way by pinpointing all the necessary information. It also provides hints and solutions, along with a smart answer sheet for your self-evaluation. You can assess your shortcomings and work accordingly on areas that may require more of your attention.

EduGorilla promises to help you succeed in your examination and accomplish your dream goals. We believe in our aspirants and see them at the top of the merit list. And the first step towards the top is to start preparing with us. EduGorilla's "RBI Grade B Officer : Phase 2 (Mains) Exam" includes the following attributes.

➤ Well-Researched Content

➤ Top-Notch Quality

➤ Detailed Answers and Analysis

➤ Smart Answer Sheet

➤ Exam Relevant Questions

Therefore, EduGorilla fortifies your preparation and makes it durable enough to help you stand tall and beat the examination.

RBI Grade B Officer
Scan QR code for Eligibility, Exam Pattern, Syllabus and more.

Book ID: 0149

TABLE OF CONTENTS

Q.1 Which of the following countries is not a member of BIMSTEC?

A. China
B. Bhutan
C. Nepal
D. Myanmar
E. None of these

Q.2 "National Consumer Rights Day" is observed on which among the following?

A. 24 December
B. 24 January
C. 24 February
D. 24 March
E. None of these

Q.3 Ad Valorem Tax is levied on the basis of which among the following?

A. Volume
B. Value
C. Production
D. Export
E. None of these

Q.4 Which among the following is the single largest cottage industry of Manipur state of India?

A. Sericulture Industry
B. Handloom Industry
C. Leather Industry
D. Jute Industry
E. None of these

Q.5 The price fixed in very short period is called

A. market price
B. normal price
C. sub normal price
D. secular price
E. None of these

Q.6 Interest Rate Policy is a part of which of the following?

A. Fiscal Policy
B. Monetary policy
C. Industrial Policy
D. Both (A) and (B)
E. None of these

Q.7 For which of the following commodities Price Stabilization Fund Scheme was launched in 2003?

A. Tea & Coffee
B. Tea , Coffee , Rubber & Tobacco
C. Tea, Coffee & Rubber
D. Tea, Coffee , Rubber, Tobacco & Coconut
E. None of these

Q.8 A number of factors are responsible for poverty in India. Which among the following is not the economic factor contributing to poverty?

A. Inequalities of Income
B. Mass illiteracy
C. Low productivity in Agriculture
D. Fast Rise in Population
E. None of these

Q.9 Which among the following programme was related to training of youths?

A. CAPART
B. TRYSEM
C. NEREGA
D. SGSA
E. None of these

Q.10 Which among the following are called "Breton Wood Twins"?

A. IBRD & IMF
B. IDA & IFC
C. IDA & MIGA
D. IMF & IDA
E. None of these

Q.11 When did the Government of India pass the Regional Rural Banks Act?

A. 1988
B. 1992
C. 1987
D. 1976
E. None of these

Q.12 Which among the following is the most abundant human resource in India?

A. High Skilled Labor in Organized Sector
B. High Skilled Labor in Unorganized Sector
C. Low skilled Labor in Organized sector
D. Low skilled Labor in Unorganized sector
E. None of these

Q.13 Round Tripping is normally used in context with which of the following ____?

A. Capital Markets
B. Foreign Direct Investments
C. Cash Deposits
D. Foreign Remittances
E. None of these

Q.14 In which year Physical coins and banknotes were introduced for the first time in Euro?

A. 1995
B. 2000
C. 2002
D. 2005
E. None of these

Q.15 Which among the following comes under economic overheads?

A. Hospitals
B. Schools
C. Sanitation facilities
D. Road and Railways
E. None of these

Q.16 Who among the following will be benefited by Deflation?

A. Salary Earners
B. pensioners
C. Equity Holders
D. Debtors
E. None of these

Q.17 Which among the following index is available on Quarterly Basis?

A. WPI
B. CPI-IW
C. CPI-AL/RL
D. GDP Deflator
E. None of these

Q.18 Annada, rasi & Kalinga-3 are the seed varieties for profitable intercrops for which of the following grains?

A. Mustard   **B.** Rice
C. Gram   **D.** wheat
E. None of these

Q.19 In which year Aid India Club was established?

A. 1951   **B.** 1953
C. 1955   **D.** 1960
E. None of these

Q.20 Indira Gandhi Institute of Development Research (IGIDR) located in Mumbai is funded by which of the following?

A. Ministry of Earth Sciences
B. Ministry of Urban Development and Planning
C. Ministry of Commerce
D. Reserve Bank of India
E. None of these

Q.21 India's first operational special economic zone (SEZ) is located at?

A. Ahamadabad   **B.** Surat
C. Jaipur   **D.** Indore
E. None of these

Q.22 The time required to process and execute an order is called?

A. allowed time   **B.** lead time
C. accepted time   **D.** fixed time
E. None of these

Q.23 Which among the following is / are instances of payment of Direct Tax?

1.VAT paid during purchase of a tyre tube for a vehicle
2.Service Tax paid while making payments of dinner in a restaurant
3.Duty paid while importing a machinery from abroad
Choose the correct option from the codes given below:

A. Only 1 & 2   **B.** Only 2
C. Only 2 & 3   **D.** Only 2
E. None of these

Q.24 Exchange Earners' Foreign Currency Account (EEFC) is an account maintained in foreign currency with an Authorised Dealer i.e. a bank dealing in foreign exchange. What is the benefit of maintain an EEFC account by an Indian Exporter / Importer ?

A. An EEFC account can be held in the form of a Savings account. Thus, interest is payable on EEFC accounts.
B. The account holder does not have to convert foreign exchange into Rupees and vice versa, thereby minimizing the transaction costs
C. The EEFC account balances cannot be hedged.
D. SEZ Units can also open EEFC Accounts.
E. None of these

Q.25 Which among the following is / are correct statements with respect to the Sales Tax and Excise duty in India?

1. Excise duty on alcohol and alcoholic preparations are collected by the State Governments
2. Excise duty on narcotic substances is collected by Central Government
3. While Sales Tax is a direct tax, Excise duty is an indirect tax
Select the correct option from the codes given below:

A. Only 1   **B.** Only 1 & 2
C. Only 1 & 3   **D.** 1, 2 & 3
E. None of these

Ques (26-30): Direction : Read the following passage carefully and answer the question:

The last great war, which nearly shook the foundations of the modern world, had little impact on Indian literature beyond aggravating the popular revulsion against violence and adding to the growing disillusionment with the 'humane pretensions' of the Western World. This was eloquently voiced in Tagore's later poems and his last testament, Crisis in Civilization. The Indian intelligentsia was in a state of moral dilemma.

On the one hand, it could not help sympathizing with England's dogged courage in the hour of peril, with the Russians fighting with their backs to the wall against the ruthless Nazi hordes, and with China groaning under the heel of Japanese militarism; on the other hand, their own country was practically under military occupation of their own soil, and an Indian army under Subhas Bose was trying from the opposite camp to liberate their country. No creative impulse could issue from such confusion of loyalties. One would imagine that the achievement of Indian independence in 1947, which came in the wake of the Allies' victory and was followed by the collapse of colonialism in the neighboring countries of South-East Asia, would have released an upsurge of creative energy.

No doubt it did, but unfortunately it was soon submerged in the great agony of partition,with its inhuman slaughter of the innocents and the uprooting of millions of people from their homeland, followed by the martyrdom of Mahatma Gandhi. These tragedies, along with Pakistan's invasion of Kashmir and its later atrocities in Bangladesh, did indeed provoke a poignant writing, particularly in the languages of the regions most affected, Bengali, Hindi, Kashmiri, Punjabi, Sindhi and Urdu. But poignant or passionate writing does not by itself make great literature. What reserves of enthusiasm and confidence survived these disasters have been mainly absorbed in the task of national reconstruction and economic development. Great literature has always emerged out of chains of convulsions. Indian literature is richer today in volume, range and variety than it ever was in the past.

Q.26 Which among the following is / are parts of Current Account?

1. Balance of trade
2. Net factor income
3. Net transfer payments
Select the correct option from the codes given below:

A. Only 1 & 2   **B.** Only 2 & 3
C. Only 1 & 3   **D.** 1, 2 & 3
E. None of these

Q.27 According to the monetarists, money supply constitutes

A. currency + demand deposits

B. currency + demand deposits + time deposits

C. currency + demand deposits + time deposits + equity shares

D. currency + all kinds of bank deposits + deposits with other institutions + borrowing

E. None of these

Q.28 Which of the following is / are correct observations about the Land Holdings in India?

1. Most of the land holdings in India are medium holdings with size between 4 to 10 hectares

2. Large holdings account for fewer than 1% of total land holdings in India

Select the correct option from the codes given below:

A. Only 1

B. Only 2

C. Both 1 & 2

D. Neither 1 nor 2

E. cannot be determined

Q.29 Which among the following is / are Capital Receipts of Government of India:

Market Loans

Borrowings from RBI

Loans received from foreign governments

Loans recovered by central government from state governments

Select the correct option from the codes given below:

A. Only 1

B. Only 1 & 2

C. Only 1, 2 & 3

D. 1, 2, 3 & 4

E. None of these

Q.30 Which among the following is used by the Government as a last resort in Deficit Financing?

A. Borrowing from Foreign Sources

B. Borrowing from Domestic Sources

C. External Grants

D. Printing of Currency

E. None of these

Q.31 Under which among the following headings, the proceeds of government bonds come in the budget ?

A. Capital outlay

B. Current expenditure

C. Capital receipts

D. Revenue expenditure

E. None of these

Q.32 As per the latest statement by finance ministry India's tax-to-GDP ratio is about __?

A. 15.5%

B. 22.2%

C. 16.7%

D. 20.3%

E. None of these

Q.33 Which of the following is not a specialized sub market of the money market?

A. Collateral loan market

B. Discount market

C. Bond market

D. Acceptance market

E. None of these

Q.34 International Monetary Fund:

1. has permanent observer status at the United Nations

2. provides concessional loans only to low-income member countries

3. headquartered in Washington DC, United States

Which of the above statements is/are correct?

A. Only 1 & 2

B. Only 1 & 3

C. Only 2 & 3

D. 1, 2 & 3

E. None of these

Q.35 India is suffering from the menace of Transfer pricing. What is "Transfer Pricing"?

A. It is a method of tax-dodging by illicit capital flows outside the country.

B. It is a factor responsibleÂ forÂ continuous price rise of food items in India.

C. It is a newÂ phenomenonÂ that emerged responsible for bad loans of Indian banks.

D. It is a global phenomenon responsible for devaluation of Indian currency in comparison to reserve currencies.

E. None of these

Q.36 Which of the following would increase India's external debt?

1. Increased NRI deposits

2. Increased Inward remittances

3. Increased External commercial borrowing

4. Increased grants from international organisations

5. Depreciation of the US dollar against the rupee

Select the correct option from codes given below:

A. Only 1, 2 & 3

B. Only 1 & 3

C. Only 1, 3 & 5

D. Only 2, 3, 4 & 5

E. None of these

Q.37 Which of the following is not a Centrally Sponsored Scheme?

A. Urban Rejuvenation Mission

B. Pradhan Mantri Krishi Sinchai Yojana

C. Pradhan Mantri Kisan Sampada Yojana

D. Pradhan Mantri Awas Yojna

E. Mahatma Gandhi National Rural Employment Guarantee Programme

Q.38 Consider the following countries:

1. Russia

2. Turkey

3. Iran

4. India

Which of the above are the founding members of the International North–South Transport Corridor?

A. Only 1, 2 & 3

B. Only 2, 3 & 4

C. Only 1, 3 & 4

D. 1, 2, 3 & 4

E. None of these

Q.39 Which of the following is / are correct statements with respect to the Indian Depository Receipts (IDRs)?

1. They allow investors abroad in Indian Companies

2. They are denominated in Indian Rupees

3. They are issued by a domestic depository in India

4. They cannot be listed in stock exchanges

Select the correct statements from the codes given below:

A. 1, 2 & 3   **B.** 2 & 3

C. 2, 3 & 4   **D.** 1, 2, 3 & 4

E. None of these

Q.40 Consider the following:

1. Endowment funds

2. Insurance funds

3. Pension funds

Which among the above are generally considered long-term investors?

A. Only 1 & 2   **B.** Only 2 & 3

C. Only 1 & 3   **D.** 1, 2 & 3

E. None of these

Q.41 Child abuse include:

A. Physical, sexual, emotional

B. Physical, Sexual, religious

C. Physical, mental, emotional

D. Physical, sexual, exploitation

E. None of the above

Q.42 Which Article says that, "No child below the age of 14 years shall be employed to work in any

factory or in any hazardous employment"?

A. Article 24   **B.** Article 25

C. Article 26   **D.** Article 27

E. None of these

Q.43 Crime against means

A. Criminal violence   **B.** Domestic violence

C. Social violence   **D.** Women violence

E. All of the above

Q.44 Rape. Abduction, murder is an example of

A. Criminal violence   **B.** Domestic violence

C. Social violence   **D.** Women violence

E. All of the above

Q.45 Dowry deaths, wife battering is an example of

A. Criminal violence   **B.** Domestic violence

C. Social violence   **D.** Women violence

E. All of the above

Q.46 Female foeticide, eve-teasing is an example of

A. Criminal violence   **B.** Domestic violence

C. Social violence   **D.** Women violence

E. All of the above

Q.47 In honour killing, it is a murder committed by

A. Neighbour   **B.** Family members

C. Enemy   **D.** Unknown

E. None of these

Q.48 In which year was the National Adult Education Programme launched?

A. October, 1, 1978

B. January 26, 1978

C. August 15, 1978

D. November 14, 1978

E. None of these

Q.49 Which is a type of delinquency?

A. Individual delinquency

B. Organized delinquency

C. Situational delinquency

D. Unorganized delinquency

E. All of the above

Q.50 The low point in the business cycle is referred to as the

A. Expansion   **B.** Boom

C. trough   **D.** peak

E. None of these

Q.51 When was the Protection of Women from Domestic Violence Act enacted?

A. 2003   **B.** 2004   **C.** 2005   **D.** 2006

E. 2007

Q.52 Which five-year plan marked the beginning of Economic Liberalization?

A. 6th FYP   **B.** 9th FYP

C. 10th FYP   **D.** 8th FYP

E. 7th FYP

Q.53 What is the full form of IMFL?

A. Indian Made Foreign Liquor

B. International Made Foreign Liquor

C. International Market for Foreign Liquor

D. Indian Market for Foreign Liquor

E. None of these

Q.54 Choose the correct pairs of the event and the date.

(A) World Health Day – 8th April

(B) World Ozone Day-16th September

(C) World Environment Day- 5th June

(D) World Population Day-10th July

A. B only   **B.** A and D only

C. B and C only   **D.** D only

E. None of these

Q.55 What is the treatment for alcoholics?

A. Detoxification in hospitals

B. Role of family

C. Alcoholic Anonymous

D. Stay hydrated

E. All of the above

Q.56 Which summit was conducted to decide ways to achieve economic growth in a sustainable way without damaging the environment?
A. Copenhagen Conference, 1992
B. Cancun Conference, 2010
C. Rio +20 Summit, 2012
D. Durban Summit, 2011
E. None of these

Q.57 Full form of EDI-
A. electronic data interface
B. elctric device interface
C. electronic data interchange
D. electronic design interface
E. None of these

Q.58 _______denotes an error in a computer program.
A. Bit
B. Bug
C. Spam
D. Virus
E. None of these

Q.59 The purpose of value education is best served by focusing on
A. Cultural practices prevailing in the society.
B. Norms of conduct laid down by a social group.
C. Concern for human values.
D. Religious and moral practices and instructions.
E. None of these

Q.60 Which of the following are the goals of higher education in India?
a) Access
b) Equity
c) Quality and Excellence
d) Relevance
e) Value based education
f) Compulsory and free education
A. a, b and e only
B. a, b, e and f
C. a, b, c, d and e
D. a, b, c, d, e and f
E. None of these

Q.61 Which of the following hypotheses are tested by a regression function?
A. Inter-relation between two or more variables is significantly different from zero.
B. The degree and direction of inter relations between two or more variables are non-zero and goodness of fit of the regression function is satisfactory.
C. Degree of influence exercised by systematic explanatory factors is greater/lesser/equal to the influence exercised by random factors.
D. Both (A) and (B)
E. All of the above

Q.62 The phenomenon of an increase in economic integration among nations is known as:
A. Privatization
B. Globalization
C. Professionalization
D. Liberalization
E. None of the Above

Q.63 A general increase in the prices of goods and services in an economy is known as:
A. Deflation
B. Inflation
C. Disinflation
D. Hyperinflation
E. None of the Above

Q.64 The total sum of the goods and services produced in a country in a year, minus depreciation is called as:
A. Gross domestic product
B. Gross national Product
C. Gross national income
D. Net domestic product
E. Net national Product

Q.65 In the presence of heteroscedasticity, which of the following statements is incorrect?
A. Heteroscedasticity does not alter the unbiasedness and consistency properties of OLS estimators.
B. The OLS estimator is one that has a minimum variance.
C. BLUE estimators are provided by the method of weighted least squares.
D. 'T' and 'F' tests based on standard assumptions of classical linear regression model may not be reliable.
E. None of these

// Smart Answer Sheet //

Correct Indicates percentage of students who answered questions correctly.

Skipped Indicates percentage of students who skipped questions.

Q.	Ans.	Correct / Skipped
1	A	27.13 % / 14.57 %
2	A	30.77 % / 8.91 %
3	B	27.13 % / 20.64 %
4	B	22.27 % / 12.95 %
5	A	24.29 % / 23.89 %
6	B	31.58 % / 25.91 %
7	B	23.08 % / 19.43 %
8	A	12.55 % / 23.89 %
9	B	23.08 % / 22.26 %
10	A	31.58 % / 24.7 %
11	D	17.81 % / 26.32 %
12	D	31.58 % / 22.27 %
13	B	21.05 % / 26.72 %

Q.	Ans.	Correct / Skipped
14	B	21.46 % / 19.03 %
15	D	31.58 % / 26.72 %
16	A	16.6 % / 22.27 %
17	D	27.53 % / 22.27 %
18	B	17.0 % / 28.34 %
19	B	14.57 % / 27.13 %
20	D	26.72 % / 8.1 %
21	D	15.79 % / 19.03 %
22	B	31.17 % / 15.39 %
23	B	13.36 % / 27.13 %
24	B	33.6 % / 9.72 %
25	A	8.5 % / 27.13 %
26	D	17.41 % / 27.53 %

Q.	Ans.	Correct / Skipped
27	B	15.38 % / 27.13 %
28	B	18.62 % / 14.58 %
29	D	14.57 % / 27.94 %
30	D	17.41 % / 17.41 %
31	C	25.91 % / 25.91 %
32	A	14.98 % / 23.48 %
33	C	20.65 % / 21.05 %
34	D	23.89 % / 12.95 %
35	A	15.79 % / 26.72 %
36	B	14.98 % / 22.67 %
37	B	12.55 % / 22.27 %
38	C	15.79 % / 27.93 %
39	B	12.15 % / 27.12 %

Q.	Ans.	Correct / Skipped
40	D	23.48 % / 27.53 %
41	A	26.32 % / 27.93 %
42	A	36.84 % / 18.63 %
43	E	28.34 % / 27.53 %
44	A	38.06 % / 21.86 %
45	B	23.48 % / 28.34 %
46	C	17.0 % / 18.63 %
47	B	35.63 % / 27.12 %
48	A	17.41 % / 25.1 %
49	E	23.08 % / 28.74 %
50	C	36.03 % / 27.53 %
51	C	23.08 % / 26.72 %
52	A	17.81 % / 21.06 %

Q.	Ans.	Correct / Skipped
53	A	17.0 % / 19.44 %
54	C	33.6 % / 27.53 %
55	E	36.03 % / 25.91 %
56	C	30.36 % / 24.7 %
57	C	19.03 % / 27.93 %
58	B	38.06 % / 27.12 %
59	C	31.58 % / 25.91 %
60	C	22.67 % / 24.7 %
61	E	12.15 % / 19.83 %
62	B	38.06 % / 27.93 %
63	B	48.18 % / 26.72 %
64	D	29.96 % / 25.1 %
65	B	7.29 % / 27.53 %

Performance Analysis

Avg. Score (%)	13.0%
Toppers Score (%)	98.0%
Your Score	

//Hints and Solutions//

1. Members of BIMSTEC (Bay of Bengal Initiative for Multi-Sectoral Technical and Economic) are Bangladesh, India, Myanmar, Sri Lanka, Thailand, Bhutan and Nepal.

Hence, the correct option is (A).

2. In India, 24th December is observed as National Consumer Day. On this day the Consumer Protection Act, 1986 had received the assent of the President.

World Consumer Rights Day is observed on 15th March every year.

Hence, the correct option is (A).

3. Ad valorem tariff is calculated on the basis of the value of the imported good, expressed as a percentage of such value. For example, an ad valorem tariff of 10% on an imported car worth US$ 10000 would lead to a requirement to pay US$ 1000 as customs duty.

Hence, the correct option is (B).

4. Handloom Industry is the single largest cottage industry of Manipur state of India.

Hence, the correct option is (B).

5. Refers to a time period in which quantity supplied of a product cannot be increased with increase in its demand. In simple terms, in very short period of time, the supply of a product is fixed. The price determined in very short period is known as market price.

Hence, the correct option is (B).

6. Interest Rate Policy is a part of Monetary policy.

Hence, the correct option is (B).

7. Tea , Coffee , Rubber & Tobacco commodities Price Stabilization Fund Scheme was launched in 2003.

Hence, the correct option is (B).

8. A number of factors are responsible for poverty in India. Inequalities of Income is not the economic factor contributing to poverty.

Hence, the correct option is (A).

9. Training of Rural Youth for Self-Employment (TRYSEM) was started in 1979.

Hence, the correct option is (B).

10. The planners at Breton Woods established the International Monetary Fund (IMF) and the International Bank for Reconstruction and Development (IBRD), which today is part of the World Bank Group.

Hence, the correct option is (A).

11. The Government of India passed the Regional Rural Banks Act in 1976.

Regional Rural Banks were established on the recommendations of the Narasimha Committee on Rural Credit. The committee was of the view that RRBs would be much better than commercial banks or cooperative banks to meet the needs of rural areas. Keeping in view the recommendations of the committee, the Government of India passed the Regional Rural Banks Act. At least 25 RRBs were set up in different parts of India after the Act was passed within a year.

Hence, the correct option is (D).

12. Low skilled Labor in Unorganized sector is the most abundant human resource in India.

Hence, the correct option is (D).

13. Round Tripping is normally used in context with Foreign Direct Investments.

Hence, the correct option is (B).

14. Establishment. The euro, which was established in 1992, introduced in non-physical form in 1999 and finally rolled out in 2002, is used by 19 of the 27 member states of the European Union. This group of 19 countries is otherwise known as the eurozone or euro area.

Hence, the correct option is (B).

15. Road and Railways comes under economic overheads.

Hence, the correct option is (D).

16. Salary Earners will be benefited by Deflation.

Hence, the correct option is (A).

17. GDP Deflator index is available on Quarterly Basis.

Hence, the correct option is (D).

18. Annada, rasi & Kalinga-3 are the seed varieties for profitable intercrops for Rice grains.

Hence, the correct option is (B).

19. 1953 year Aid India Club was established.

Hence, the correct option is (B).

20. Indira Gandhi Institute of Development Research is an advanced research and educational institution in Mumbai. This includes economics, energy and environmental policy. This is funded by Reserve Bank of India (RBI).

Hence, the correct option is (D).

21. India's first operational special economic zone (SEZ) is located at Indore.

Hence, the correct option is (D).

22. The time required to process and execute an order is called lead time. Lead time is the amount of time that passes from the start of a process until its conclusion.

23. Direct taxes include income tax, property tax, corporate tax, estate tax, gift tax, value-added tax (VAT), sin tax, and taxes on assets. There are also indirect taxes, such as sales taxes, where a tax is levied on the seller but paid by the buyer.

Hence, the correct option is (B).

24. An EEFC account can be held only in the form of a current account. No interest is payable on EEFC accounts. The account holders do not have to convert foreign exchange into Rupees and vice versa, thereby minimizing the transaction costs. There is no restriction on withdrawal in Rupees of funds held in an EEFC account. However, the amount withdrawn in Rupees shall not be eligible for conversion into foreign currency and for re-credit to the account. SEZ Units cannot open EEFC Accounts. The EEFC account balances can be hedged.

The account holder does not have to convert foreign exchange into Rupees and vice versa, thereby minimizing the transaction costs.

Hence, the correct option is (B).

25. Excise duty is a tax on manufacture or production of goods. Excise duty on alcohol, alcoholic preparations, and narcotic substances is collected by the State Government and is called "State Excise" duty. The Excise duty on rest of goods is called "Central Excise" duty and is collected in terms of Section 3 of the Central Excise Act, 1944. Sales Tax is different from the Excise duty as former is a tax on the act of sale while the latter is a tax on the act of manufacture or production of goods.

Hence, the correct option is (A).

26. 1. Balance of trade

2. Net factor income

3. Net transfer payments

Hence, the correct option is (D).

27. The monetarists, money supply constitutes currency + demand deposits + time deposits. Monetarism, school of economic thought that maintains that the money supply (the total amount of money in an economy, in the form of coin, currency, and bank deposits) is the chief determinant on the demand side of short-run economic activity. The monetarist approach became influential during the 1970s and early '80s.

Hence, the correct option is (B).

28. There are five kinds of Land Holdings in India, depending on various sizes as follows:

Marginal holdings: Size 1 hectare or less

Small holdings: Size 1 to 2 hectares

Semi-medium holdings : Size 2 to 4 hectares

Medium holdings: Size 4 to 10 hectares

Large holdings: Size above 10 hectare

Maximum number of operational land holdings in India is marginal holdings. According to Census 2011, 67 per cent of holdings were classified as marginal (less than one hectare) and 18 per cent were classified as small (one-two hectare). Large holdings were estimated to be only 0.7%. Operational Land Holdings include only those units which are used either in farm production or farm production + livestock and poultry products (primary) and/or pisciculture or for only livestock and poultry products (primary) and/or pisciculture.

Hence, the correct option is (B).

29. •Capital Budget consists of capital receipts and payments.

•The main items of capital receipts are loans raised by Government from public which are called Market Loans, borrowings by Government from Reserve Bank and other parties through sale of Treasury Bills, loans received from foreign Governments and bodies and recoveries of loans granted by Central Government to State and Union Territory Governments and other parties.

•Capital payments consist of capital expenditure on acquisition of assets like land, buildings, machinery, equipment, as also investments in shares, etc., and loans and advances granted by Central Government to State and Union Territory Governments, Government companies, Corporations and other parties. Capital Budget also incorporates transactions in the Public Account.

Hence, the correct option is (D).

30. Printing of Currency is used by the Government as a last resort in Deficit Financing.

Hence, the correct option is (D).

31. Government Bonds indicate government borrowing from public, which shall come under capital receipts.

Hence, the correct option is (C).

32. Tax-to-GDP ratio is the total government tax collections divided by the country's GDP. India has very low tax-to-GDP ratio. The tax-to-GDP ratio for the central government is 10 percent and state plus centre is about 15.5 percent.

Hence, the correct option is (A).

33. It is on account of this reason that these loans are called 'call money' or call loans. The investment of funds in the call market meets the need of liquidity but not that of profitability because the rate of interest on call. It is another specialized sector of the money market. All these four sub-markets form the money market.

Hence, the correct option is (C).

34. All of the above are correct statements.

Hence, the correct option is (D).

35. Commercial transactions between the different parts of the multinational groups may not be subject to the same market forces shaping relations between the two independent firms. One party transfers to another goods or services, for a price. That price is known as "transfer price". It is mainly done for tax-dodging in a country.

Hence, the correct option is (A).

36. Increased NRI deposits are an external debt. Inward remittance is not because it is not to be repaid back. ECBs are again external debt. Grants are never debt because they don't need to be paid back. Depreciation of US dollar against the rupee will reduce external debt as rupee getting stronger.

Hence, the correct option is (B).

37. Government of India has approved a new Central Sector Scheme – Pradhan Mantri Kisan SAMPADA Yojana (Scheme for Agro-Marine Processing and Development of Agro-Processing Clusters) with an allocation of Rs. 6,000 crore for the period 2016-20 coterminous with the 14th Finance Commission cycle. The scheme will be implemented by Ministry of Food Processing Industries.

Hence, the correct option is (B).

38. Turkey is not the founding member of the International North–South Transport Corridor. Russia, Iran and India signed the agreement for the NSTC project on the 16th of May 2002.

Hence, the correct option is (C).

39. An IDR is a mechanism that allows investors in India to invest in listed foreign companies, including multinational companies, in Indian rupees. IDRs give the holder the opportunity to hold an interest in equity shares in an overseas company. IDRs are denominated in Indian Rupees and issued by a Domestic Depository in India. They can be listed on any Indian stock exchange. Anybody who can invest in an IPO (Initial Public Offer) is/are eligible to invest in IDRs. In other words, what ADRs/GDRs are for investors abroad with respect to Indian companies, IDRs are for Indian investors with respect to foreign companies.

Hence, the correct option is (B).

40. 'Long-term investors' include SEBI-registered 'sovereign wealth funds' (SWFs), multilateral agencies, endowment funds, insurance funds, pension funds and foreign central banks.

Hence, the correct option is (D).

41. Child abuse is when a parent or caregiver, whether through action or failing to act, causes injury, death, emotional harm or risk of serious harm to a child. There are many forms of child maltreatment, including neglect, physical abuse, sexual abuse, exploitation and emotional abuse.

Hence, the correct option is (A).

42. According to Article 24, no child below the age of 14 years shall be employed to work in any factory or in any hazardous employment.

Hence, the correct option is (A).

43. Criminal offenses which usually involve bodily harm, the threat of bodily harm, or other actions committed against the will of an individual.

Hence, the correct option is (E).

44. Rape, abduction, murder is an example of criminal violence.

Hence, the correct option is (A).

45. Dowry deaths, wife battering is an example of domestic violence.

Hence, the correct option is (B).

46. Female foeticide, eve-teasing is an example of social violence.

Hence, the correct option is (C).

47. In honour killing, it is a murder committed by family members.

Hence, the correct option is (B).

48. October, 1, 1978 year was the National Adult Education Programme launched.

Hence, the correct option is (A).

49. Delinquency, crimes committed by minors, which are dealt with by the juvenile courts and justice system.

Hence, the correct option is (E).

50. Trough. The lowest point of real GDP reached during the business cycle is known as the trough. Troughs can be for varying amounts of time.

51. 2005 the Protection of Women from Domestic Violence Act enacted.

Hence, the correct option is (C).

52. The Sixth Five-Year Plan marked the beginning of economic liberalisation. Price controls were eliminated and ration shops were closed. This led to an increase in food prices and an increase in the cost of living. This was the end of Nehruvian socialism. The National Bank for Agriculture and Rural Development was established for development of rural areas on 12 July 1982 by recommendation of the Shivaraman Committee.

Hence, the correct option is (A).

53. Indian Made Foreign Liquor

Hence, the correct option is (A).

54. World Health Day – 7th April

World Ozone Day-16th September

World Environment Day- 5th June

World Population Day-11th July

Hence, the correct option is (C).

55. Treatment involves counselling by a healthcare professional. A detoxification programme in a hospital or medical facility is an option for those who need additional assistance. Medications are available that reduce the desire to drink.

Hence, the correct option is (E).

56. • The aim of the Rio + 20 summit was to agree on ways to achieve economic growth in a sustainable manner.

• The aim of Copenhagen Conference, 1992- to phase out of CFC by 1996, Halons by 2000.

• The aim of Cancun Conference ,2010-to create a green climate fund.

• The aim of Durban Summit, 2011 to create a green climate fund up to 2016.

Hence, the correct option is (C).

57. Electronic Data Interchange (EDI) is the computer-to-computer exchange of business documents in a standard electronic format between business partners.

Hence, the correct option is (C).

58. Bug is a term used in a computer science to denote an error in a particular program that is used to run a software.

Hence, the correct option is (B).

59. The purpose of value education is best served by focusing upon the concern for human values and these values can be achieved by following the various aims of education:

a) to make individual to give moral value to each other.

b) to prepare individuals for future challenges and to fulfill personal goals and achievements.

c) to prepare responsible youth for the society, nation and for the world.

Hence, the correct option is (C).

60. Higher Education in India has certain goals to achieve:

• Access – Education is the right to every individual. So, higher education institutes have the duty to ensure education access to every learner.

• Equity, Quality and Excellence – The first and the foremost motive of every higher education institute is to ensure quality and proper infrastructure to the students.

• Relevance and value-based education – The higher education institutes must provide value through education.

Hence, the correct option is (C).

61. Hypotheses tested by a regression function are:

Inter-relation between two or more variables is significantly different from zero.

The degree and direction of inter relations between two or more variables are non-zero and goodness of fit of the regression function is satisfactory.

Degree of influence exercised by systematic explanatory factors is greater/lesser/equal to the influence exercised by random factors.

Hence, the correct option is (E).

62. Globalization has always been there in the economic sense of the term though it always had its political dimensions. It is defined as an increase in economic integration among nations. Even before the nation-states were born, the countries around the world had gone for globalization i.e. a closer integration among economies. It lasted from 1800 to 1930. The concept was popularized again in the mid-1980s.

Hence, the correct option is (B).

63. Inflation is defined as the rise in the general level of prices of goods and services in an economy. If the price of one goods has gone up, it is not termed as inflation but for it, to be counted as inflation, the prices of most of the goods should go up. On the other hand, when the general level of prices is falling, it is known as deflation.

Hence, the correct option is (B).

64. The net domestic product (NDP) equals the gross domestic product (GDP) minus depreciation on a country's capital goods. Net domestic product accounts for capital that has been consumed over the year in the form of housing, vehicle, or machinery deterioration.

Hence, the correct option is (D).

65. The existence of heteroscedasticity is a major concern in regression analysis and the analysis of variance, as it invalidates statistical tests of significance that assume that the modelling errors all have the same variance. While the ordinary least squares estimator is still unbiased in the presence of heteroscedasticity, it is inefficient and generalized least squares should be used instead.

Hence, the correct option is (B).

Q.1 Risks in the business arise because of
A. Introduction of the new products
B. Uncertain policy of rival firms
C. Changes in tastes
D. Both (A) and (B)
E. All of the above

Q.2 Indifference curves are convex to the origin because
A. Two goods are perfect substitutes
B. Two goods are imperfect substitutes
C. Two goods are perfect complementary goods
D. Two goods are imperfect complementary goods
E. None of these

Q.3 Which of the following is the most widely used method of calculating correlation?
A. Scatter diagram   B. Karl Pearson's
C. Charles Spearman's   D. Both (A) and (B)
E. None of these

Q.4 Standard of living of a country can be raised if it increases
A. Labour force   B. Production
C. Money supply   D. Exports
E. None of these

Q.5 According to Malthus, population increases by progression of which kind?
A. Systematic   B. Arithmetic
C. Geometric   D. Automatic
E. None of these

Q.6 Profit is maximum when
A. Slope of MC and Mr is the same
B. Slope of TC and TR is the same
C. Slope of AC and AR is the same
D. Slope of BC and BR is the same
E. None of these

Q.7 Excise tax is a part of
A. Fixed cost   B. Variable cost
C. Implicit cost   D. Is not a part of cost
E. None of these

Q.8 The labour force participation rate is the
A. Proportion of population that is working
B. Proportion of population working or looking for work
C. Proportion of skilled workers population
D. Proportion of female workers to male workers
E. None of these

Q.9 The human effort applied to the production of goods is called in economics
A. Labour   B. Skill
C. Experience   D. Service

E. None of these

Q.10 Normal profit is
A. Part of total cost
B. Part of economic profit
C. Total revenue minus total cost
D. Total revenue minus implicit cost
E. None of these

Q.11 As output increases
A. MC curve initially falls and then rises
B. MC initially rises and then falls
C. MC continuously rises
D. MC continuously falls
E. None of the above

Q.12 He described economics as a science of material welfare
A. Robbins   B. Marshall
C. Ricardo   D. Keynes
E. None of these

Q.13 Economic profit is
A. Part of total cost
B. Total revenue minus total cost
C. Total revenue minus explicit cost
D. Total variable cost minus total fixed cost
E. None of these

Q.14 Which statement relates to macroeconomics?
A. Oil prices are rising in Pakistan
B. Profit rate is high on textile industry
C. The firms try to make huge profits
D. The government has failed to control inflation
E. None of these

Q.15 A firm earns economic profit when total profit exceeds?
A. Normal profit   B. Implicit costs
C. Explicit costs   D. Variable costs
E. None of these

Q.16 Who is the 'father of economics'?
A. Max Muller   B. Adam Smith
C. Karl Marx   D. Galileo Galilei
E. None of these

Q.17 For inferior commodities, income effect is
A. Zero   B. Negative
C. Infinite   D. Positive
E. None of these

Q.18 Mixed economy means an economy where
A. Both agriculture and industry are equally promoted by the state
B. There is co-existence of public sector along with private sector

C. There is importance of small scale industries along with heavy industries

D. Economy is controlled by military as well as civilian rulers

E. None of these

Q.19 When total utility becomes maximum, then marginal utility will be

A. Minimum
B. Average
C. Zero
D. Negative
E. None of these

Q.20 Utility means

A. Power to satisfy a want
B. Usefulness
C. Willingness of a person
D. Harmfulness
E. None of these

Q.21 Marginal utility is equal to average utility at that time when average utility is

A. Increasing
B. Maximum
C. Falling
D. Minimum
E. None of these

Q.22 Which one of the following is the task of the Planning Commission?

A. Preparation of the plan
B. Implementation of the plan
C. Financing of the plan
D. Execution of the plan
E. None of these

Q.23 At the point of satiety, marginal utility is

A. Zero
B. Positive
C. Maximum
D. Negative
E. None of these

Q.24 Total utility of a commodity is measured by which price of that commodity?

A. Value in use
B. Value in exchange
C. Value in interchange
D. Both (A) and (B)
E. None of these

Q.25 Which of the following bodies finalizes the Five Year Plan Proposals?

A. Planning Commission
B. Union Cabinet
C. National Development Council
D. Ministry of Planning
E. None of these

Q.26 What implication does resource scarcity have for the satisfaction of wants?

A. Not all wants can be satisfied
B. We will never be faced with the need to make choices
C. We must develop ways to decrease our individual wants
D. The discovery of new natural resources is necessary to increase our ability to satisfy wants
E. None of these

Q.27 Which one of the following is true about Planning Commission?

A. It is a Ministry
B. It is a Government Department
C. It is an Advisory Body
D. It is an Autonomous Corporation
E. None of these

Q.28 A firm encounters its 'shutdown point' when

A. Average total cost equals price at the profit-maximizing level of output
B. Average variable cost equals price at the profit-maximizing level of output
C. Average fixed cost equals price at the profit-maximizing level of output
D. Marginal cost equals price at the profit-maximizing level of output
E. None of these

Q.29 Larger production of ___ goods would lead to higher production in future

A. Consumer goods
B. Capital goods
C. Agricultural goods
D. Public goods
E. None of the above

Q.30 Economic survey is published by

A. Ministry of Finance
B. Planning Commission
C. Government of India
D. Indian Statistical Institute
E. None of these

Q.31 The economic analysis expects the consumer to behave in a manner which is

A. Rational
B. Irrational
C. Emotional
D. Indifferent
E. None of these

Q.32 Consumer surplus is highest in case of

A. Necessities
B. Luxuries
C. Comforts
D. Conventional necessities
E. None of these

Q.33 The law of variable proportions come into being when

A. There are only two variable factors
B. There is a fixed factor and a variable factor
C. All factors are variable
D. Variable factors yield less
E. None of these

Q.34 ____ is an implicit cost of production

A. Wages of the labour
B. Charges for electricity
C. Interest on owned money capital
D. Payment for raw material

E. None of these

Q.35 Excess capacity is not found under
A. Monopoly
B. Monopolistic competition
C. Perfect competition
D. Oligopoly
E. None of these

Q.36 Which of the following schemes have not been launched by the Ministry of Human Resource Development to maintain equity?
A. Ishan Vikas
B. Saksham
C. Sakshar Bharat
D. Swayam
E. PAHAL

Q.37 Which of the following items are used to determine the poverty line in India by the NSSO?
A. Clothing
B. Footwear
C. Durable goods
D. Education
E. All of the above

Q.38 In which of the following migration occurs from more developed areas to less developed but more environmentally suitable areas?
A. Push migration
B. Hike migration
C. Out migration
D. In migration
E. Perverse migration

Q.39 Name the online portal launched by RBI to ease the process of customer complaints?
A. Ombudsman Portal
B. National Portal of India
C. Complaint management System
D. Complaint RBI
E. None of the above

Q.40 Central Government has set up a new body Rice Export Promotion Forum to give impetus to rice exports under the aegis of _____.
A. Department of Agriculture, Cooperation & Farmers Welfare
B. Agricultural and Processed Foods Export Promotion Development Authority (APEDA)
C. Department of Agricultural Research and Education
D. National Agricultural Cooperative Marketing Federation of India (NAFED)
E. None of these

Q.41 Which of the following is correct regarding Export Processing Zones?
A. EPZ encourage and generate the economic development
B. It encourages FDI
C. It helps in the growth of Indian export commodities
D. It ensures world class quality of products
E. All of the above

Q.42 As the union budget 2020-21, the National Gas Grid shall be expanded from 16,200 km to how many km?
A. 24000
B. 25000
C. 26000
D. 27000
E. 28000

Q.43 Jan Swasthya Abhiyan was launched in which of the following year?
A. 2005
B. 2015
C. 2001
D. 2012
E. 2017

Q.44 Poverty is defined in India on the basis which of the following factor?
A. Income of family
B. Living standard of people
C. Number of people in a family
D. Calorie Consumption
E. Tax paid by a family

Q.45 Which of the following statements is correct with regards to 'Global Environment Facility'?
A. Global Environment Facility is an agency under OECD to facilitate the transfer of technology and funds to underdeveloped countries with specific aim to protect their environment.
B. Global Environment Facility (GEF) was established in October 1999.
C. Global Environment Facility serves as financial mechanism for Convention on Biological Diversity' and 'United Nations Framework Convention on Climate Change'
D. Global Environment Facility undertakes scientific research on environmental issues at global level
E. None of these

Q.46 Which of the following is not a source of income for Panchayti Raj institutions?
A. Public support and money contribution
B. Tax, fees and penalty
C. Grants
D. License fees on transport
E. Loans

Q.47 Income tax of India for any particular individual can be described by which of the following taxation nature?
A. Proportionate taxation
B. Progressive taxation
C. Regressive taxation
D. Degressive taxation
E. None of these

Q.48 Which of the following is not a part of fiscal deficit?
A. Internal debt
B. Government's external debt
C. Liability of Central Government to states
D. Liability to RBI
E. None of these

Q.49 What is the Modified Mixed reference period for clothing, footwear, education, institutional medical care, and durable goods as per Rangarajan Committee?
A. 7 Days
B. 365 Days
C. 30 Days
D. 180 Days
E. 100 Days

Q.50 The National Family Health Survey (NFHS)gets the financial assistance from which of the following organizations?
A.   WHO and UNICEF
B.   UNICEF and UNFPA
C.   UNICEF and USAID
D.   WHO and UNESCO
E.   IMF and WTO

Q.51 For the success of the penetration price policy, which one of the following is not desirable?
A.   Short-run demand for the product to have elasticity greater than unity.
B.   Availability of economies of large scale production.
C.   Product to have very low cross-elasticity of demand.
D.   Easy acceptance and adoption of the product by the consumers.
E.   None of these

Q.52 Match the following and select the correct answer from the codes given below:

Group - I	Group - II
(a) Asian Drama	(i) A. K. Sen
(b) Choice of Technique	(ii) W. W. Rostow
(c) Stages of Economic Growth	(iii) Gunnar Myrdal
(d) Strategy of Economic Development	(iv) A.O. Hirschman
	(v) Leibenstein

A. (i), (ii), (iv), (iii)   B. (iii), (i), (ii), (iv)
C. (i), (ii), (iii), (iv)   D. (v), (iii), (ii), (i)
E. None of these

Q.53 What is the shape of the long - run Philips curve?
A.   Horizontal Straight line
B.   Vertical Straight line
C.   Upward Sloping
D.   Downward Sloping
E.   None of these

Q.54 Consumption sub - model was introduced in Indian Planning for the first time in preparing which plan:
A. Third Plan   B. Fourth Plan
C. Fifth Plan   D. Sixth Plan
E. None of these

Q.55 According to the Sustainable Development Goal (SDG) India Index 2018, which state among the following has the highest SDG Index score?
A. Himachal Pradesh   B. Goa
C. Andhra Pradesh   D. Tamil Nadu
E. None of these

Q.56 Which of the following are the demerits of globalization of higher education?
1) Exposure to global curriculum
2) Promotion of elitism in education
3) Commodification of higher education
4) Increase in the cost of education
A. 1 and 4   B. 1, 3 and 4
C. 2, 3 and 4   D. 1, 2, 3 and 4

E.   None of these

Q.57 Research has shown that the most frequent symptom of nervous instability among teachers is
A.   Digestive upsets
B.   Explosive behaviour
C.   Fatigue
D.   Worry
E.   None of these

Q.58 As Chairman of an independent commission on education, Jacques Delors report to UNESCO was titled:
A.   International Commission on Education Report
B.   Millennium Development Report
C.   Learning: The Treasure Within
D.   World Declaration on Education for all
E.   None of these

Q.59 Apart from food and water which is another important factor from the point of view of good health?
A. Sleep   B. Fats
C. Vitamins   D. Minerals
E. None of these

Q.60 To make sure that your heart keeps healthy all the time, have a whole some _______ .
A. Meal   B. Carbohydrates
C. Water   D. Fats
E. None of these

Q.61 How many glasses of water are essential for maintaining a good rate of metabolism?
A. 1 to 1   B. 10 to 12
C. 3 to 4   D. 5 to 6
E. None of these

Q.62 Certain hormones those are essential for making antibodies that are capable of fighting against diseases and infections are released by our body in which situation
A. Sleeping   B. Walking
C. Happiness   D. Breathing
E. None of these

Q.63 Which of the following options reveals the meaning of the following sentence in the most right manner?
A.   In order to be happy you must try to be healthy.
B.   You can only be happy when you are healthy.
C.   A happy heart is the indication that the person is healthy.
D.   When you are not happy you are not healthy.
E.   None of these

Q.64 Keynesian revolution's central aspects was
A.   change in theory concerning the factors determining employment levels in the overall economy
B.   change in theory concerning the factors determining agricultural levels in the overall economy
C.   change in theory concerning the factors determining Production levels in the overall economy
D.   None of the above
E.   a and b both

Q.65 WTO was established in 1995 to replace General
Agreement on Tariffs and Trade (GATT) after Uruguay Round of
talks. What was the name of the agreement through which
WTO came into being?

A. GATT Agreement
B. Uruguay Agreement
C. Vienna treaty
D. Marrakesh Agreement
E. None of these

// Smart Answer Sheet //

Correct   Indicates percentage of students who answered questions correctly.

Skipped   Indicates percentage of students who skipped questions.

Q.	Ans.	Correct / Skipped
1	E	88.56 % / 10.35 %
2	B	80.28 % / 16.77 %
3	B	86.44 % / 10.34 %
4	B	81.05 % / 18.77 %
5	C	88.54 % / 11.36 %
6	B	77.54 % / 21.6 %
7	B	82.55 % / 17.27 %
8	C	89.4 % / 10.37 %
9	A	81.21 % / 11.86 %
10	A	82.55 % / 16.63 %
11	A	83.68 % / 12.39 %
12	B	81.12 % / 13.51 %
13	B	79.28 % / 19.83 %

Q.	Ans.	Correct / Skipped
14	D	78.98 % / 17.25 %
15	A	78.85 % / 10.81 %
16	B	85.31 % / 13.89 %
17	B	77.41 % / 19.64 %
18	B	88.15 % / 10.15 %
19	C	89.62 % / 10.04 %
20	A	82.13 % / 15.47 %
21	B	76.77 % / 21.75 %
22	A	84.19 % / 11.58 %
23	B	87.04 % / 11.71 %
24	A	85.01 % / 13.2 %
25	C	77.08 % / 22.27 %
26	A	86.03 % / 12.33 %

Q.	Ans.	Correct / Skipped
27	C	89.73 % / 10.17 %
28	B	80.6 % / 14.64 %
29	B	83.31 % / 10.2 %
30	A	82.57 % / 13.9 %
31	A	86.29 % / 11.41 %
32	A	83.39 % / 15.06 %
33	B	86.91 % / 10.38 %
34	C	79.61 % / 18.52 %
35	C	86.06 % / 11.03 %
36	E	77.4 % / 13.57 %
37	E	81.7 % / 18.02 %
38	E	89.35 % / 10.46 %
39	C	88.07 % / 10.23 %

Q.	Ans.	Correct / Skipped
40	B	78.45 % / 13.54 %
41	E	76.51 % / 12.18 %
42	D	86.86 % / 12.7 %
43	C	79.82 % / 20.07 %
44	D	85.84 % / 11.7 %
45	C	85.43 % / 11.97 %
46	E	87.09 % / 10.84 %
47	B	88.22 % / 11.58 %
48	C	82.18 % / 14.63 %
49	B	88.56 % / 10.31 %
50	C	89.2 % / 10.5 %
51	C	85.38 % / 13.78 %
52	B	89.78 % / 10.12 %

Q.	Ans.	Correct / Skipped
53	B	81.02 % / 18.59 %
54	C	79.5 % / 11.74 %
55	A	84.09 % / 11.26 %
56	C	85.27 % / 10.88 %
57	B	88.12 % / 11.15 %
58	C	82.9 % / 16.56 %
59	A	89.74 % / 10.21 %
60	A	85.53 % / 13.33 %
61	B	78.27 % / 15.76 %
62	C	85.22 % / 12.53 %
63	C	88.17 % / 10.23 %
64	A	84.46 % / 11.36 %
65	D	87.89 % / 10.25 %

Performance Analysis

Avg. Score (%)	46.0%
Toppers Score (%)	59.0%
Your Score	

//Hints and Solutions//

1. Risks in the business arise because of Introduction of the new products, Uncertain policy of rival firms and Changes in tastes.

2. Indifference curves are convex to the origin because two goods are imperfect substitutes.

3. Karl Pearson's Correlation Coefficient. Pearson is the most widely used correlation coefficient. Pearson correlation measures the linear association between continuous variables.

4. Standard of living of a country can be raised if it increases a) Labour force b) Production c) Money supply d) Exports.

5. According to Malthus, population increases by progression of Geometric.

6. Profit is maximum when Slope of TC and TR is the same. To obtain the profit maximizing output quantity, we start by recognizing that profit is equal to total revenue (TR) minus total cost (TC).

7. Excise tax is a part of Variable cost. Excise duty is an indirect tax. That means the tax amount is included as part of the selling price. Excise duty, also known as excise tax, is ultimately passed on and paid by the consumer when he makes a purchase.

8. The labour force participation rate is the proportion of skilled workers population. It refers to the number of people who are either employed or are actively looking for work.

9. The human effort applied to the production of goods is called Labour in economics. Labor is the human effort that can be applied to the production of goods and services.

10. Normal profit is Part of total cost. Normal profit is an economic term that describes when a company's total revenues are equal to its total costs in a perfectly competitive market.

11. As output increases when MC curve initially falls and then rises. The Marginal Cost curve is U shaped because initially when a firm increases its output, total costs, as well as variable costs, start to increase at a diminishing rate. Then as output rises, the marginal cost increases.

12. Marshall described economics as a science of material welfare. Marshall's view is that economics studies all the actions that people take in order to achieve economic welfare. In the words of Marshall, "man earns money to get material welfare."

13. Economic profit is Total revenue minus total cost. Economic profit is the monetary costs and opportunity costs a firm pays and the revenue a firm receives. Economic profit = total revenue – (explicit costs + implicit costs).

14. The government has failed to control inflation relates to macroeconomics. Governments can use wage and price controls to fight inflation, but that can cause recession and job losses. Governments can also employ a contradictory monetary policy to fight inflation by reducing the money supply within an economy via decreased bond prices and increased interest rates.

15. A firm earns economic profit when total profit exceeds Normal profit. Economic profit is the profitability measurement that calculates the amount that revenues received from selling a product exceeds opportunity costs incurred from using resources to make and sell these products.

16. Adam Smith is the 'father of economics'. Adam Smith is called the father of economics for his work on The Wealth of Nations which he published in 1776.

17. For inferior commodities, income effect is Negative. When price of an inferior good falls, its negative income effect will tend to reduce the quantity purchased, while the substitution effect will tend to increase the quantity purchased.

18. Mixed economy means an economy where there is co-existence of public sector along with private sector. All modern economies are mixed where the means of production are shared between the private and public sectors. Also called dual economy.

19. When total utility becomes maximum, then marginal utility will be Zero. It is based in the law of diminishing marginal utility which says 'as more and more units of a good are consumed, MU i.e level of satisfaction derived from each successive unit goes on falling because desire for that commodity tend to fall.

20. Utility means power to satisfy a want. It is a quality possessed by a commodity or service to satisfy human wants. Utility can also be defined as value-in-use of a commodity because the satisfaction which we get from the consumption of a commodity is its value-in-use.

21. Marginal utility is equal to average utility at that time when average utility is maximum.

22. Preparation of the plan is the task of the Planning Commission. The Planning Commission is charged with the responsibility of making assessment of all resources in the country, augmenting deficient resources, formulating plans for the most effective and balanced utilisation of resources and determining priorities.

23. At the point of satiety, marginal utility is positive. Goods where there is a point of satiety. This situation is common in food. To the point of satiety, the marginal utility is positive; after that point, the marginal utility is negative.

24. Total utility of a commodity is measured by value in use price of that commodity. The utility theory of value was the belief that price and value were solely based on how much "use" an individual received from a commodity.

25. National Development Council finalizes the Five Year Plan Proposals.

26. Resource scarcity for the satisfaction of wants implicates that not all wants can be satisfied. The classification of human wants is not a rigid concept.

27. Planning Commission is an Advisory Body. The Planning Commission is a non-constitutional and non-statutory body and is responsible to formulate five years plan for social and economic development in India.

28. A firm encounters its 'shutdown point' when average variable cost equals price at the profit-maximizing level of output.

29. Larger production of Capital goods goods would lead to higher production in future. If investment in capital good increases ,in turn it further increases the production of consumer goods in the long run. So, if an economy is investing more in capital goods, it shows signs of growth in near future, an increase in GDP.

30. The Department of Economic Affairs, Finance Ministry of India presents the Economic Survey in the parliament every year, just before the Union Budget.It is prepared under the guidance of the Chief Economic Adviser, Finance Ministry. It is the ministry's view on the annual economic development of the country.

31. The economic analysis expects the consumer to behave in a manner which is Rational. The assumption of rational behavior implies that people would rather be better off than worse off. Most conventional economic theories are based on the assumption that all individuals taking part in an action or activity are behaving rationally.

32. Consumer surplus is highest in case of necessities. Consumer surplus happens when the price that consumers pay for a product or service is less than the price they're willing to pay.

33. The law of variable proportions come into being when there is a fixed factor and a variable factor. The law of variable proportions states that as the quantity of one factor is increased, keeping the other factors fixed, the marginal product of that factor will eventually decline.

34. Interest on owned money capital is an implicit cost of production. The costs in which there is no cash outlay, is known as Implicit Cost.

35. Excess capacity is not found under Perfect competition. Under perfect competition, each firm produces at the minimum point on its LAC curve and its horizontal demand curve is tangent to it at that point. Its output is ideal and there is no excess capacity in the long-run.

36. Swayam - Study Webs of Active Learning for Young Aspiring Minds is a programme of the Ministry of Human Resource Development, Government of India, that enables professors and faculties of centrally funded institutions like IITs, IIMs, Central University Of Haryana to offer online courses.

• Ishan Vikas - Ishan Vikas is a program organised by MHRD of Govt of India to provide financial assistance for Advancement of Girls participation in Technical Education and to introduce school children from the North-Eastern states into close contact with the IITs and IISERs during their vacation periods.

• Saksham - Saksham is a Ministry of Human Resource Development (MHRD) Scheme being implemented by All India Council for Technical Education (AICTE) aimed at providing encouragement and support to specially-abled children to pursue Technical Education. This is an attempt to give every young student, who is otherwise specially-abled, the opportunity to study further and prepare for a successful future.

• Saakshar Bharat – Saakshar Bharat Programme goes beyond '3' R's (i.e. Reading, Writing & Arithmetic) ; for it also seeks to create awareness of social disparities and a person's deprivation on the means for its amelioration and general well being. This programme was formulated in 2009 by MHRD with the objective of achieving 80% literacy level at national level, by focusing on adult women literacy seeking – to reduce the gap between male and female literacy to not more than 10 percentage points.

37. From 1999-2000 onwards, the NSSO switched to a method known as the Mixed Reference Period (MRP). The MRP measures consumption of five low-frequency items (clothing, footwear, durables, education and institutional health expenditure) over the previous year, and all other items over the previous 30 days. That is to say, for the five items, survey respondents are asked about consumption in the previous one year. For the remaining items, they are asked about consumption in the previous 30 days.

38.

- Perverse migration is the migration which is from more developed areas to less developed but more environmentally suitable areas.

- This has the perverse effect of causing migration and investment to centre on more developed areas, leaving other areas abandoned and in decline. This has the perverse effect of causing migration and investment to centre on more developed areas, leaving other areas abandoned and in decline.

39. RBI launched the online portal "Complaint management System"(CMS) to ease the process of customer complaints. CMS contemplates improved customer convenience by, providing a single window on RBI's website for lodging complaints against any regulated entity.

40.

- Centre set up a new body Rice Export Promotion Forum to give impetus to rice exports under the aegis of Agricultural and Processed Foods Export Promotion Development Authority (APEDA).

- The Constitution of Rice Export Promotion Forum has been done considering the importance of exporting rice and inherent the potentials and multifarious issues faced in the exportation.

41. Export Processing Zones of India were established to help the growth of Indian export commodities, especially from the fast-growing sectors.

42.

- While presenting union budget 2020-21, the Finance Minister Nirmala Sitharaman proposed a plan for the expansion of National Gas Grid to 27,000 km from the present 16,200 km.

- Currently, around 7,000 km of pipeline is under construction. Besides, the city gas distribution projects are expected to add several thousand more kilometres of steel pipeline.

43.

- The Jan Swasthya Abhiyan (JSA) was formed in 2001, with the coming together of 18 national networks that had organised activities across the country in 2000, in the lead up to the First Global Peoples Health Assembly, in Dhaka, in December 2000. The JSA forms the Indian regional circle of the global People's Health Movement (PHM).

- The important areas of immediate concern and continuing activities include –

- Strengthening the Public Sector

- Women's health rights and gender equity

44.

- The Planning Commission of India has defined a poverty line on the basis of recommended nutritional requirements of 2,400 calories per person per day for rural areas and 2,100 calories for urban areas.

- The average calorie requirement is estimated by taking into account the population composition by age, sex and occupation categories together with the corresponding calorie norms by the Indian Council of Medical Research.

45.

- GEF funds are available to developing countries and countries with economies in transition to meet the objectives of the international environmental conventions and agreements.

- The Global Environment Facility (GEF) was established in October 1991 to provide new and additional grants and concessional funding to cover additional costs associated with transforming a project with national benefits into one with global environmental benefits. The GEF unites 180 member governments in partnership with international institutions, nongovernmental organizations and the private sector.

46.

- The main sources of income for Panchayats are local cess, house tax, profession tax, vehicle tax, duty on transfers of property, a portion of entertainments tax, house tax, matching grant and development rates levied under Section 119(3) of the Madras Panchayats Act, 1958.

- The taxes imposed by the Panchayats are important source of income of Panchayats, such as: Taxes on land and houses, the custom duty, the toll tax, License fees on transport and communication etc.

47. Individual income tax increases with income up to a limit but after that it becomes flat. So, this is mix of progressive and proportionate taxation, which is termed as degressive taxation.

• A progressive tax imposes a greater percentage of taxation on higher income levels, operating on the theory that high-income earners can afford to pay more.

• A progressive tax has more of a financial impact on higher-income individuals and businesses than on low-income earners.

• A regressive tax is thought to be disproportionately difficult on lower-income individuals because it's the same percentage of products or goods purchased regardless of the buyer's income.

48.

- The fiscal deficit is the total liability of a single budgetary year. But issued securities to Food Corporation of India and liability of central government to state governments will not be included in this.

- The fiscal deficit is the difference between the government's total expenditure and its total receipts (excluding borrowing).

- The elements of the fiscal deficit are the revenue deficit, which is the difference between the government's current (or revenue) expenditure and total current receipts (that is, excluding borrowing) and capital expenditure. The fiscal deficit can be financed by borrowing from the Reserve Bank of India (which is also called deficit financing or money creation) and market borrowing (from the money market, that is mainly from banks).

49.

- Modified Mixed reference period: Instead of Mixed reference Period (MRP) Rangarajan Committee recommended Modified Mixed Reference Period (MMRP) in which reference periods for different items were taken as:

- 365- days for clothing, footwear, education, institutional medical care, and durable goods.

- 7-days for edible oil, egg, fish and meat, vegetables, fruits, spices, beverages, refreshments, processed food, pan, and tobacco

- 30-days for the remaining food items, fuel and light, miscellaneous goods and services including non-institutional medical rents and taxes.

50. The National Family Health Survey (NFHS) is a large-scale, multi-round survey conducted in a representative sample of households throughout India.

51. Conditions for market penetration pricing strategy:
• Short-run demand for the product to have elasticity more than unity.
• Availability of economies of large scale production.
• The market is highly price-sensitive and low prices stimulate market growth.
• Low price reduces actual and potential competition
• Easy acceptance and adoption of the product by the consumers.

52. Asian Drama- Gunnar Myrdal.

Choice of Technique- A. K. Sen.

Stages of Economic Growth- W. W. Rostow.

Strategy of Economic Development- A.O. Hirschman.

53. The long-run Phillips curve is a vertical line at the natural rate of unemployment, but the short-run Phillips curve is roughly L-shaped. The inverse relationship shown by the short-run Phillips curve only exists in the short-run; there is no trade-off between inflation and unemployment in the long run.

54. From 1947 to 2017, the Indian economy was premised on the concept of planning. This was carried through the Five-Year Plans, developed, executed, and monitored by the Planning Commission (1951-2014) and the NITI Aayog (2015-2017). With the prime minister as the ex-officio chairman, the commission has a nominated deputy chairman, who holds the rank of a cabinet minister. Montek Singh Ahluwalia is the last deputy chairman of the commission (resigned on 26 May 2014). The Twelfth Plan completed its term in March 2017. Prior to the Fourth Plan, the allocation of state resources was based on schematic patterns rather than a transparent and objective mechanism, which led to the adoption of the Gadgil formula in 1969.

55. According to the SDG India Index 2018, these states which have the highest SDG Index scores- Himachal Pradesh (69), Kerala (69), Goa (64), Andhra Pradesh (64) and Tamil Nadu (62).

56. Demerits of globalization of higher education are as follows:

• Promotion of elitism in higher education

• Commodification of higher education (It has become as saleable commodity)

• Increase in the cost of education (not affordable by everyone to study abroad)

57. Research has shown that the most frequent symptom of nervous instability among teachers is Explosive beaviour.

Teaher frustration triggers hostile-aggressive behavior. Frustration with others or oneself is dealt with through physical or verbal aggression or vandalism. With this behavior, the teacher gains negative attention from the student or peers.

58. Jacques Delors is the Chairman of the International Commission on Education. The report, which was submitted to UNESCO was titled as "Learning: The Treasure Within". In this report, Jacques Delors proposes that the society should aim to move towards the situation where the talent of the people should not go untapped.

59. Apart from food and water sleep is another important factor from the point of view of good health

As we seen in last paragraph 'Sleep is another important factor with regards to health. Along with proper liquid and solid food supply you also need to sound and sufficient sleep to keep you fresh all the day'

60. As we seen in first paragraph 'Another important point that you should always keep in mind is that you cannot stay healthy by skipping meals'.

So, to make sure that your heart keeps healthy all the time, have a whole some meal.

61. According to the given passage, You must drink at least 10 to 12 glasses of water in the entire day. This maintains a very rate of metabolism.

Thus, option (b) is correct answer.

62. According to the given passage, Certain hormones those are essential for making antibodies that are capable of fighting against diseases and infections are released by our body when we are happy . Thus, option C is the correct answer.

63. From the given passage we conclude that a happy heart is the indication that the person is healthy is correct explanation of the given statement.

64. •Keynesian revolution was a change in theory concerning the factors determining employment levels in the overall economy.

•In 1936, Keynesian Revolution took place in the publication of Keynes' General Theory.

•In Keynesian view, employers will be able to make a profit by employing all available workers as long as workers drop their wages below the value of the total output they are able to produce

65. The WTO officially commenced on 1 January 1995 under the Marrakesh Agreement, signed by 123 nations on 15 April 1994, replacing the General Agreement on Tariffs and Trade (GATT), which commenced in 1948.

Q.1 The term discovered small field (DSF), which was recently making news is related to which of the following ?

A. Petroleum Sector **B.** Nuclear Minerals
C. Quantum Science **D.** (A) and (B) both
E. none of these

Q.2 What is the number of members in the Monetary Policy Committee (MPC)?

A. 4 **B.** 5
C. 6 **D.** 7
E. none of these

Q.3 A persistent fall in the general price level of goods and services is known as __:

A. Deflation **B.** Disinflation
C. Stagflation **D.** Depression
E. none of these

Q.4 In which year Bombay Stock Exchange was established?

A. 1865 **B.** 1875
C. 1880 **D.** 1890
E. none of these

Q.5 Which among the following is a most suitable example of double counting in national income ?

A. Wages of bus and train drivers
B. Cotton output and cotton cloth output
C. Electricity output and water output
D. Tax receipts and earnings of inland revenue officials
E. none of these

Q.6 In September 1999, which organization established the Poverty Reduction and Growth Facility (PRGF) to make the objectives of poverty reduction and growth more central to lending operations in its poorest member countries?

A. Asian Development Bank
B. International Monetary Fund
C. World Bank
D. US Federal Bank
E. none of these

Q.7 Which among the following is a direct tax?

A. Excise Duty **B.** Sales Tax
C. VAT **D.** Income Tax
E. none of these

Q.8 Which among the following is an anti-inflationary measure?

A. Stagflation **B.** Hyper inflation
C. Disinflation **D.** Deflation
E. none of these

Q.9 The name of UTI bank ltd was changed in 2007 as which of the following?

A. AXIS bank **B.** YES Bank
C. Indian Bank **D.** Federal Bank
E. none of these

Q.10 Which among the following body in India requires to protect the interests of consumers against anti-competitive practices of all market entities?

A. National Consumer Forum
B. Competition Commission of India
C. National Consumer Disputes Redressal Commission
D. Central Vigilance Commission
E. none of these

Q.11 Which among the following is assisted by Safety Review Committee for Operating Plants (SARCOP) for its functioning in India?

A. Atomic Energy Regulatory Board
B. Coconut Development Board
C. National Dairy Development Board
D. National Science & Technology Entrepreneurship Development Board
E. none of these

Q.12 Which of the following agency is helping India's Integrated Coastal Zone Management (ICZM) Project?

A. JICA: Japan International Cooperation Agency
B. ADB: Asian Development Bank
C. WB: World Bank
D. DIDA : Danish International Development Agency
E. A and B both

Q.13 Which of the following Five year Plans set the lowest growth target?

A. 1st **B.** 2nd
C. 3rd **D.** 4th
E. none of these

Q.14 Many a times we read in the newspapers about margin requirements. Which of the following correctly indicates margin requirements?

A. Margin requirements aim at the regulation of the volume of credit as well as flow of the credit
B. Margin requirements imply that every bank has to keep certain minimum cash reserves with the reserve bank of India
C. Margin requirements imply that every bank has to keep certain proportion of its total deposits in the form of cash with it self
D. Margin requirements imply to a cushion against the decline in the value of the security
E. none of these

Q.15 Who among the following is the chairman of "Takeover Regulations Advisory Committee"?

A. C Achuthan **B.** Deepak Parekh

C. Kiran Karnik	**D.** Rajesh Mehra

E. none of these

Q.16 Year 1921 is known as a year of "Great Divide" in the demographic history of India. After that in which decade there was a slight dip in the rate of decadal population growth in India?

A. 1921-31	**B.** 1931-41

C. 1941-51	**D.** 1951-61

E. none of these

Q.17 Any banking company can undertake any business other than the banking business in accordance with the provisions contained in which among the following acts?

A. Reserve Bank of India Act

B. Negotiable Instruments Act

C. Banking Regulation Act

D. (A) and (B) both

E. none of these

Q.18 Which of the following is / are correct statements regarding Narrow Banking?

1. In Narrow Banking, Banks just accept deposits and provide loans.

2. In Narrow Banking, there is rarely Asset Liability Mismatch.

Select the correct option from the codes given below:

A. Only 1 is correct

B. Only 2 is correct

C. Both 1 & 2 are correct

D. Neither 1 nor 2 is correct

E. can't be determine

Q.19 Which among the following state has highest number of Export Oriented Units in India?

A. Tamil Nadu	**B.** Maharastra

C. Karnataka	**D.** Andhra Pradesh

E. none of these

Q.20 Many a times, we read in the newspapers about a term "contra funds". Which among the following is a correct statement about the contra funds?

A. Contra funds are likely to perform well in the long run, but not in the short term

B. Contra funds are likely to perform well in the short run, but not in the long term

C. Contra funds are come with a guaranteed return and issued as a contract

D. Contra funds are those funds in which ONLY corporate investors are allowed to invest

E. none of these

Q.21 Which among the following is the correct fullform of NCPR — a modified version of Trai's 'Do Not Call Registry' list.?

A. National Consumer Protection Register

B. National Customer Privacy Registry

C. National Customer Protection Registry

D. National Customer Preference Registry

E. none of these

Q.22 Portfolio risk is best measured by the___________.

A. expected value

B. portfolio beta

C. weighted average of individual risk

D. standard deviation

E. none of these

Q.23 The focal point of financial management in a firm is _______.

A. the number and types of products or services provided by the firm

B. the minimization of the amount of taxes paid by the firm

C. the creation of value for shareholders

D. the dollars profits earned by the firm

E. none of these

Q.24 Consider the following Statements:

1. Core Inflation is essentially demand driven.

2. Core Inflation includes items that face volatile price movement.

Which of the following Statement(s) given above is/are correct?

A. Only 1	**B.** Only 2

C. Both 1 and 2	**D.** Neither 1 nor 2

E. can't be determine

Q.25 With reference to the CTS 2010 (cheque truncation system), consider the following statements:

1. CTS 2010 provides faster, more secure and more cost effective clearing of cheques

2. CTS cheques are payable at par at all branches of the originating bank

Which among the above statements is / are correct ?

A. Only 1	**B.** Only 2

C. Both 1 & 2	**D.** Neither 1 nor 2

E. can't be determine

Q.26 Which of the following is / are correct statements about market capitalization?

1. It is total value of authorized shares of a publicly traded company

2. It is a robust indicator of economic growth

3. It is a measure of investors' wealth

Select the correct option from the codes given below:

A. Only 1 & 2	**B.** Only 1 & 3

C. Only 2 & 3	**D.** Only 3

E. none of these

Q.27 With respect to Bharatiya Mahila Bank consider the following statements:

1. It is the first specialised bank in the world for women

2. The board has all woman directors

3. It prioritises lending to women and their empowerment

Which of the above statements is/are correct?

A. Only 1 & 3	**B.** Only 2 & 3

C. Only 3	**D.** 1, 2 & 3

E. none of these

Q.28 The IMF quota system was created to raise funds for loans by its member states. Which among the following decide the quota for a member?

1. GDP
2. Openness of the Economy
3. International reserves
4. Human Development Index

Select the correct option from the codes given below:

A. Only 1 & 2   **B.** Only 2 & 3
C. Only 1, 2 & 3   **D.** 1, 2, 3 & 4
E. none of these

Q.29 With which of the following neighbours, India has an Inland water transit and trade protocol?

A. Sri Lanka   **B.** Bangladesh
C. Pakistan   **D.** Myanmar
E. none of these

Q.30 The Annual percentage yield (APY) reflecting the total amount of interest paid on __:

1. Current Account
2. Saving Account
3. Certificates of Deposits

Which among the above is / are correct?

A. Only 1   **B.** Only 2 & 3
C. Only 3   **D.** 1, 2 & 3
E. none of these

Q.31 The green shoe option is a clause in the underwriting agreement of an IPO, which allows to ___?

A. Sell additional shares
B. Record Investor demands
C. Purchase the shares back from Investors
D. Both (A) and (B)
E. None of them

Q.32 With reference to the deposit accounts facilities to the NRIs, which among the following is / are rupee-denominated accounts?

1. NRE account
2. NRO account
3. FCNR account

Select the correct option from the codes given below:

A. Only 1 & 2   **B.** Only 2 & 3
C. Only 1 & 3   **D.** 1, 2 & 3
E. none of these

Q.33 In banking language, which among the following is called Contingent Liability of the banks?

A. Fund based lending
B. Non fund based lending
C. Priority sector lending
D. Statutory pre-emptions
E. None of these

Q.34 Recently, the prime minister of India announced some incentives for the MSME sector. MSME Sector in India accounts for more than half of India's __:

1. Total number of industrial enterprises
2. Industrial production in rupee terms
3. Gross Domestic Product

Select the correct option from the codes given below:

A. Only 1   **B.** Only 1 & 2
C. Only 1 & 3   **D.** 1, 2 & 3
E. None of these

Q.35 Which of the following bodies procures, distributes, exports and imports agricultural commodities?

A. FCI   **B.** NAFED
C. NABARD   **D.** (A) and (B) both
E. None of these

Q.36 Which among the following activities can result in widening of revenue deficit of the government?

1. Government approves the revised pay scale as per 7th Pay commission
2. Government announces a waiver of farm loans
3. Oil prices decrease sharply
4. Government launches successful auction of coal mines

Select the correct option from the codes given below:

A. Only 1 & 2   **B.** Only 2 & 3
C. Only 1, 2 & 3   **D.** 1, 2,3 & 4
E. None of these

Q.37 Consider the following countries:

1. China
2. India
3. Japan
4. Russia

Which of the above is/are NOT members of G4 nations?

A. 1 and 2 Only   **B.** 2 and 3 Only
C. 1 and 4 Only   **D.** 3 and 4 Only
E. None of these

Q.38 Goldilocks Economy is characterized by:

1. low unemployment rate
2. low inflation
3. steady GDP growth

Which of the above statements is/are correct?

A. 3 Only   **B.** 2 and 3 Only
C. 1, 2 and 3   **D.** (A) and (B) only
E. None of these

Q.39 Which of the following is/are the major objectives of National Rural Livelihood Mission?

1. Poverty alleviation
2. Promoting self employment
3. Organize the poor into Self Help Groups

Select the correct answer from the codes given below:

A. Only 1 & 2   **B.** Only 2 & 3
C. Only 1 & 3   **D.** 1, 2 & 3
E. None of these

Q.40 Consider the following fruit capitals with fruits they are known for:

1. Kotgarh – Apples
2. Mahabaleshwar – Strawberry
3. Siliguri – Pineapples

Which of the above is/are correct?

A. 1 & 2 Only   **B.** 3 Only
C. 2 & 3 Only   **D.** 1, 2 & 3
E. None of these

Q.41 Which of the following is not a merit of Well Irrigation?

A. Cheapest
B. Independent
C. Reliable
D. Draw neighbour area water
E. None of these

Q.42 Consider the following differences between the Credit and Debit card:

1. While credit card can be used with zero balance in the account, to use debit card one must have balance in saving/current account
2. While a credit card is connected to the bank or financial institution that issued the card, debit card is connected to a personal bank account

Which of the above statements is/are correct?

A. 1 Only   **B.** 2 Only
C. Both 1 & 2   **D.** Neither 1 nor 2
E. Can't be determine

Q.43 Consider the following statements about the Small Finance Bank:

1. It can undertake basic banking activities of accepting deposits and lending to small businesses
2. Foreign Direct Investment is permitted in Small Finance Banks

Which of the above statements is/are correct?

A. 1 Only   **B.** 2 Only
C. Both 1 & 2   **D.** Neither 1 nor 2
E. can't be determine

Q.44 Consider the following indexes:

1. CPI Agricultural Labour
2. CPI Industrial Labour
3. CPI Urban Non-Manual Employees

Which of the above is/are published by the Labour Bureau?

A. 1 & 2 Only   **B.** 3 Only
C. 2 & 3 Only   **D.** 1, 2 & 3
E. None of these

Q.45 The Sugamya Bharat Abhiyaan programme:

A. envisages to built friendly physical and infrastructure environment for Persons with Disabilities.
B. provides easy short term loans to unemployed youth for entrepreneurship.
C. envisages to generate awareness about clean and green society, and use of technologies to treat the waste material.
D. aims to uplift of urban and rural poor through enhancement of livelihood opportunities.
E. None of these

Q.46 Though India has registered significant decline in Maternal Mortality Ratio (MMR) in recent years, yet it is a grave health concern for the country. In this context, which of the following is / are correct observations?

1. In India Hemorrhage accounts for more than one-third maternal mortality
2. The largest reason of death in Indian women post delivery is due to anaemia

Select the correct option from the codes given below:

A. Only 1   **B.** Only 2
C. Both 1 & 2   **D.** Neither 1 nor 2
E. Can't be determine

Q.47 Which of the following countries collaborated with Bhilai Steel plant for its establishment?

A. Britain   **B.** USA
C. Russia   **D.** Japan
E. None of the above

Q.48 FFC stands for which of the following?

A. Foreign Finance Corporation
B. Federation of Football Council
C. Film Finance Corporation
D. Flood Forecasting Centre
E. None of the above

Q.49 In which type of economy is government interference is limited?

A. Socialist economy   **B.** Market Economy
C. Mixed Economy   **D.** (A) and (B) Both
E. None of the above

Q.50 Which of the below problems occur in an economy?

A. What to produce?
B. How to produce?
C. For whom to produce?
D. (A) and (B) Both
E. All of the above

Q.51 Which of the following statements is true regarding a mixed economy?

A. Private property is not encouraged
B. Monopoly doesn't exist in market
C. The government play a role in the production and distribution of resources
D. Consumers choice is limited
E. None of these

Q.52 What was the Indian economy share in the world economy after Independence?
A. 2.3%   B. 3.2%   C. 3.3%   D. 3.8%
E. 7.8%

Q.53 What is the full form of the initiative AIM, launched by NITI Aayog?
A. Atal Indian Mission
B. Atal Innovation Mission
C. Atal Inovative Mind
D. Atal Indian Medicine
E. None of these

Q.54 Which three states partnered with NITI Aayog to improve healthcare delivery?
A. Uttar Pradesh,bihar,Odisha
B. Uttar Pradesh,karnataka,Odisha
C. Uttar Pradesh,bihar,Karnataka
D. Uttar Pradesh,Assam,Karnataka
E. None of these

Q.55 What is the FDI allowed under direct route for food product e-commerce?
A. 100%   B. 51%   C. 43%   D. 75%
E. 98%

Q.56 Which of the following are reasons for Farm Crisis in India?
1. Monsoon Failure
2. Lack of remunerative price
3. Lack of proper Irrigation facilities
4. Unavailability Formal banking
5. High Input cost
Choose the correct option from the codes given below:
A. 1,2 and 4 only   B. 1,2 and 5 only
C. 1,2,3 and 5 only   D. 1,2 and 3 only
E. All the above

Q.57 Which of the following is not a category of seeds?
A. Breeder   B. Foundation
C. Certified   D. Edged
E. None of these

Q.58 What is the chemical composition of Urea?
A. Carbamide   B. Carbide
C. Creatinine   D. (A) and (B) Both
E. None of the above

Q.59 Which of the following is not a problem in the Indian agricultural sector?
A. Low productivity
B. Lack of modernization
C. Land reforms
D. Low dependence of people
E. None of these

Q.60 Which among the following is caused by a lack of proper infrastructure?
A. Low Export cost
B. Less devlopment of interior region
C. More imports
D. High Cost of goods
E. None of these

Q.61 Which Five-year plan oversaw the beginning of economic liberalization?
A. 5th   B. 6th
C. 7th   D. 8th
E. None of these

Q.62 How many SDG's are selected by NITI Aayog for the SDG index?
A. 14   B. 13
C. 15   D. 12
E. None of these

Q.63 Which Indian organization launched the Samvesh initiative?
A. Niti Aayog
B. Department of Science and technology
C. Department of Bio technology
D. PMO
E. None of these

Q.64 Which among the following is a Kharif Crop?
A. Wheat   B. Tobacco
C. Mustard   D. Jute
E. None of these

Q.65 What is the Horticulture premium in the PM Fasal Bima Yojna?
A. 5%   B. 2%
C. 4%   D. 6%
E. None of these

// Smart Answer Sheet //

Correct Indicates percentage of students who answered questions correctly.

Skipped Indicates percentage of students who skipped questions.

Q.	Ans.	Correct / Skipped
1	A	77.87 % / 19.55 %
2	C	89.17 % / 10.67 %
3	A	85.93 % / 11.72 %
4	B	85.87 % / 13.0 %
5	B	77.09 % / 22.31 %
6	B	82.72 % / 11.04 %
7	D	76.49 % / 19.72 %
8	C	82.51 % / 12.83 %
9	A	76.49 % / 18.02 %
10	B	78.6 % / 20.57 %
11	A	87.19 % / 12.01 %
12	C	79.32 % / 16.31 %
13	A	90.0 % / 10.0 %
14	D	85.24 % / 10.91 %
15	A	88.31 % / 10.16 %
16	C	83.11 % / 15.32 %
17	C	82.45 % / 16.47 %
18	B	77.02 % / 21.94 %
19	C	89.51 % / 10.15 %
20	A	82.94 % / 13.15 %
21	D	83.83 % / 12.32 %
22	C	87.74 % / 10.1 %
23	C	82.08 % / 11.82 %
24	A	86.51 % / 11.61 %
25	C	80.76 % / 13.17 %
26	D	85.57 % / 11.22 %
27	B	81.6 % / 10.5 %
28	C	84.54 % / 13.12 %
29	B	81.34 % / 15.33 %
30	B	87.73 % / 11.97 %
31	A	78.71 % / 13.96 %
32	A	76.09 % / 11.52 %
33	B	86.13 % / 10.62 %
34	A	83.93 % / 11.1 %
35	B	77.02 % / 16.4 %
36	A	86.78 % / 11.75 %
37	C	83.08 % / 11.36 %
38	C	83.47 % / 12.76 %
39	D	89.88 % / 10.08 %
40	D	87.84 % / 11.71 %
41	D	86.4 % / 10.08 %
42	C	81.78 % / 17.24 %
43	C	80.96 % / 11.04 %
44	A	78.54 % / 21.37 %
45	A	82.52 % / 13.97 %
46	C	78.86 % / 16.06 %
47	C	80.45 % / 14.85 %
48	C	84.93 % / 13.11 %
49	B	87.52 % / 12.15 %
50	E	77.25 % / 10.69 %
51	C	77.19 % / 11.71 %
52	D	85.6 % / 10.02 %
53	B	78.31 % / 14.0 %
54	D	89.24 % / 10.62 %
55	A	77.76 % / 11.97 %
56	E	85.26 % / 13.76 %
57	D	80.38 % / 19.39 %
58	A	76.98 % / 11.63 %
59	D	76.96 % / 10.46 %
60	B	80.04 % / 18.94 %
61	B	84.43 % / 11.37 %
62	B	84.37 % / 13.21 %
63	A	88.28 % / 10.11 %
64	D	83.2 % / 10.37 %
65	A	79.82 % / 17.32 %

Performance Analysis	
Avg. Score (%)	43.0%
Toppers Score (%)	63.0%
Your Score	

//Hints and Solutions//

1. Discovered small field (DSF) auction happened recently. The term is related to oil sector.

2. MPC has all six members.

3. Inflation refers to rise in general price level of goods and services, deflation is fall in general price level of goods and services. Deflation is inflation in negative zone, i.e. a decrease in the general price level of goods and services.

4. The Bombay Stock Exchange (BSE) is the first and largest securities market in India and was established in 1875 as the Native Share and Stock Brokers' Association.

5. Cotton output and cotton cloth output is a most suitable example of double counting in national income .

6. In September 1999, International Monetary Fund organization established the Poverty Reduction and Growth Facility (PRGF) to make the objectives of poverty reduction and growth more central to lending operations in its poorest member countries.

7. Direct tax is a tax directly paid to the government by the individuals or organizations on whom it is imposed. The main examples of Direct Taxes are Income Tax, Gift Tax, Wealth Tax, Property Tax etc.

8. Disinflation is an anti-inflationary measure.

9. The name of UTI bank ltd was changed in 2007 as AXIS bank.

10. The Competition Commission of India (CCI) was set up to replace the anachronistic Monopolies and Restrictive Trade Practices Commission (MRTPC). It was established to eliminate practices that adversely affect competition in different industries/areas and protect interests of consumers and ensure freedom of trade. The Competition Act of 2002 called for the creation of CCI. However, it was established in 2003 and became fully functional only by 2009. The CCI is a quasi-judicial body which gives opinions to statutory authorities and also deals with other cases. It has one chairman and six members. It is the youngest and the only cross-sector regulator in India.

11. Atomic Energy Regulatory Board is assisted by Safety Review Committee for Operating Plants (SARCOP) for its functioning in India.

12. WB: World Bank agency is helping India's Integrated Coastal Zone Management (ICZM) Project.

13. Five year Plans set the lowest growth target 1st.

14. Option 1: Quantitative control aim at the regulation of the volume of credit as well as flow of the credit, qualitative control aim at the regulation of flow of the credit.

Option 2 : every bank has to keep certain minimum cash reserves with the reserve bank of India – Cash Reserve Requirements,

3- every bank has to keep certain proportion of its total deposits in the form of cash with it self-Statutory Liquidity ratio,

Option 4 – certain rate at which it discounts the bills of exchange of the commercial bank -Bank Rate .

Margin requirements imply to a cushion against the decline in the value of the security

15. C Achuthan is the chairman of "Takeover Regulations Advisory Committee".

16. Year 1921 is known as a year of "Great Divide" in the demographic history of India. After that in 1941-51 decade there was a slight dip in the rate of decadal population growth in India.

17. Any banking company can undertake any business other than the banking business in accordance with the provisions contained in Banking Regulation Act acts.

18. Narrow Banking involves mobilizing the large part of the deposits in Risk Free assets such as Government Securities. It does not mean that the banks limit their activities to only accepting deposits and providing loans. Thus first statement is incorrect. Since large part of deposits are in government securities, there is rarely asset liability mismatch. Thus, option 2 is correct.

19. Karnataka state has highest number of Export Oriented Units in India.

20. A contra fund is defined by its against-the-wind kind of investing style. The manager of a contra fund bets against the prevailing market trends by buying assets that are either under-performing or depressed at that point in time.

 Contra funds are likely to perform well in the long run, but not in the short term.

21. Fullform of NCPR is National Customer Preference Registry.

22. Portfolio risk is best measured by the weighted average of individual risk. Portfolio risk is a chance that the combination of assets or units, within the investments that you own, fail to meet financial objectives.

23. The focal point of financial management in a firm is the creation of value for shareholders.

24. Manufacturing inflation, also known as 'core inflation', is essentially driven by demand and makes up the non-food basket of the wholesale price index.

Core inflation is a measures of inflation that excludes items that face volatile price movement, notably food and energy. It is, therefore, a preferred tool for framing long-term policy.

25. 1. CTS 2010 provides faster, more secure and more cost effective clearing of cheques

2. CTS cheques are payable at par at all branches of the originating bank

26. Market capitalization (or market cap) is the total value of the issued shares of a publicly traded company; it is equal to the share price times the number of shares outstanding. As outstanding stock is bought and sold in public markets, capitalization could be used as a proxy for the public opinion of a company's net worth and is a determining factor in some forms of stock valuation. It's a measure of investor's health.

27. India is the third country in the world to have a bank especially for women, after Pakistan and Tanzania.

28. Quota involves several economic criteria such as- Member's GDP, Its openness to trade, its volume of Current Account Transactions and its level of official revenues.

29. An Inland water transit and trade protocol exists between India and Bangladesh under which inland vessels of one country can transit through the specified routes of the other country. The existing protocol routes are (i) Kolkata-Pandu-Kolkata, (ii) Kolkata-Karimganj – Kolkata, (iii) Rajshahi-Dhulian-Rajshahi and (iv) Pandu-Karimganj-Pandu. For inter-country trade, four ports of call have been designated in each country namely; Haldia, Kolkata, Pandu and Karimganj in India and Narayanganj, Khulna, Mongla and Sirajganj in Bangladesh. Under the Protocol, 50:50 cargo sharing by Indian and Bangladeshi vessels is permitted both for transit and inter country trade.

30. The Annual percentage yield (APY) reflecting the total amount of interest paid on Saving Account and Certificates of Deposits.

31. The green shoe option is a clause in the underwriting agreement of an IPO, which allows to sell additional shares, usually 15%, to the public if the demand exceeds expectations and the stock trades above its offering price. This option, also known as the over-allotment provision. It gets its name from the Green Shoe company, which was the first company to allow such an option.

32. Both NRE and NRO accounts are rupee dominated accounts, which means funds in the NRO/ NRE account are maintained in Indian Rupees. This means that the foreign currency is converted to Indian rupees at the prevailing foreign exchange rates when the money is deposited into the account.

33. In Non-fund based lending, bank does not make any funds outlay but only gives assurance. The "letter of credit" and "bank guarantees" fall into the category of non-funding loans. The non-funding loan can be converted to a fund-based advance if the client fails to fulfil the term of contract with the counterparty. In banking language, the non-funding advances are called Contingent Liability of the banks.

34. MSMEs in India account for over 95% of the total number of industrial enterprises. Thus first statement is correct. MSME contributes about 45% of the industrial production and 37.5% of the national GDP. Thus, second and third statements are not correct. Further, MSME accounts for 40% of the total l exports from India.

35. NAFED is the apex body in cooperative sector and deals in procurement , distribution, export and import of selected agricultural commodities.

36. From Finance Commission Report Union Government undertook several fiscal expansionary measures such as revision of pay scales based on the recommendations of the Sixth Pay Commission, waiver of farm loans and the expansion of the Mahatma Gandhi National Rural Employment Guarantee Act (MGNREGA) to all districts from the 200 districts it was originally slated to cover. In addition, oil prices escalated sharply, leading to a rise in subsidy. It then rose to 5.2 per cent in 2009-10 because of a substantial increase in revenue expenditures on subsidies, interest payments and salaries and pensions.

37. The G4 nations includes India, Japan, Germany and Brazil.The G4's primary aim is the permanent member seatson the Security Council.

38. Goldilocks is an economy that is not so hot that it causes inflation, and not so cold that it causes a recession. There are no exact markers of a Goldilocks economy, but it is characterized by a lowunemployment rate, increasing asset prices (stocks, real estate, etc.), low interest rates, brisk but steady GDP growth and low inflation.

39. National Rural Livelihood Mission (NRLM) is a poverty alleviation project implemented by Ministry of Rural Development. This scheme is focused on promoting self-employment and organization of rural poor. The basic idea behind this programme is to organize the poor into SHG (Self Help Groups) groups and make them capable for self-employment.

40. All of the above given pairs are correctly matched.

Siliguri is situated in the plains at the base of the Himalayan Mountains in West Bengal. The place is well known for cultivation of pineapples. Kotgarh is a famous place near Shimla and is very famous for its good quality apples. Mahabaleshwar an acclaimed hill station is also the Strawberry capital of India.

41. Well irrigation is the simplest, cheapest, and independent source of irrigation and can be used as and when the necessity arises. It is more reliable during periods of drought when surface water dries up.

Tubewells can draw a lot of groundwater from its neighboring areas and make the ground dry and unfit for agriculture. This is a demerit.

42. Both are correct statements

Credit cards are lines of credit. When we use a credit card, the issuer puts money toward the transaction. While when we use a debit card to buy something, money is deducted from our bank account. While there is a the credit limit set by the credit issuer in case of credit card, there is no such limit in case of debit card and it can be used as per sum available in the account linked to debit card.

43. Both are correct statements

Small Finance Bank aims to provide a whole suite of basic banking products such as deposits and supply of credit mainly to small farmers, micro and small industries, and other unorganised sector entities through high technology-low cost operations.

44. Labour Bureau publishes the CPI Numbers for Agricultural Labourers & CPI Numbers for Industrial Workers. CPI Urban Non-Manual Employees is published by Central Statistical Organization.

45. First option is the correct answer.Department of Empowerment of Persons with Disabilities (DEPwD), Ministry of Social Justice and Empowerment, has formulated the Accessible India Campaign (Sugamya Bharat Abhiyan), as a nation-wide campaign for achieving universal accessibility for Persons with Disabilities. It will provide for:Ramps in public buildings; Provision of toilets for wheelchair user;Braille symbols and auditory signals in elevators or lifts and Ramps in hospitals, primary health centres and other rehabilitation centres etc.

46. Maternal Mortality is a cause of great concern. The major causes of these deaths have been identified as hemorrhage (both ante and post partum), toxemia (Hypertension during pregnancy), anemia, obstructed labour, puerperal sepsis (infections after delivery) and unsafe abortion.

47. The Bhilai plant and the Bokaro Steel Plant in Jharkhand were commissioned to collaborate with Russia. The agreement for constructing Bhilai plant was signed with the Soviet Union in 1955 after Indian Prime Minster Jawaharlal Nehru visited Magnitogorsk, the capital of Russian iron and steel works.

48. The Film Finance Corporation (FFC), is India's state funding body for films. The 1927 Indian Cinematograph Committee recommended such a state-sponsored agency in its Report of the Indian Cinematograph Committee.

49. Market economy or capitalist economy works on the laissez-faire principle where there is limited gov and market forces of demand and supply plays a key role in its functioning.

50. The limited resources is the main reason for the problems in economy. This leads to a question of

What to produce?

How to produce ?

And How much to produce ?

51. In a mixed economic system, there is a cross between a market economy and the Socialist economy. In the most common types of mixed economies, the market is more or less free of government ownership except for a few key areas like transportation or sensitive industries like defense and railroad.

52. India's economy had a 3.8% share of world income in 1952 after Independence from the British empire. Currently, India's share in the world economy is 7.5% of world GDP.

53. Atal Innovation Mission(AIM) is a flagship initiative set up by the NITI Aayog to promote innovation and entrepreneurship across the length and breadth of the country, based on a detailed study and deliberations on innovation and entrepreneurial needs of India in the years ahead.

54. NITI Aayog has selected Uttar Pradesh, Assam, and Karnataka to improve healthcare delivery and key outcomes in these States. It is part of the Cooperative federalism. It was launched in 2017.

55. The Government of India has allowed 100 percent FDI in the marketing of food products and in food product e-commerce under the automatic route.

56. The farm crisis in India is mainly due to back-to-back monsoon failures and falling crop prices. All the above-mentioned options are the other reasons.

57. There are four generally recognized classes of seeds:

1. Breeder seed

2. Foundation seed

3. Registered seed

4. Certified seed

58. Carbamide chemical name and the composition of Urea is $CO(NH_2)_2$.

59. Indian agriculture sector has many problems like low agricultural productivity, lack of modernisation and lack of diversification in its output, high dependence are some of the problems. APMC reforms are an issue in India but recently e-nam has been introduced.

60. The lack of infrastructure creates a lot of problems mainly regarding the development of interior regions. The two most vital sectors i.e. agriculture and industry could not make much headway in the absence of proper infrastructural facilities in the country. Moreover, due to the absence of proper infrastructural facilities, the development potential of different regions of the country largely remains under-utilized.

61. The Sixth Five-Year Plan from 1980-85 marked the beginning of economic liberalization. Price controls were eliminated and ration shops were closed. This led to an increase in food prices and an increase in the cost of living. Family planning was also expanded in order to prevent overpopulation.

62. The SDG index by NITI Aayog has been constructed spanning across 13 out of 17 SDGs (leaving out Goals 12, 13, 14, and 17). It tracks the progress of all the States and Union Territories (UTs) on a set of 62 National Indicators, measuring their progress on the outcomes of interventions and schemes of the Government of India.

63. 'Samavesh' is a program launched by the NITI Aayog to link together various lead Knowledge and Research Institutions to catalyze development processes, enhance institutional capacity development and enable a field level interface with the community for mutual enrichment.

64. Kharif season is from June to November. Rice, Maize, millets, cotton, jute, sugarcane, groundnut are some of the Kharif crops.

65. The PM Fasal Bima Yojna is launched to provide crop insurance to farmers. Ministry of agriculture is implementing it. All crops are covered in it. Kharif premium is 2%, RAbi is 1.5% and Horticulture is 5%.

Q.1 If the value of coefficient of determination is 0.64, then what is the value of coefficient of correlation?

A. 0.4   **B.** 0.8   **C.** 0.04   **D.** 0.08
E. 0.09

Q.2 Which state has launched a Ama Gaon, Ama Vikas (Our Village, our development) scheme to reach out to the people in rural areas and involve themselves in the developmental activities?

A. Uttar Pradesh   **B.** Bihar
C. Andhra Pradesh   **D.** Odisha
E. Madhya Pradesh

Q.3 Which of the following rates is closest to Marginal standing facility rate?

A. Liquid adjustment facility rate
B. Repo rate
C. SLR
D. Reverse repo rate
E. Call money rate

Q.4 Under Union Budget 2018, Government has allocated how much amount for rural infrastructure?

A. Rs 10 lakh crore   **B.** Rs 11 lakh crore
C. Rs 12.6 lakh crore   **D.** Rs 14.3 lakh crore
E. None of the above

Q.5 An Non-Resident Ordinary Rupee Account for non-resident Indians has a limit of ___.

A. $50000   **B.** $1 million
C. $100000   **D.** $2.5 million
E. $1.5 million

Q.6 According to the 2011 Census, the population of India was 121 crores with a decadal growth rate of

A. 9.82%   **B.** 12.3%   **C.** 15.19%   **D.** 17.64%
E. 20.21%

Q.7 In the long run, ______ plays a dominant role in determination of price

A. demand
B. supply
C. factors of production
D. climate
E. All of the above

Q.8 "India Development Update" is released by _______.

A. NITI Aayog
B. World Bank
C. International Monetary Fund
D. Department Economic Affairs
E. Central Statistics Office

Q.9 Name the premier institution that is taking care of the financial needs of importers and exporters of our country which was established in the year 1981.

A. EXPO Bank
B. Export Import Bank (EXIM)
C. Merchant Bank
D. ECGC
E. None of the above

Q.10 The Bharat Sanchar Nigam Limited (BSNL) and Vihaan Networks Limited (VNL) have signed MoU to launch ________ service to provide disaster management in India.

A. "Relief 111"   **B.** "Relief 181"
C. "Relief 123"   **D.** "Relief 99"
E. "Relief 100"

Q.11 Name the bank that has recently launched 'Project Nishchay' in partnership with the Boston Consulting Group (BCG) to accelerate its turnaround program and improve financial performance.

A. Canara Bank   **B.** IndusInd Bank
C. PNB   **D.** ICICI Bank
E. IDBI Bank

Q.12 The Asian Development Bank has announced to increase its annual lending to India to a maximum of __________ between 2018 and 2022 to help fasten inclusive economic transformation.

A. $4.0 billion   **B.** $4.5 billion
C. $3.8 billion   **D.** $3.5 billion
E. $3.2 billion

Q.13 The Insolvency and Bankruptcy Board of India (IBBI) has registered National E-Governance Services Limited (NeSL) as a/an ___________ under the IBBI Regulations, 2017.

A. Service Provider
B. Technical Assistance Unit
C. Internal Utility Service
D. Artificial Intelligence Unit
E. Information Utility

Q.14 The U.S. Federal Reserve fined HSBC Holdings PLC _______ million for "unsafe and unsound practices" in its foreign exchange trading business.

A. $175 million   **B.** $150 million
C. $100 million   **D.** $200 million
E. None of these

Q.15 Name the lender that has recently announced a new home loan scheme that overs borrowers the benefit of 1% cashback on every EMI, for the entire tenure of the loan.

A. State Bank of India
B. HDFC Bank
C. IndusInd Bank

D. Oriental Commerce Bank

E. ICICI Bank

Q.16 Name the state government for which India and the World Bank signed a $200 million Loan Agreement for the state's Agribusiness and Rural Transformation Project.

A. Tamil Nadu   **B.** Meghalaya

C. Assam   **D.** Tripura

E. Karnataka

Q.17 Name the lender that has announced the sanction of credit facilities amounting to Rs.2,317 crore to corporate for financing Grid Connected Rooftop Solar projects under the bank's program with World Bank.

A. State Bank of India

B. Reserve Bank of India

C. Syndicate Bank

D. Allahabad Bank

E. Bank of Baroda

Q.18 Which of the following bank has signed an agreement with the government to provide Rs 1,000 crore financing for food processing projects?

A. SBI   **B.** Dena Bank

C. Yes Bank   **D.** Axis Bank

E. ICICI Bank

Q.19 Central Board of Direct Taxes (CBDT) clarified that farmers do not need to quote Permanent Account Number (PAN) for cash sale of their produce up to Rs.___ lakh a day.

A. Rs 1 lakh   **B.** Rs 2 lakh

C. Rs 3 lakh   **D.** Rs 4 lakh

E. Rs 5 lakh

Q.20 A decrease in Cash Reserve Ratio (CRR) can lead to which among the following ?

1. increase in cash availability of the banks

2. increase in repo rate

3. decrease in SLR

Select the correct answer

A. 1 only   **B.** 1 and 2 only

C. 1 and 3 only   **D.** 1,2 and 3

E. None of these

Q.21 The WTO follows the principle of 'self selection'. This means :

A. countries decides to which agreement they want to be party.

B. countries decide the rate of tariff and tariff reduction

C. countries themselves decide whether they want to be in developed or developing categories.

D. (A) and (B) both

E. None of these

Q.22 Which of the following also acts as a mechanism for government lending.

1. CRR

2. Repo rate

3. Reverse repo rate

4. SLR

Select the correct answer using the codes given below.

A. 1 and 3 only   **B.** 1, 2 and 4 only

C. 1 and 4 only   **D.** 4 only

E. None of these

Q.23 With reference to foreign portfolio investments (FPI), consider the following statements :

1. FPIs are more volatile than loans from international financial institutions.

2. Foreign Direct Investments are part of FPIs.

Which of the statements given above is/are correct ?

A. 1 only   **B.** 2 only

C. Both 1 and 2   **D.** Neither 1 nor 2

E. Can't be determine

Q.24 India's central bank, RBI performs various functions. Which of these are its functions according to the RBI act, 1934.

1. managing inflation

2. acting as banker's bank

3. managing India's Forex

4. handling government's borrowing program

Select the correct answer using the codes given below.

A. 2, 3 and 4 only   **B.** 1, 2 and 3 only

C. 2 and 3 only   **D.** 1, 2, 3 and 4

E. None of these

Q.25 Which among the following can result in 'demand pull inflation' ?

1. increase in subsidy on LPG

2. increase in fuel prices

3. decrease in income tax rates

Select the correct answer using the codes given below.

A. 1 and 2 only   **B.** 1 and 3 only

C. 2 and 3 only   **D.** 1, 2 and 3

E. None of these

Q.26 The term 'narrow banking' is best described as :

A. banks acting only as payment banks

B. banking by non-banking financial companies

C. limited areas of operation by banks

D. banks lending only to risk free sectors

E. None of these

Q.27 If indirect taxes in an economy are increased, then which of the following can occur ?

1. GDP at factor cost increases

2. GDP at factor cost decreases

3. GDP at market price increases

4. GDP at market price decreases

Select the correct answer using the codes given below.

A. 1 only   **B.** 2 and 3 only

C. 3 only   **D.** 4 only

E. None of these

Q.28 Equity market instruments help in financing a firm. Which of these is/are equity market instruments ?

1. Bonds

2. Shares

3. Debentures

Select the correct answer using the codes given below.

A. 1 and 2 only
B. 2 only
C. 2 and 3 only
D. 1, 2 and 3
E. None of these

Q.29 An economy pursuing an expansionary fiscal policy can witness :

1. increase in fiscal deficit

2. increase in wages of labour

3. increase in rate of income tax

Select the correct answer using the codes given below.

A. 1 only
B. 1 and 2 only
C. 1 and 3 only
D. 1,2 and 3
E. None of these

Q.30 What is the rate of interest on Kisan Vikas Patra?

A. 7.5%
B. 7.2%
C. 7.3%
D. 7.7%
E. None of these

Q.31 In PMMY (Pradhan Mantri MUDRA Yojana), what does 'R' in MUDRA stands for?

A. Rate
B. Refinancing
C. Ratio
D. Registered
E. None of these

Q.32 Which of these states secured First Prize in 100 day work Program for Promoting Livelihoods?

A. Bengal
B. Punjab
C. Assam
D. Rajasthan
E. None of these

Q.33 In the Universal debt relief scheme, people with annual income of Rs _______ or less, outstanding loans of Rs 35,000 or less, and assets worth Rs 20,000 or less may be eligible.

A. 40,000
B. 50,000
C. 60,000
D. 70,000
E. None of these

Q.34 In which of the following schemes, the localisation condition has been incorporated by the NITI Aayog to avail the benefits of the scheme?

A. FAME – I Scheme
B. FAME – II Scheme
C. Green Urban Transport Scheme (GUTP)
D. (A) and (B) both
E. None of these

Q.35 Which of the following will be the first Indian state to roll out Universal Basic Income scheme?

A. Punjab
B. Sikkim
C. Himachal Pradesh
D. Gujarat
E. None of these

Q.36 As per the interim budget 2019, the Government will make how many villages into Digital Villages over next five years?

A. 50 thousand
B. 3 lakh
C. 80 thousand
D. 1 lakh
E. None of these

Q.37 When does an account become Inactive ?

A. Not operated for more than 12 months
B. Not operated for more than 24 months
C. Not operated for more than 48 months
D. Not operated for more than 6 months
E. None of these

Q.38 Reduction in loan amount over a period of time is called as?

A. Arbitrage
B. Alteration
C. Annuity
D. Amortization
E. None of these

Q.39 What is the reason for cost push inflation?

A. Increase in wage rate
B. Increase in interest rate
C. Increase in the price of raw material
D. Increase in indirect tax
E. None of these

Q.40 Consider following statement regarding brown label ATM

i) Brown label ATMs have the logo of outsourcing bank which has outsourced the work

ii) The company is required to install 1/3rd of white label ATMs in semi urban and rural areas.

iii) RBI is directly involved with the set up of brown label ATM

iv) Indicash was the first brown label ATM opened in India

Which of the following statement is incorrect?

A. ii, iii and iv only
B. ii and iii only
C. i, ii and iii only
D. iv only
E. None of these

Q.41 Co - operative banks in India do not finance rural areas under

A. Farming
B. Cattle
C. Milk
D. Industries
E. None of these

Q.42 Debit cards

A. Are plastic cards embedded with electro magnetic identification

B. Are issued by banks to its customers who could use them to pay for their purchases or services at specified points of sale terminals

C. Facilitate the customers to effect the transactions on their accounts, remotely

D. (A) and (B) both

E. All of these

Q.43 Which of the following is/are true regarding the North East in the interim budget of 2019?

A. Allocation to be increased by 21% to Rs. 58,166 crore in

2019-20.
B. Arunachal Pradesh came on the air map recently.
C. Meghalaya, Tripura and Mizoram came on India's rail map for the first time.
D. (A) and (B) both
E. All of these

Q.44 Which of the following statements is/are correct regarding Electoral Bond Scheme 2018?
A. A citizen of India or incorporated or established in India can purchase the Electoral Bonds.
B. An individual either singly or jointly with other individuals can purchase the Electoral Bonds.
C. A political party can encash the Electoral Bonds only through a bank account with an authorised bank.
D. (A) and (B) both
E. All of the above

Q.45 A report titled 'Sand and Sustainability: finding new solutions for environmental governance of global sand resources' was released by the United Nations Environment Programme. India ranked at what position in the report?
A. 2   **B.** 5
C. 4   **D.** 3
E. None of these

Q.46 Women and Child Development Ministry has approved projects worth over Rs _______ crore under the Nirbhaya fund for eight major cities to make them safer for women.
A. 1,968   **B.** 1,863
C. 2,900   **D.** 2,568
E. None of these

Q.47 The 2020s are set to be the Asian decade, with the continent dominating an exclusive list of economies expected to sustain growth rates of around _______%.
A. 5   **B.** 6
C. 7   **D.** 8
E. None of these

Q.48 'NISM' established by which institute?
A. IRDAI   **B.** RBI
C. SEBI   **D.** NABARD
E. None of these

Q.49 Read the following statements:-
1. The Union Cabinet has approved the North East Industrial Development Scheme (NEIDS), 2017.
2. In order to promote employment in the North East States, Government is incentivizing primarily the MSME Sector through this scheme.
3. The newly introduced scheme shall promote industrialization in the States of the North Eastern Region and will boost employment and income generation.

Which of the following above statement/statements is/are true?
A. Only 1   **B.** Only 2
C. Only 3   **D.** 1 and 2 only

E. All of the above

Q.50 Regional Rural Banks (RRBs) were established in
A. 1956   **B.** 1950
C. 1980   **D.** 1975
E. None of these

Q.51 The agency which is related to mutual funds is
A. SEBI   **B.** IRDA
C. RBI   **D.** AMFI
E. None of these

Q.52 Initial coin offering is related to which of the following?
A. Equity
B. Stock shares
C. Bonds and securities
D. Digital currencies
E. None of these

Q.53 Which one statement is incorrect about Securities and Exchange Board of India?
A. It was established in the year 1992
B. The chairman who is nominated by Union Government of India.
C. One member from the Reserve Bank of India.
D. The present chairman is U.K.Sinha
E. None of these

Q.54 What does CAGR mean when it is used in relation to a company stock?
A. Compound Annual growth rate.
B. Company Annual growth rate
C. Componud accumulated growth rate
D. Company accelerated growth rate
E. None of these

Q.55 Industrial output contracted _______% in March 2019 due to slowdown in the manufacturing sector.
A. 0.1   **B.** 0.2
C. 0.3   **D.** 0.4
E. None of these

Q.56 What does R stands in the term 'INROADS"
A. Real   **B.** Reserve
C. Repo   **D.** Risk
E. None of these

Q.57 The objectives of setting up SIDBI are
A. To initiate steps for technological upgradation and modernization of existing units
B. Supply of agricultural and other production requirements
C. To promote employment - oriented industries in semi - urban areas and to check migration of population to big cities
D. (A) and (B) both
E. All of the above

Q.58 Which of the following is a money market instrument?
A. Certificates of Deposit
B. Commercial Paper

C. Bills of exchange

D. (A) and (B) both

E. All of the above

Q.59 Which among the following is/are Prospective Investors in Mutual Funds?

A. Non-Banking Finance Companies

B. Insurance Companies

C. Provident Funds

D. (A) and (B) both

E. All of the above

Q.60 Morgan Stanley has downgraded Reliance Industries Limited's (RIL) stock to 'equal weight' (EW), leading to a ________% fall in the company's shares to ₹1,255.15.

A. 2.86   **B.** 3.41

C. 4.32   **D.** 5.12

E. None of these

Q.61 The government of India has prohibited Import of second-hand or refurbished electronics and IT goods without registration with the ________.

A. International Organization for Standardization

B. BSI Group

C. Bureau of Indian Standards

D. Ministry of Electronics and Information Technology

E. None of these

Q.62 Which of the following fintech startups has announced its foray into merchant services with a new app in May 2019?

A. BharatPe   **B.** FINO PayTech

C. ItzCash   **D.** Citrus Pay

E. None of these

Q.63 Which country has emerged as the third largest foreign direct investor in India during 2017-18?

A. USA   **B.** Singapore

C. China   **D.** Netherlands

E. None of these

Q.64 Many a times, we read a term 'SEPA' in financial newspapers. What is the full form of the SEPA?

A. Single exchange processing Agency

B. Single Euro Payments Area

C. Single Electronic Processing Agency

D. Super Electronic Purchase Agency

E. None of these

Q.65 Zubair has a special taste for college canteen's hotdogs. The owner of the canteen doubles the prices of hotdogs. Zubair did not respond to the increase in prices and kept on demanding the same quantity of hotdogs. His demand for hotdogs is

A. Perfectly elastic   **B.** Perfectly inelastic

C. Elastic   **D.** Less elastic

E. None of these

// Smart Answer Sheet //

Correct Indicates percentage of students who answered questions correctly.

Skipped Indicates percentage of students who skipped questions.

Q.	Ans.	Correct / Skipped	Q.	Ans.	Correct / Skipped	Q.	Ans.	Correct / Skipped	Q.	Ans.	Correct / Skipped	Q.	Ans.	Correct / Skipped
1	B	85.23 % / 12.06 %	14	A	84.07 % / 14.85 %	27	C	80.69 % / 12.19 %	40	A	86.67 % / 12.28 %	53	D	89.25 % / 10.55 %
2	D	89.97 % / 10.02 %	15	E	78.19 % / 12.65 %	28	B	83.21 % / 14.32 %	41	D	76.75 % / 14.71 %	54	A	89.45 % / 10.07 %
3	A	78.45 % / 18.18 %	16	C	78.83 % / 17.86 %	29	B	89.58 % / 10.39 %	42	E	77.77 % / 14.43 %	55	A	85.29 % / 12.07 %
4	D	77.34 % / 11.2 %	17	A	89.67 % / 10.29 %	30	D	76.02 % / 17.63 %	43	E	85.81 % / 13.53 %	56	D	76.22 % / 18.74 %
5	B	78.85 % / 14.85 %	18	C	83.56 % / 11.97 %	31	B	88.07 % / 10.64 %	44	E	81.95 % / 13.59 %	57	E	83.4 % / 10.96 %
6	D	84.58 % / 14.53 %	19	B	86.63 % / 11.82 %	32	A	79.99 % / 15.59 %	45	A	83.06 % / 14.45 %	58	E	82.08 % / 10.03 %
7	B	84.96 % / 14.68 %	20	A	83.56 % / 14.74 %	33	C	87.39 % / 11.57 %	46	C	88.81 % / 11.03 %	59	E	81.49 % / 17.11 %
8	B	85.44 % / 13.24 %	21	C	86.64 % / 10.01 %	34	B	87.12 % / 12.64 %	47	C	78.96 % / 10.68 %	60	B	82.21 % / 10.83 %
9	B	76.73 % / 17.7 %	22	D	81.08 % / 11.9 %	35	B	77.38 % / 13.14 %	48	C	86.81 % / 10.86 %	61	C	84.14 % / 13.12 %
10	C	79.69 % / 14.32 %	23	A	83.78 % / 10.24 %	36	D	83.96 % / 14.56 %	49	D	83.3 % / 14.18 %	62	A	76.88 % / 13.04 %
11	E	88.54 % / 10.04 %	24	D	76.97 % / 14.61 %	37	A	81.92 % / 15.9 %	50	D	80.05 % / 14.24 %	63	D	89.67 % / 10.22 %
12	A	88.05 % / 11.55 %	25	B	88.54 % / 10.11 %	38	D	84.28 % / 14.55 %	51	D	80.4 % / 18.2 %	64	B	76.67 % / 17.16 %
13	E	89.63 % / 10.08 %	26	D	89.17 % / 10.48 %	39	C	89.47 % / 10.11 %	52	D	80.62 % / 18.78 %	65	B	87.39 % / 10.21 %

Performance Analysis

Avg. Score (%)	50.0%
Toppers Score (%)	72.0%
Your Score	

//Hints and Solutions//

1. In this example the coefficient of determination is 0.64 or 64%. The coefficient of determination is symbolized by r-squared, where r is the coefficient of correlation. Hence, a coefficient of determination of 0.64 or 64% means that the coefficient of correlation was 0.8 or 80%.

2. Odisha has launched a Ama Gaon, Ama Vikas (Our Village, our development) to reach out to the people in rural areas and involve themselves in the developmental activities. CM flagged off wi-fi enabled mobile video wall vans through which people can send their grievances directly to the CM's office. With this initiative the administration will solve the the grievances of the people quickly.

3. LAF is a monetary policy to which allows banks to borrow money through repurchase agreements. MSF refers to the penal rate at which banks can borrow money from the central bank over and above what is available to them through the LAF window. So the two are practically the same

4. Arun Jaitley said that the government has allocated ₹14.3 lakh crore to be spent for rural infrastructure. He said every block with more than 50% ST population and at least 20,000 tribal people will have a model residential school by 2022. He added social security will be provided to aged, widows, and orphaned children.

5. An Non-Resident Ordinary Rupee Account has a limit of $1 million. When an Indian national or person of Indian origin residing in India leaves India for a foreign country for taking up employment, business or vocation outside India, or for any other purpose, indicating his intention to say outside India permanently or for an indefinite period, he becomes a person resident outside India. His bank account, if any, in India is designated as an Ordinary Non-resident Account (NRO Account).

6. As per the provisional report published during 31st March, 2011, India showed a decadal growth rate of 17.64 % for the entire population as compared to 21.15 % in Census 2001. The report says, during the last decade of 2001 to 2011, population in India grew by 181 million.

7. In the long-run, as compared to the demand force the supply force becomes a dominant factor in determining the equilibrium price. The long-run price is also described as the normal price.

8. According to the World Bank's "India Development Update", India's economic growth will accelerate to 7.3% in 2018-19, from 6.7% in 2017-2018. The World Bank said sustaining a growth rate higher than 7.5% will require contributions from all domestic sectors and support from the global economy. The report also highlights several challenges facing the Indian economy that need attention.

9. Export–Import Bank of India is the premier export finance institution in India, established in 1982 under Export-Import Bank of India Act 1981. Since its inception, Exim Bank of India has been both a catalyst and a key player in the promotion of cross border trade and investment.

10. Domestic telecom equipment provider Vihaan Networks Limited (VNL) signed a Memorandum of Understanding (MoU) with Bharat Sanchar Nigam Limited (BSNL) to launch "Relief 123" service to provide disaster management in India.

11. IDBI Bank has launched 'Project Nishchay' in partnership with The Boston Consulting Group (BCG) to accelerate its turnaround programme and improve financial performance.

12. The Asian Development Bank will increase its annual lending to India to a maximum of $4billion between 2018 and 2022 to help fasten inclusive economic transformation towards upper middle income status.

13. For the first time, the Insolvency and Bankruptcy Board of India (IBBI) registered National e-Governance Services Limited (NeSL) as an information utility. This registration is valid for five years from the date of registration, the ministry of corporate affairs said in a statement.

14. The US Federal Reserve has fined HSBC Holdings PLC and HSBC North America Holdings Inc USD175 million for "unsafe and unsound practices" in its foreign exchange trading business.

15. ICICI Bank announced a new home loan scheme that overs borrowers the benefit of 1% cashback on every EMI, for the entire tenure of the loan. The offer will be valid for home loans with a minimum tenure of 15 years and maximum tenure of 30 years.

16. India signed a $200 million loan agreement with the World Bank to promote agri businesses and climate-resilient farming in the north-eastern state of Assam.

17. State Bank of India announced sanction of credit facilities amounting to Rs2,317 crore to corporates for financing Grid Connected Rooftop Solar projects under an SBI-World Bank program.

18. Private sector lender Yes Bank signed an agreement with the government to provide Rs 1,000 crore financing for food processing projects.

19. The revenue department said that the farmers do not need to quote PAN for cash sale of their produce up to Rs 2 lakh a day.

20. 1 only.Under CRR a certain percentage of the total bank deposits has to be kept in the current account with RBI which means banks do not have access to that much amount for any economic activity or commercial activity. Banks can't lend the money to corporates or individual borrowers, banks can't use that money for investment purposes.In short, CRR is the amount in cash which banks have to keep with RBI. Any decrease in CRR will therefore increase cash availability with the banks. Repo rate and SLR would not be affected by changes in CRR. They r separate mechanisms, the rate of which is decided by RBI.

21. countries themselves decide whether they want to be in developed or developing categories. There are no WTO definitions of "developed" or "developing" countries. Developing countries in the WTO are designated on the basis of self-selection although this is not necessarily automatically accepted in all WTO bodies.

22. 4 only. SLR, statutory liquidity ratio is the amount of money that is invested in certain specified securities predominantly central government and state government securities. Investing in government securities by bank is one way of fulfilling the requirement of SLR. In this way, SLR acts as a lending mechanism to government. Repo rate is a rate at which banks borrow from RBI for short periods up to 7 or 14 days but predominantly overnight.

23. 1 only. FPI is also called Foreign institutional Investments (FIIs). Because of their volatility they are also called hot money. Loans from international financial institutions are given for a fixed tenure and hence are stable. FDI is not part of FPI, but are accounted separately.

24. RBI's functions – acting as banker's bank, managing India's Forex and handling govt's borrowing programme

These three are well defined, no confusion over this.

Now let's read more on inflation management by RBI . Before march 2015, the Reserve Bank was not formally an inflation targeting central bank. The defining features of an inflation targeting central bank are a precise mandate, a single instrument (the policy interest rate) in its armoury, a single minded devotion to achieving this target and a principal-agent relationship with the Government.

So, even though RBI was informally helping manage inflation, it was not it's function as defined by the RBI Acvt, 1934

However, in March 2015 it was formally decided that from now, RBI will have the official mandate to manage inflation.

For this the RBI Act, 1934 will be amended. The amendment has yet not happened, because passing a legislation takes some time. But it has been now fully agreed that such an amendment will be made.

25. Increase in subsidy of LPG will reduce the pocket expenditure of people on LPG, making more money available with them, thereby increasing demand and pulling inflation. Similar will be the effect of decrease of income tax rates – more money availability. Increase in fuel prices will lead to cost-push inflation.

26. A 'Narrow Bank' can be defined as the system of banking under which a bank places its funds in risk-free assets with maturity period matching its liability maturity profile, so that there is no problem relating to asset liability mismatch and the quality of assets remains intact without leading to emergence of sub-standard assets.

27. GDP (market price) = GDP (factor cost) + indirect taxes – subisdies. This equation makes it clear that any increase in indirect taxes will increase the GDP at market prices.

28. Shares are equity instruments, while bonds and debentures are debt instruments. Debt instruments are assets that require a fixed payment to the holder, usually with interest. Examples of debt instruments include bonds (government or corporate), debentures and mortgages. Equity financing allows a company to acquire funds (often for investment) without incurring debt, eg shares.

29. Expansionary fiscal policy is a macroeconomic policy that seeks to expand the money supply to encourage economic growth or combat inflation (price increases). One form of expansionary policy is fiscal policy, which comes in the form of tax cuts, rebates and increased government spending. Expansionary policies can also come from central banks, which focus on increasing the money supply in the economy. Such a

fiscal policy will increase the expenditure, thereby increasing fiscal deficit. Increase in wages of labour is unrelated. There can be a decrease (not increase) in income tax rates, so statement 3 is false.

30.

- The rate of interest in Kisan Vikas Patra (KVP) is 7.7%. It is a saving scheme was first launched by India Post in the year 1988 and then relaunched in the year 2014.

- Based on the current rate of interest, it would double the principal in 112 months(9 years 4 months). The KVP certificates are available in ₹ 1000, ₹ 5000, ₹ 10000 and ₹ 50000. Maturity period is 30 months. Premature encashment of KVP is not allowed.

31. Pradhan Mantri Mudra Yojana (PMMY) scheme of Government of India was launched on April 8, 2015. It provides loans up to ₹ 10 lakh to the non-corporate small business sector from all banks Public Sector Banks, Regional Rural Banks and Cooperative Banks, Foreign banks and Non-Banking Financial Companies (NBFC's). Under this Scheme, a new institution named, MUDRA (Micro Units Development & Refinance Agency Ltd.) would look after the loans given under PMMY.

32. West Bengal has been selected for 1st prize in 100 day work program for promoting livelihood.

33.

- India has begun work on a universal debt relief scheme for small borrowers aimed at micro enterprises, small farmers and artisans.

- Individuals below a specified income and asset threshold will be eligible for debt relief.

- People with annual income of Rs 60,000 or less, outstanding loans of Rs 35,000 or less, and assets worth Rs 20,000 or less may be eligible.

34.

- NITI Aayog led committee Inter-Ministerial Steering Committee of the National Mission for Transformative Mobility has decided to incorporate localisation conditions to avail benefits under the FAME-II Scheme.

- The steering committee has mandated that only companies that meet the 50% localisation threshold will be eligible for the incentives.

- The incentives will be available under the Faster Adoption and Manufacturing of Hybrid and Electric Vehicles (FAME-II) scheme to boost electric mobility as well as the 'Make in India' initiative.

35.

- Sikkim will be the first Indian state to roll out Universal Basic Income (UBI) scheme by 2022.

- The decision was taken by Sikkim's ruling party the Sikkim Democratic Front (SDF).

- UBI is a programme for providing all citizens of a country or other geographic area/state with a given sum of money, regardless of their income, resources or employment status.

36.

- As per the interim budget 2019, the Government will make 1 lakh villages into Digital Villages over next five years.
- It will be done with the help of Common Service Centres.
- CSCs, is a public-private initiative that offers digital services to villagers.

37. An account becomes inactive when not operated for more than 12 months and if no transactions are performed for 24 months then it becomes a dormant account.

38. Amortization simply means the balancing out of a loan over a period of time. It is the paying the amount loan in a certain time. During a loan tenure, the first few months contains more interest and less principal and as time gradually proceeds, the amount of principal gradually increases and at the final month, The EMI contains full principal and zero interest. This process is called amortization.

39. Cost push inflation is inflation caused by an increase in prices of inputs like labour, raw material, etc. The increased price of the factors of production leads to a decreased supply of these goods.

40. In case of brown label ATM, ATM has the logo of the outsourcing bank whereas in case of white label ATM, there is no logo of any sponsoring bank.

There is no compulsion regarding opening up of a specific number of brown label ATMs in different areas of the country.

RBI is not directly involved with the set up of brown label ATM, while in case of white label ATMs, RBI provides license.

Indicash was the first white label ATM which was opened in India and now brown label ATM.

41. The co - operative banks in rural areas mainly finance agricultural based activities including farming, cattle, milk, hatchery, personal finance etc., along with some small scale industries and self - employment driven activities.

42. Debit cards are plastic cards embedded with electro magnetic identification. It is called plastic card because if one loses this card, then on informing the concerned bank the card can be deactivated and hence losing all the value.

The debit card can be used at Point of sale terminal to pay for purchase or sale or to do any monetary activities, instead of using physical cash. Once a customer does transaction, the addition or subtraction of money happens in his/her account ensuring remote access to the bank account. One does not have to go physically to a bank to access the account.

43. All are true regarding the North East in the interim budget of 2019.

- Allocation to be increased by 21% to Rs. 58,166 crore in 2019-20.
- Arunachal Pradesh came on the air map recently.
- Meghalaya, Tripura and Mizoram came on India's rail map for the first time.

- Container cargo movement through improved navigation capacity of the Brahmaputra.

44.

- The Electoral Bond Scheme 2018 was notified on January 2, 2018 by the central government.
- The provisions of the Electoral Bond Scheme are:
- The electoral bonds may be purchased by a person, who is a citizen of India or incorporated or established in India.
- A person being an individual can buy electoral bonds, either singly or jointly with other individuals.
- A political party must be registered under the Section 29A of the Representation of the People Act, 1951 to get the benefit of the Electoral Bond Scheme 2018.
- The eligible and registered political parties must secure not less than one% of votes polled in the last general election to the House of the People or the Legislative Assembly of the State, shall be eligible to receive electoral bonds.
- An eligible political party can encash the Electoral bonds only through a bank account with an authorized bank.

45.

- A report titled 'Sand and Sustainability: finding new solutions for environmental governance of global sand resources' was released by the United Nations Environment Programme.
- India and China top a list of countries where illegal sand mining has become a major environmental problem.
- In 2017, China recorded the highest use of cement in the world.
- India came second followed by the USA.

46. Women and Child Development Ministry has approved projects worth over Rs 2,900 crore under the Nirbhaya fund for eight major cities to make them safer for women. These cities are Delhi, Mumbai, Kolkata, Chennai, Bengaluru, Hyderabad, Ahmedabad and Lucknow. The decision was taken after a meeting of Empowered Committee, which is headed by Women and Child Development Secretary.

47.

- The 2020s are set to be the Asian decade, with the continent dominating an exclusive list of economies expected to sustain growth rates of around 7%.
- Ethiopia and Côte d'Ivoire are also likely to reach the 7% growth pace.
- India, Bangladesh, Vietnam, Myanmar and the Philippines should all meet that benchmark, according to a research note.

48.

- The abbreviation of NISM is National Institute of security Markets.

- Its headquarters is in Navi Mumbai.
- It is an educational initiative undertaken by SEBI.
- It is an Indian public trust and also trains staff for SEBI and it was established in 2006.

49. The Union Cabinet has approved the North East Industrial Development Scheme (NEIDS), 2017. In order to promote employment in the North East States, Government is incentivizing primarily the MSME Sector through this scheme. The newly introduced scheme shall promote industrialization in the States of the North Eastern Region and will boost employment and income generation.

50. Regional Rural Banks were established under the provisions of an Ordinance passed in September 1975 and the RRB Act 1976 to provide sufficient banking and credit facility for agriculture and other rural sectors.

51. The Association of Mutual Funds in India is an industry standards organisation in India in the mutual funds sector. It was formed in 1995. Most mutual funds firms in India are its members.

52. An initial coin offering is similar to Initial public offerings where it acts as a crowdfunding source for the digital currency, which can be used as a capital for the start - up companies. In ICO, the coin offerings are in the form of tokens, which are provided to the investors.

53. Ajay Tyagi is the present chairman of SEBI is appointed byUnion Government of India on 10th January 2017 replacing U.K Sinha.

54. When dealing with investments (including stocks), CAGR describes the average growth of an investment over a period of time. The acronym stands for Compound Annual Growth Rate.

55.

- Industrial output contracted 0.1% in March 2019 due to slowdown in the manufacturing sector.
- Factory output as measured in terms of the Index of Industrial Production (IIP) had expanded 5.3% in March 2018.
- During the entire 2018-19 fiscal, industrial output witnessed a 3.6% growth as against 4.4% in the previous fiscal.

56. INROADS stands for Indian Risk Oriented And Dynamic **Rating** System.

57. Small Industries Development Bank of India was set up on April 2, 1990 through an act of parliament aiming to aid the growth and development of micro, small and medium - scale enterprises in India.

The main purpose of SIDBI is to provide refinance facilities and short term lending to industries. SIDBI also focuses to promote employment - oriented industries in semi - urban areas and to check migration of population to big cities.

SIDBI also aims to expand channels for marketing of SSI sector products in India & abroad and initiate's steps for technological upgradation and modernization of existing units.

58. Money markets operate through a number of instruments, some of them are:

1. Certificates of Deposit - Certificates of deposit are short term instruments issued by commercial banks and financial institutions to the individuals, corporations and companies. They are unsecured and negotiable.

2. Treasury Bills - Treasury bills, also known as Zero Coupon Bonds are the instrument of short term borrowing with maturity period of less than one year. This instrument is issued by Reserve Bank of India on behalf of the Central Government for fulfilling short term requirements of funds. They are issued at discount and are paid at par.

3. Commercial Paper - Commercial Paper is a short term unsecured promissory note with maturity period of 15 days to one year. Since it is unsecured, it is issued by the large and creditworthy companies to meet their short term fund requirements. It is negotiable and transferable by endorsement.

4. Bills of Exchange - It is an unconditional order in writing, addressed by one person to another, signed by the person giving it requiring the person to whom it is addressed to pay on demand, or at a fixed or determinable future time, a sum certain in money to or to the order of a specified person, or to a bearer.

59. Mutual fund is a mechanism for pooling the resources by issuing units to the investors and investing funds in securities in accordance with objectives as disclosed in offer document. Investments in securities are spread across a wide cross-section of industries and sectors and thus the risk is reduced.

60.

- Morgan Stanley has downgraded Reliance Industries Limited's (RIL) stock to 'equal weight' (EW), leading to a 3.41% fall in the company's shares to ₹1,255.15.
- With this fall, the company has again lost the tag of India's most-valued firm to Tata Consultancy Services (TCS).
- RIL's market capitalisation fell to ₹7,98,628.55 crore compared with TCS's ₹8,13,779.67 crore.

61. The government of India has prohibited Import of second-hand or refurbished electronics and IT goods without registration with the Bureau of Indian Standards.

Under the Electronics and IT Goods (Requirement of Compulsory Registration) order 2012, imports of these goods is allowed through the registration with the BIS or on specific exemption letter from the ministry of IT and electronics.

62.

- BharatPe, a fintech startup enabling payments for merchants through interoperable UPI QR codes, has announced its foray into merchant services with a new app.
- The app allows merchants to record their cash/credit (udhar) sales customer wise, request accounts receivable from customers via SMS payment links, and keep track of accounts payable to suppliers.

63.

- The Netherlands has emerged as the third largest foreign direct investor in India during 2017-18.

- The Netherlands was also the second largest destination for foreign investment by Indian companies, after Singapore, with investments worth $12.8 billion in 2017.

- During 2017-18, the bilateral trade topped $ 8.77 billion while the Indian exports to the Netherlands grew at 14.7%.

64. Single Euro Payments Area (SEPA) is a payment-integration initiative of the European Union for simplification of bank transfers denominated in euro. As of 2015, SEPA consists of the 28 member states of the European Union. It aims to improve the efficiency of cross-border payments and turn the fragmented national markets for euro payments into a single domestic one.

65. Zubair has a special taste for college canteen's hotdogs. The owner of the canteen doubles the prices of hotdogs. Zubair did not respond to the increase in prices and kept on demanding the same quantity of hotdogs. His demand for hotdogs is perfectly inelastic.

Q.1 The total sum of the goods and services produced in a country in a year, minus depreciation is called as –

A. Gross domestic product
B. Gross national Product
C. Gross national income
D. Net domestic product
E. Net national Product

Q.2 Under the NITI Aayog 15-years vision plan, three years 'Action agenda' is created to boost economic growth. The duration of three-year action plan is ?

A. 2017-18 to 2019-20458
B. 2018-19 to 2020-21
C. 2016-17 to 2018-19
D. 2019-20 to 2021-22
E. None of these

Q.3 What is India's rank in human development index 2016?

A. 122nd   B. 130th   C. 132nd   D. 131st
E. 121st

Q.4 Under union Budget 2017-18, 'Income tax' on annual income of 2.5 lakh to 5 lakh has been reduced from 10 percent to ?

A. 8%   B. 7%   C. 7.5%   D. 6%
E. 5%

Q.5 Second nationalization of commercial banks in India took place in?

A. 1930   B. 1948   C. 1970   D. 1950
E. 1980

Q.6 Asian development bank projected India's economic growth rate for 2017-18?

A. 7.4%   B. 7.7%   C. 7.2%   D. 7.8%
E. 7.6%

Q.7 World economic outlook is released by ?

A. WEF   B. World Bank
C. IBRD   D. IMF
E. IFSC

Q.8 The 1967 Industrial licensing policy inquiry committee was set up under Chairmanship of?

A. K.C. Dasgupta   B. Dr. R.K. Hazari
C. Mr. Subimal Dutt   D. R. Narsimhan
E. TSR Subramaniam

Q.9 The policy to deal with the taxation and expenditure decision of government is ?

A. Investment policy   B. Monetary policy
C. Tax policy   D. Fiscal policy
E. None of these

Q.10 The formation of NAA to ensure that the benefits that accrue to entities due to reduction in costs passed by on to customers. What is the full form of NAA?

A. New anti-profiteering association
B. New anti-profiteering authority
C. National anti-profiteering association
D. National anti-profiteering authority
E. Other than given options

Q.11 What is India's rank on the 2017 World happiness index?

A. 131st   B. 132nd   C. 122nd   D. 121st
E. 130th

Q.12 IFM is established to solve the problems related to EU investment in India what is the full form of IFM?

A. International fund management
B. Investment fund management
C. Investors fund managementD. Investment facilitation mechani
D. Investment facilitation mechanism
E. Indian fund management

Q.13 Which country has ratified automatic exchange of financial account information with India and 40 other countries?

A. United states of America
B. Singapore
C. Europe
D. Britain
E. Switzerland

Q.14 Recently, Maternity amendment bill 2016 is passed by Parliament. Under this the maternity benefits raised form 12 weeks to ?

A. 20 weeks   B. 18 weeks
C. 22 weeks   D. 24 weeks
E. 26 weeks

Q.15 An increase in aggregate demand over the available output leads to a rise in the price level. This kind of inflation is known as ?

A. Cost-push inflation
B. Demand pull inflation
C. Credit inflation
D. Walking Inflation
E. Galloping inflation

Q.16 Rejuvenation, Modernization and Technology Upgradation has been renamed as?

A. Coir industry upgradation
B. Coir udyami yojana
C. Coir vikas yojana
D. Coir upradation scheme
E. None of these

Q.17 The platform aimed at addressing common man' grievances and simultaneously monitoring and reviewing important programmes.

A. EVIN
B. UIP
C. PRAGATI
D. SWAYAM
E. NRTP

Q.18 World Thalassemia day is celebrated on ?

A. May 8
B. May 4
C. May 10
D. May 16
E. May 30

Q.19 Under the housing scheme the EPFO allowed its subscriber to withdraw how much percentage of its EPF accumulations to buy homes?

A. Upto 69%
B. Upto 75%
C. Upto 82%
D. Upto 90%
E. Upto 79%

Q.20 Inflation in the double or triple digit range of 20, 100 or 200 p.c. a year is termed as -

A. Walking inflation
B. Creeping inflation
C. Galloping inflation
D. Credit inflation
E. Mild inflation

Q.21 Who headed the committee setup to recommend ways to deal with employment data discrepancies and its reliable solutions –

A. Arvind Mayaram
B. R. Ranarajan
C. Shekar Basu
D. Arvind Panagariya
E. Ashok Lavasa

Q.22 Central statistics office has changed the base year of Index of Industrial Production (IIP) from 2004-05 to –

A. 2010-11
B. 2009-10
C. 2012-14
D. 2015-16
E. 2011-12

Q.23 Which of the following about SEZ is incorrect?

A. It is a duty free enclave to be treated as foreign territory for the trade operations and duties and tarrifs.
B. No manufacturing activities are allowed in SEZ
C. For SEZ developers there is Zero tax and duty on raw material
D. Both (A) and (B)
E. None of these

Q.24 What is the budget allocation for recapitalization of bank in lines with the Indhradhanush roadmap?

A. 5,000 crores
B. 10,000 crores
C. 15,000 crores
D. 20,000 crores
E. 25,000 crores

Q.25 It is a manned service delivery point which is open for at least four hours a day and at least five days a week.

A. Samadhan kendra
B. Banking ombudsman
C. Seva kendra
D. Nirakaran kendra
E. Banking outlet

Q.26 It is an international financial institution that provides loan to the countries of the world for capital programs ?

A. World bank
B. International monetary fund
C. World economic forum
D. Bank for International settlement
E. European central bank

Q.27 What is the title of India economy survey 2017 released by OECD –

A. Strong reforms and boosting inclusive growth
B. Women and developing country
C. Empowering India, educating India
D. Inclusive growth, Employment and education
E. Empowering India – Inclusive growth, women empowerment

Q.28 According to Swachh Survekshan 2017, which city is declared as cleanest city in India?

A. Vishakhapatnam
B. Bhopal
C. Idduki
D. Indore
E. Surat

Q.29 During Inflation who gains and profited?

A. Lenders
B. Borrowers
C. Salaried peoples
D. Bond holders
E. None of these

Q.30 What is the theme for Technotex 2017?

A. Textile – future growth sector
B. Technical Textiles: Towards future
C. Technology and textiles
D. Textile growth with technology
E. Future of textile with technology

Q.31 The third edition of G20 Framework Working Group (FWG) meeting was held in?

A. Hyderabad
B. Varanasi
C. New Delhi
D. Gujarat
E. Pune

Q.32 Wholesale price Index is released by –

A. Central statistics office
B. Office of economic advisor, Department of Industrial policy and promotion
C. Reserve bank of India
D. Chief Economic advisor
E. Government of India

Q.33 'Mission 41k' is related to ?

A. Railways
B. Electricity
C. Education
D. Banking
E. Mining

Q.34 It is a digital payment platform for merchants to receive digital payments from customers over the counter through Aadhar authentication.

A. BHIM
B. E-Pay
C. E-aadhar
D. Aadhar Pay

E. E- merchant

Q.35 Which among the following organizations make major credit policies for the Regional Rural Banks (RRBs)?
A. NABARD
B. Asian Development Bank
C. World Bank
D. State Bank of India
E. None of the above

Q.36 In Budget estimates of 2017-18 the fiscal deficit stands at __ of GDP
A. 4%   **B.** 3%   **C.** 3.5%   **D.** 3.2%
E. 4.5%

Q.37 According to WTO provisions India has to stop the payment of subsidy to exporters by –
A. 2017   **B.** 2018   **C.** 2019   **D.** 2020
E. 2021

Q.38 What is real income?
A. The net part of wage one is free to use which is derived after deducting the directtaxes
B. The wage someone gets in hand per day or per month
C. The net part of wage one is free to use which is derived after deducting the indirect taxes
D. The wage someone gets in hand per day or per month minus the present-day rate of inflation - adjusted in percentage form
E. None of these

Q.39 A comprehensive plan launched by government for recapitalization of public sector lenders with a view to make sure they remain solvent and fully comply with the global capital adequacy norms, Basel-III.
A. Industrial revolution 4.0
B. Industrial revolution 3.0
C. Indradhanush 2.0
D. Indradhanush 3.0
E. None of these

Q.40 Public enterprises survey 2015-16 is released by ?
A. CSO
B. RBI
C. DIPP
D. Department of Public enterprises
E. Union government

Q.41 NCCT is recently in news, What does 'T' stands for in NCCT?
A. Task   **B.** Territories
C. Term   **D.** Trade
E. Tourism

Q.42 Which five-year plan is also known as Liberalization of Economy?
A. 5th FYP   **B.** 9th FYP
C. 10th FYP   **D.** 8th FYP
E. 7th FYP

Q.43 RBI reconstituted an oversight 5 five-member panel for bad loan solutions who headed the committee?
A. Pradeep Kumar
B. Prabhas Kumar jha
C. Uday kotak
D. Arvind mayaram
E. Kewal Kumar sharma

Q.44 Twenty-point Programme was launched in?
A. 1960   **B.** 1975   **C.** 1970   **D.** 1980
E. 1982

Q.45 The term Seignorage is related to ?
A. Insurance   **B.** Recession
C. Inflation   **D.** Internet Banking
E. None of these

Q.46 In union budget 2017-18 the specific relaxation with respect to holding period for treating it as long term asset has been given to ?
A. Debt funds
B. Real estates
C. Gold exchange funds
D. Unlisted equities
E. None of these

Q.47 Nirvan fund was set up to help?
A. Youths of Nomadic tribe
B. Displaced Kashimiri Pandits
C. Old age people having no means of livelihood
D. Ventures of selected candidates trained under PMKVY but don't get any job
E. None of these

Q.48 NITI Aayog has recommended 'Price deficiency system' in three year action plan. The system is a –
A. Measure to boost food processing industries
B. Measure to boost banking industry
C. Measure to boost handicraft industry
D. Measure to boost export subsidies
E. Reform to minimum support price system in agricultural marketing.

Q.49 Recession is defined as ?
A. a downturn in the aggregate demand on overall fall in the demand
B. general fall in demand as economic activities takes a downturn, Industries resort
C. 'price cuts' to sustain their business
D. the economy heats up and a demand supply lag is visible
E. demand goes upward, inflation also moves upward making borrowing cheaper for investors

Q.50 In an economy, if the share of its primary sector is 50% or more in the total output of the economy it is called as ?
A. Industrial economy   **B.** Service economy
C. Agrarian economy   **D.** Command economy
E. Mixed economy

Q.51 A tax-exempt bond issued by federally qualified organizations or by municipalities for the development of brownfield sites is termed as?

A. Masala Bond   **B.** Climate Bond
C. Green Bond   **D.** Social Impact Bond
E. None of these

Q.52 In PMMY, loan range for Tarun category is ?

A. Loan up to Rs 50,000
B. Rs 50,000 to 5 lakhs
C. Rs 50,000 to 15 lakhs
D. Rs 5 lakh to Rs 10 lakh.
E. Rs 5 lakh to Rs 20 lakh.

Q.53 What is India's place in crude steel production?

A. First   **B.** Second   **C.** Third   **D.** Fourth
E. Fifth

Q.54 The purest form of the income of the Nation is –

A. Net National income
B. Gross National Income
C. Gross National Product
D. Net National product
E. None of these

Q.55 Who headed the committee set up by RBI to suggest the measures to tackle the cyber security challenges?

A. Meena Hemchandra
B. S S Mundra
C. Kewal Kumar Sharma
D. Nandita Chatterjee
E. Amar Sinha

Q.56 Recently AQR is in news, what is R in AQR?

A. Restructure   **B.** Ratio
C. Review   **D.** Retailed
E. Research

Q.57 The new revised Indian Standard on Gold hallmarking, gold jewellery will be available in three grades and these are ?

A. 14, 18 and 22   **B.** 11, 15 and 21
C. 12, 15 and 22   **D.** 12, 15 and 24
E. 14, 18 and 24

Q.58 E-NIKSHAY platform is related to ?

A. Crime record portal
B. Banking complaints
C. Platform for TB patient database
D. Tax portal
E. GST

Q.59 Under new National steel policy 2017, the domestic steel production capacity will be doubled by the year –

A. 2019-20   **B.** 2021-22   **C.** 2025-26   **D.** 2029-30
E. 2030-31

Q.60 According to the 2nd advance estimates of production of major crops for 2016-17, the total food grain production is estimated at ?

A. 108.99 million tonnes
B. 271.98 million tonnes
C. 309.98 million tonnes
D. 439.86 million tonnes
E. 108.86 million tonnes

Q.61 Global economic prospect report is published by ?

A. World bank
B. IMF
C. World Economic forum
D. United Nation
E. UNESCO

Q.62 The independent Banking industry watchdog that protects consumers of banking services in India.

A. RBI
B. FMC
C. BCSBI
D. BSBDA
E. Banking Ombudsman

Q.63 Committee on 7th CPC recommendation on allowances headed by ?

A. AP shah   **B.** ESL Narsimhan
C. Shaktikanta Das   **D.** Arvind Panagariya
E. Ashok Lavasa

Q.64 What is Net National Product?

A. It is calculated after adjusting the weight of the value of 'depreciation'
B. It is calculated as the GDP of a country added with its 'income from abroad'.
C. The GNP after deducting the loss due to 'depreciation.
D. The GDP of a country after deducion its 'income from abroad'.
E. None of these

Q.65 In Keynes General Theory, investment and savings are brought to equality primarily through changes in the

A. rate of interest
B. income velocity of money
C. national income
D. level of prices
E. None of the above

// Smart Answer Sheet //

Correct   Indicates percentage of students who answered questions correctly.

Skipped   Indicates percentage of students who skipped questions.

Q.	Ans.	Correct / Skipped
1	D	81.2 % / 18.04 %
2	A	88.93 % / 10.93 %
3	D	80.49 % / 12.38 %
4	E	79.07 % / 15.96 %
5	E	86.43 % / 12.43 %
6	A	79.27 % / 19.72 %
7	D	79.12 % / 12.47 %
8	C	88.32 % / 11.39 %
9	D	77.84 % / 14.54 %
10	D	78.41 % / 21.35 %
11	C	89.34 % / 10.06 %
12	D	87.76 % / 11.23 %
13	E	77.48 % / 14.59 %

Q.	Ans.	Correct / Skipped
14	E	77.52 % / 11.68 %
15	B	85.02 % / 11.92 %
16	B	80.82 % / 17.87 %
17	C	77.28 % / 20.55 %
18	A	89.54 % / 10.36 %
19	D	84.77 % / 12.16 %
20	C	82.23 % / 15.1 %
21	D	86.71 % / 10.77 %
22	E	79.57 % / 19.69 %
23	B	85.45 % / 11.09 %
24	C	86.33 % / 13.59 %
25	E	87.96 % / 11.75 %
26	A	80.06 % / 17.59 %

Q.	Ans.	Correct / Skipped
27	A	86.42 % / 10.36 %
28	D	86.79 % / 11.48 %
29	B	81.72 % / 15.05 %
30	B	88.86 % / 10.38 %
31	B	85.69 % / 14.02 %
32	B	86.76 % / 11.06 %
33	A	81.69 % / 15.94 %
34	D	76.7 % / 20.6 %
35	A	89.1 % / 10.13 %
36	D	86.64 % / 10.32 %
37	B	78.03 % / 14.02 %
38	D	88.87 % / 11.06 %
39	C	82.45 % / 10.34 %

Q.	Ans.	Correct / Skipped
40	D	80.78 % / 18.31 %
41	B	76.28 % / 18.58 %
42	D	79.1 % / 10.88 %
43	A	81.88 % / 14.15 %
44	B	85.04 % / 14.64 %
45	C	87.35 % / 10.63 %
46	B	83.06 % / 15.32 %
47	D	77.52 % / 16.86 %
48	D	81.67 % / 15.34 %
49	B	80.56 % / 14.94 %
50	C	85.42 % / 11.74 %
51	B	85.63 % / 12.46 %
52	D	88.67 % / 10.46 %

Q.	Ans.	Correct / Skipped
53	B	89.35 % / 10.38 %
54	D	89.75 % / 10.14 %
55	A	78.86 % / 20.91 %
56	C	77.28 % / 20.99 %
57	A	85.24 % / 11.68 %
58	C	87.37 % / 11.58 %
59	E	86.3 % / 11.71 %
60	B	79.21 % / 19.68 %
61	A	84.86 % / 10.09 %
62	C	88.27 % / 10.01 %
63	D	77.44 % / 10.31 %
64	C	88.27 % / 11.0 %
65	A	89.38 % / 10.21 %

Performance Analysis	
Avg. Score (%)	44.0%
Toppers Score (%)	57.0%
Your Score	

//Hints and Solutions//

1. Net Domestic Product

2. NITI Aayog drafted a 15 year vision plan to boost the economic growth of the country to more than three times as compared to present day. As a National development agenda a three year 'Action agenda' was created from 2017-18 to 2019-20.

3. Human Development Index (HDI) is a measure for assessing progress in three basic dimensions of human development – a long healthy life, access to basic standard of living and access to knowledge.

4. In the Union Budget of 2017-18, Finance Minister Arun Jaitley relaxed the chargeable tax rates. The income tax for personal income in Rs. 25 lakh to 5 lakh bracket was reduced to 5% from the former 10%. This would bring more people into the tax net.

5. On 19th of July 1969 14 private banks were nationalised. This was the first nationalization of commercial banks in India. In the year 1980 the second nationalization of commercial banks in India took place where another 6 private banks were nationalised.

6. Asian Development Bank released the Asian development outlook 2017 in which it had cut India's projection to 7.4% for 2017-18 from an earlier projection estimate of 7.8%.

7. The World Economic Outlook (WEO) is a survey conducted and published by the International Monetary Fund. It is published biannually and partly updated twice a year. It portrays the world economy in the near and medium context, with projections for up to four years into the future.

8. The 1967 Industrial licensing policy inquiry committee was also known as the Dutt Committee. It also recommended the classification of industries into sectors like core sector, non-core sector, reserve sector etc.

9. Fiscal policy is the means by which a government adjusts its spending levels and tax rates to monitor and influence a nation's economy. It is the sister strategy to monetary policy throughwhich a central bank influences a nation's money supply.

10. The National Anti-profiteering Authority (NAA) is the institutional mechanism under GST law to check the unfair profit-making activities by the trading community. The Authority's core function is to ensure that the benefits of the reduction is GST rates on goods and services made by GST Council and proportional change in the Input tax credit passed on to the ultimate consumers and recipient respectively by way of reduction in the prices by the suppliers.

11. India ranked at 122 out of 155 countries in the World Happiness Report 2017 published by the UN Sustainable Development Solutions Network on the eve of International Day of Happiness (20th March).

12. European Union (EU) and India established an Investment Fund Mechanism (IFM) which will

allow for a close coordination between EU and Government of India with the aim to promote and

facilitate EU investment in India.

13. Switzerland has ratified automatic exchange of financial account information through which it can share information about suspected black money with India and 40 other countries.

14. The Maternity Benefit (Amendment) Bill, 2016 amended the Maternity Benefit Act, 1961. The Act

states that every woman will be entitled to maternity benefit of 12 weeks. The Bill increases this to

26 weeks.

15. Demand-pull inflation is asserted to arise when aggregate demand in an economy outpaces

aggregate supply. It involves inflation rising as real gross domestic product rises and

unemployment falls. This is commonly described as "too much money spent chasing too few

goods."

16. Coir Udyami yojana is a credited linked subsidy scheme introduced by the Government of India to establish coir units. Coir is a fibrous mass extracted out from the coconut husk.

17. PRAGATI (Pro-Active Governance And Timely Implementation), is a multi-purpose and multimodal platform that is aimed at addressing common man's grievances, and simultaneouslymonitoring and reviewing important programmes and projects of the Government of India as wellas projects flagged by State Governments..

So, Option C is correct.

18. World Thalassemia day is celebrated on 'May 8'. Thalassemia is a genetic blood disorder with no cure except for bone marrow transplant.

19. EPFO signed an MoU with Housing and Urban development Corporation to enable its members to avail subsidy and intervention under PMAY.

20. Galloping Inflation is a type of inflation that occurs when the prices of goods and services increase at two-digit or three-digit rate per annum. It is an extreme form of inflation when an economy gets shattered.

21. The government set up a task force headed by Niti Aayog Vice-Chairman Arvind Panagariya to recommend ways to deal with employment data discrepancies and come up with reliable solutions to promote job creation.

22. Index of Industrial Production (IIP) is a composite indicator that measures the changes in the volume of production of a basket of industrial products during a given period with respect to the volume of production in a chosen base period. The base year for the IIP is 2011-12.

23. SEZ is Special Economic Zone in which the business and trade laws are different from the rest of the country. Manufacturing, trading and service activities are allowed in SEZ.

24. According to the Indradhanush roadmap, Rs. 10,000 crores were allocated towards the recapitalization of public sector banks in FY2017-18.

25. A 'Banking Outlet' for a Domestic Scheduled Commercial Bank (DSCB), a Small Finance Bank

(SFB) and a Payment Bank (PB) is a fixed point service delivery unit, manned by either bank's staff

or its Business Correspondent where services of acceptance of deposits, encashment of cheques/

cash withdrawal or lending of money are provided for a minimum of 4 hours per day for at least

five days a week.

26. World Bank consists of two institutions – International Bank for reconstruction and development and International Development association

27. According to report, India's growth rate will be very high and it will be one of the strongest among G20 countries.

28. According to Swachh Survekshan 2017, Indore city is declared as cleanest city in India.

29. Borrowers gain in inflation as they have to pay less in real terms as compared to when they borrowed the amount.

30. The theme for Technotex 2017 was Technical Textiles: Towards Future. It was organized by Ministry of textiles and FICCI in Mumbai

31. The third edition of G20 Framework Working Group (FWG) meeting was held in Varanasi, Uttar Pradesh. The two-day meeting took place under the G20 German presidency, and was co-hosted by the Union Finance Ministry and the Reserve Bank of India (RBI).

32. The Wholesale Price Index (WPI) is the price of a representative basket of wholesale goods.

33. Under Mission 41k, Indian Railways will save 41000 crores expenditure on energy consumption fornext 10 years.

34. The merchant needs a smartphone and has to download his or her bank's Aadhar Pay app from theGoogle Play store and accept payment by sending a pull notification to the customer's paymentbank.

35. Major functions of NABARD include providing refinance to financial institutions for financing various activities in rural sector, coordination with govt, banks and other institutions in rural area, credit planning, implementation of development and promotional programs and supervision of rural credit institutions.

36. The Government in the Budget estimates of 2017-18 had revised the fiscal deficit target to 3.5% from the earlier estimate of 3.2%.

37. The US had requested dispute settlement consultations with India at the WTO overMerchandise Exports from India Scheme and Export Oriented Units Scheme, among others. WTOprovision require that India must stop the payment of subsidies to exporters by 2018.

38. Real income is income of individuals or nations after adjusting for inflation. It is calculated by dividing nominal income by the price level.

39. It aims to clean up the balance sheets for PSBs to ensure banks remain solvent and fully comply with global capital adequacy norms Base – III. Besides, revised program of capitalisation will also be issued as a part of it.

40. The survey is released by department of public enterprises, Ministry of heavy industries and public enterprises on the performance of central public sector enterprises.

41. NCCT – Non-Cooperative Companies and Territories. RBI prohibited Indian entities from making direct investment in any entities located in NCCT.

42. The 8th Five Year Plan is also known as Liberalisation of the Economy. The liberalisation policieswere unveiled by then Finance Minister Dr. Manmohan Singh in 1991-92.

43. The committee reconstituted by RBI of an oversight 5 five-member panel for bad loan solutions was headed by Pradeep Kumar.

44. The twenty point program was conceived for coordinated and intensive monitoring of a number ofschemes implemented by the central and state governments.

45. Seigniorage is the revenue that state enjoys by having the monopoly to issue monetarybase. Inflation tax is the loss that is sustained by the holder of real money balances and nonindexed government bonds due to inflation.

46. An individual can claim long term capital gain on selling a house property after holding it for twoyears instead of three years.

47. The 'Nirvana Fund' will gather donations made from the private sector and establish a substantial pool of capital funds. These funds will be disbursed as 'angel investments' at minimal loan interest to fund the entrepreneurial ventures of those trained under the Pradhan Mantri Kaushal Vikas Yojana-2 scheme who haven't yet landed a job.

48. Under Price Deficiency Payment, farmers are proposed to be compensated for the difference between the government announced MSPs for select crops and their actual market prices.

49. A recession is a term that refers to a significant decline in general economic activity in a region, country, or the entire world leading to a decline in GDP and other economic indicators.

50. An economy where the share of its primary sector is 50% or more in the total output of the economy is called Agrarian economy.

51. The issuer of green bond publically states that capital is being raised for green projects

52. The scheme provides loans to micro in three categories ranging from Rs. 50,000 to Rs 10 lakh.Shishu - Loan up to Rs 50,000Kishore - Rs 50,000 to 5 lakhsTarun - Rs 5 lakh to Rs 10 lakh

53. India has replaced Japan as world's second largest steel producing country, while China is the largest producer of crude steel accounting for more than 51 per cent of production, according to World Steel Association (worldsteel).

54. When we divide NNP by the population of the country we get per capita income (PCI) of that nation.

55. The Reserve Bank of India (RBI) set up an inter-disciplinary Standing Committee on cyber security to examine various threats and suggest measures to deal with it. The committee has been set up based on the recommendations of the expert panel on information technology examination and cyber security headed by Meena Hemachandra.

56. The RBI during 2015 conducted inspection of selected banks' balance sheets in random. The report from such inspection is termed as Asset Quality Review (AQR)

57. Bureau of Indian standards revised the Indian standards for gold hallmarking i.e. 14 carat, 18 carat and 22 carat.

58. E-NIKSHAY platform is an IT tool which facilitates monitoring of universal access to TB patients database.

59. Steel ministry released new draft National Steel Policy 2017 which aims to double the domestic steel production capacity to 300 million tonnes.

60. 2nd advance food grains estimate of production of major crops id released by department of agriculture, cooperation and farmer's welfare. The production during 2016-17 is higher by 14.97 million tonnes than the previous 5 years average production of food grains.

61. Global Economic Prospects is a World Bank Group flagship report that examines global economicdevelopments and prospects, with a special focus on emerging market and developing economies.It is issued twice a year, in January and June.

62. BCSBI, Banking Codes and Standards Board of India, is an independent Banking industry watchdog that protects consumers of banking services in India. It was registered as a society under the societies registration act 1960.

63. Arvind Panagariya

64. Net national product refers to gross national product, i.e. the total market value of all final goods and services produced by the factors of production of a country or other polity during a given time period, minus depreciation.

65. Keynes made it known clearly that the equality between saving and investment is brought about by the changes in the national income (and not by the rate of interest as stressed by the classicals).

Q.1 In February 2020, which state has launched the Janasevaka scheme in a few municipal corporation wards?

A. Karnataka　　　　**B.** Maharashtra
C. Kerala　　　　　　**D.** Telangana
E. Telangana

Q.2 As per statement made by Tripura CM Biplab Kumar Deb in January 2020, around how many Gram Sevaks will be recruited in the state?

A. 900　　**B.** 1000　　**C.** 1100　　**D.** 1200
E. 1300

Q.3 Among the Padma Shri award recipients for 2020, how many women from Sri Lanka received award for their pioneering contributions in their individual fields and for strengthening India-Sri Lanka ties?

A. 2　　**B.** 3　　**C.** 4　　**D.** 5
E. 6

Q.4 Who has been appointed as a member of the Monetary Policy Committee (MPC) by RBI in January 2020?

A. Sudha Balakrishnan　　**B.** Mahesh Kumar Jain
C. Janak Raj　　　　　　 **D.** Viral Acharya
E. Amitabh Chaudhry

Q.5 Who will impart free Hindi classes for Americans and foreign nationals having a keen interest to learn the language and enhance their understanding of India's culture?

A. Syed Akbaruddin　　**B.** Moxraj
C. Shivshankar Menon　　**D.** Mani Shankar Aiyar
E. Raveesh Kumar

Q.6 Who took charge as new foreign secretary succeeding Vijay Gokhale, in January 2020?

A. Navtej Sarna
B. Syed Akbaruddin
C. Vijay Keshav Gokhale
D. Harsh Vardhan Shringla
E. Shivshankar Menon

Q.7 What are the OSCs for?

A. For promotion of Swaacch Bharat
B. To promote education in rural India
C. To help violent affected women
D. To cater better health facilities in the remote areas
E. None of the above

Q.8 Who releases Consumer Price Index for Industrial Workers?

A. Central Statistical Office
B. Labour Bureau
C. Department of Economic Affairs
D. Office of Economic Adviser
E. None of the above

Q.9 What is Consumer price index (CPI)?

A. It measures changes in the price level of a market basket of consumer goods and services purchased by households.
B. Is a tool used by collectors and investors to track values of collectibles against collectors market from a specific date, calculated in form of Index. It measures the value of a section of the collectors market and computed from the prices of selected collectibles, typically a weighted average.
C. It measures changes in the prices paid for goods and services used in crop and livestock production and family living.
D. A theoretical price index that measures relative cost of living over time or regions.
E. A quarterly economic series detailing the changes in the costs of labor for businesses in the country

Q.10 Which of the following is not a series of CPI?
A. CPI UNME　　　　**B.** CPI AL
C. CPI MC　　　　　**D.** CPI IW
E. CPI RL

Q.11 Which state has lowest rural population according to census 2011?
A. Rajasthan　　　　**B.** Madhya Pradesh
C. Haryana　　　　　**D.** Punjab
E. Sikkim

Q.12 Total literacy of India according to census 2011 is?
A. 64 %　　**B.** 67.66 %　　**C.** 69.76 %　　**D.** 74.04 %
E. 78 %

Q.13 Balance of Trade is positive when _________ are more than _________.
A. Import value, Export Value
B. Services, Products
C. Products, Services
D. Export Value, Import Value
E. Loans, Investments

Q.14 Which of are the following is/are the features of foreign trade of India?
A. 68% of trade occurs through ocean
B. Deficit in balance of trade
C. Increased export of manufactured goods
D. All of the above
E. None of the above

Q.15 The term 'Laissez Faire' is mainly associated with which among the following?
A. Capitalist Economy
B. Socialist Economy
C. Mixed Economy
D. Communist Economy
E. It is not related to economy

Q.16 SEZ Act in India was passed in
A. 2005　　**B.** 2006　　**C.** 2007　　**D.** 2008

E. 2009

Q.17 The Employees Provident Fund Organisation (EPFO) aims to cover all the workers in the country under provident fund (PF), pension and life insurance by ___.

A. 2030   **B.** 2025   **C.** 2028   **D.** 2040
E. 2050

Q.18 The Fees & Allowances of the members of the ESI Corporation is prescribed by the __________.
A. Director General, ESIC
B. Financial Commissioner, ESIC
C. Central Government
D. Standing Committee on Labour of the Parliament
E. None of the above

Q.19 Consider the following schemes launched by the Government of India since independence:

I. The Drought Prone Area Programme

II. The Nehru Rozgar Yojana

III. Swarna Jayanti Shahari Rozgar Yojana

Which among the above schemes was/were launched before the economic liberalization in India?

A. Both I and II   **B.** Only III
C. Both I and III   **D.** Only I
E. Only II

Q.20 Which of these schemes have been approved by the Employees' State Insurance Corporation (ESIC) for Insured Persons covered under the Employees' State Insurance Act?
A. Ayushman Bharat-National Health Protection Mission
B. Green Revolution-Krishonnati Yojana
C. Atal Bimit Vyakti Kalyan Yojna
D. Rahstriya Krishi Vikas Yojana
E. None of the above

Q.21 Which of the following is a centrally sponsored scheme to empower adolescent boys?
A. AKSHAY   **B.** SAKSHAM
C. SABLA   **D.** UJJWALA
E. None of the above

Q.22 What is the aim of Sakhi Centres?
A. To provide medical aid to women
B. To provide police assistance to women
C. To provide psychosocial counselling to women
D. Only 1 and 2
E. 1, 2 & 3

Q.23 Sometimes seen in news, what is NARI related to?
A. Self Help group
B. Online portal
C. NGO
D. Grievance redressal center
E. None of the above

Q.24 The RBI announced a DPI to assess and capture the extent of digitalisation of payments effectively. What does 'P' stand for in DPI?

A. Panel   **B.** Payments
C. Percentage   **D.** Prospect
E. Profit

Q.25 In February 2020, Dr Amit Mitra proposed Rs. 2,55,677 cr Budget for the next fiscal in the state assembly. He is the Finance Minister of which of the following states?
A. Maharashtra   **B.** Uttar Pradesh
C. West Bengal   **D.** Bihar
E. Punjab

Q.26 In February 2020, which of the following has received permission from the National Payments Corporation of India (NPCI) to expand its pilot UPI services to 10 million users?
A. Telegram   **B.** WhatsApp
C. WeChat   **D.** Snapchat
E. AnyDesk

Q.27 Which of the following has launched an e-calculator for individuals to estimate their tax liability?
A. RBI
B. Income-Tax Department
C. NITI Aayog
D. Ministry of Corporate Affairs
E. Institute of Chartered Accountants of India

Q.28 In February 2020, RBI has increased the real GDP growth for the fiscal year 2020-21 to how much per cent?
A. 5.5   **B.** 5.8   **C.** 6.0   **D.** 6.2
E. 6.4

Q.29 What was the color of Economic Survey 2019-20 this time?
A. Pink   **B.** Sky Blue
C. Blue   **D.** Lavender
E. Stone Grey

Q.30 Which of the following launched its Android POS device for merchant partners and small businesses in India in February 2020?
A. Paytm   **B.** PhonePe
C. FreeCharge   **D.** MobiKwik
E. PayPal

Q.31 Which of the following has imposed a penalty of Rs. 1 cr each on ICICI Lombard GIC and Tata AIG General Insurance Company in January 2020 for violation of various norms?
A. SEBI   **B.** RBI
C. PFRDA   **D.** IRDAI
E. NABARD

Q.32 In January 2020, which of the following has received Sebi's approval to float its initial public offering (IPO)?
A. Burger Club
B. Cafe Zoe
C. Burger Lounge India
D. Burger King India Ltd
E. None of the above

Q.33 In January 2020, the government has announced the sale of how much per cent stake in debt-laden Air India?
A. 100   **B.** 90   **C.** 80   **D.** 70
E. 60

Q.34 In January 2020, which of the following has launched UPI-powered payments service and has started offering the feature to its subscribers?
A. Bharti Airtel   **B.** Vodafone Idea
C. Reliance Jio   **D.** BSNL
E. Xiaomi

Q.35 In January 2020, the RBI has cancelled the Certificate of Authorisation (CoA) of which of the following digital payment wallets?
A. PayUMoney
B. Vodafone m-pesa Limited
C. Mobikwik
D. Citrus
E. ICICI Pockets

Q.36 Which of the following is planning to invest over Rs. 45,000 crore over the next five years to expand the National Gas Pipeline Grid and city gas distribution network?
A. ONGC
B. GAIL India Ltd
C. Bharat Petroleum
D. Indian Oil Corporation
E. NTPC

Q.37 Which among the following is the employee's contribution rate of wages under Employees' State Insurance Scheme with effect from 01.07.2019?
A. 3.25%   **B.** 1.25%   **C.** 0.75%   **D.** 5.25%
E. 2.25%

Q.38 Which among the following is not a reason to keep buffer stock of food grains by the Government of India?
A. To meet requirements in natural calamities
B. Prize stabilisation in case of crop failures
C. to provide grains under public distribution system
D. to export grains to gain profits
E. None of the above

Q.39 Which among the following Ministries is responsible for macroeconomic data gathering and statistical record keeping in order to calculate GDP?
A. Ministry of Finance
B. Ministry of Statistics and Program Implementation
C. Ministry of Human Resources and Development
D. Ministry of Urban Development
E. Ministry of Home Affairs

Q.40 The factor cost method assesses the performance of eight different industries to calculate GDP. Which among the following is not one of the industries?
A. Agriculture   **B.** Mining
C. Transport   **D.** Insurance
E. Education

Q.41 In January 2020, the Department of Telecom (DoT) has approved raising of foreign direct investment in Bharti Airtel to how much per cent from 49 per cent allowed earlier?
A. 100   **B.** 95   **C.** 75   **D.** 60
E. 51

Q.42 In January 2020, which of the following has secured a Rs. 3,000-crore loan from State Bank of India, which will enable it to clear some vendor dues and salaries?
A. Airtel   **B.** Vodafone Idea
C. Tata Docomo   **D.** BSNL
E. MTNL

Q.43 What is the maximum amount that the Paytm Payments Bank allows to be transferred to other bank accounts through NEFT mode?
A. 2 lakhs   **B.** 1 lakh   **C.** 10 lakhs   **D.** 5 lakhs
E. 7 lakhs

Q.44 What is the maximum percentage of the tax concession to the sovereign wealth funds on investment in infrastructure projects ?
A. 80%   **B.** 90%   **C.** 100%   **D.** 20%
E. 50%

Q.45 How many crores is allocated for Skill development program in 2020-21?
A. 3000 crore   **B.** 4500 crore
C. 4000 crore   **D.** 1000 crore
E. 2000 crore

Q.46 In which district will the 8th airport of Karnataka state be operated?
A. Belagavi   **B.** Ballari
C. Bidar   **D.** Vijayapur
E. Hassan

Q.47 Who has been chosen as the Central Banker of the Year 2020 for the Asia Pacific Region by The Banker magazine?
A. Shaktikhanta Das   **B.** Mahesh Kumar Jain
C. Sudha Balakrishnan   **D.** Rajnish Kumar
E. Prashant Kumar

Q.48 Which of the following years has been set as the deadline for the Delhi-Mumbai expressway?
A. 2021   **B.** 2022   **C.** 2023   **D.** 2024
E. 2025

Q.49 National Institute of Mental Health And Neurosciences (NIMHANS) is planning to train which of the following police departments in combating stress and other psychological issues?
A. ITBP   **B.** BSF   **C.** CRPF   **D.** CISF
E. SSB

Q.50 Where did the External Affairs Minister S Jaishankar co-chair the 19th Joint Commission meeting with Foreign Minister of Iran in December 2019?
A. New Delhi   **B.** Tehran
C. Pune   **D.** Tabriz

E. Chennai

Q.51 Who has been named 'Junior Wrestler of the Year' by United World Wrestling (UWW) in December 2019?

A. Rahul Aware
B. Amit Panghal
C. Deepak Punia
D. Ravi Kumar Dahiya
E. Robin Singh

Q.52 Who has won the 'India Cyber Cop of the Year 2019' award by NASSCOM-DSCI?

A. Navajyoti Gogoi
B. BP Raju
C. Santosh Kumar
D. P.K.Pandey
E. Arun Pandey

Q.53 According to a US government agency data, what is the rank of India in terms of largest publisher of science and engineering articles?

A. 1
B. 2
C. 3
D. 4
E. 5

Q.54 In December 2019, the Goods and Services Tax or GST Council has fixed a uniform tax rate of what percent on both state-run and private lottery?

A. 28
B. 20
C. 18
D. 10
E. 5

Q.55 How much concession will be granted by the Indian Railways for the youth participating in the "Ek Bharat Shrestha Bharat" programme?

A. 40%
B. 45%
C. 50%
D. 55%
E. 60%

Q.56 Where did a two-day National Conference on 'Uniformed Women in Prisons Administration' begin in December 2019?

A. Uttar Pradesh
B. Bihar
C. Madhya Pradesh
D. Jharkhand
E. Chhattisgarh

Q.57 Who has been honoured with the World Economic Forum's 26th Annual Crystal Award for raising mental health awareness?

A. Priyanka Chopra
B. Deepika Padukone
C. Anushka Sharma
D. Katrina Kaif
E. Alia Bhatt

Q.58 How many fast track special courts are being set up by the government for expeditious trial and disposal of rape cases, including that of minors?

A. 500
B. 750
C. 1000
D. 1500
E. 2000

Q.59 In December 2019, Social Justice and Empowerment Minister launched Braille version of the book Exam Warriors written by PM Modi. Who is the Union Social Justice and Empowerment Minister?

A. Narendra Singh Tomar
B. D. V. Sadananda Gowda
C. Thawarchand Gehlot
D. Krishan Pal Gurjar
E. Ramesh Pokhriyal

Q.60 Who has been appointed as the India's Representative and Governor on board of ERIA?

A. Arun Kumar Sinha
B. Rohan Shah
C. Sanjay Gupta
D. S S Deswal
E. None of these

Q.61 In December 2019, who has taken over as the new President of The Associated Chambers of Commerce & Industry of India (Assocham)?

A. Chandru Raheja
B. Subhash Runwal
C. Niranjan Hiranandani
D. Mangal Prabhat Lodha
E. Radhe Shyam Agarwal

Q.62 Which of the following has become the 3rd Indian firm to cross $100 billion mark in market capitalisation in December 2019?

A. SBI
B. HDFC Bank
C. ICICI Bank
D. Yes Bank
E. Canara Bank

Q.63 Which among the following means transfer of ownership, management and control of public sector enterprises to the private sector?

A. Privatisation
B. Liberalisation
C. Globalisation
D. Oligopoly
E. None of the above

Q.64 Who among the following was the Prime Minister of India when Economy Policy-1991 was launched?

A. Manmohan Singh
B. I.K Gujral
C. Atal Bihari Vajpayee
D. P V Narsimha Rao
E. Indira Gandhi

Q.65 Which among the following type of economies exist in Indian Economy?

A. Mixed Economy
B. Socialist Economy
C. Capitalist Economy
D. Free Trade Economy
E. None of the above

// Smart Answer Sheet //

Correct Indicates percentage of students who answered questions correctly.

Skipped Indicates percentage of students who skipped questions.

Q.	Ans.	Correct / Skipped
1	A	80.43 % / 17.66 %
2	C	84.09 % / 10.98 %
3	A	87.22 % / 10.78 %
4	C	76.94 % / 20.47 %
5	B	88.98 % / 10.03 %
6	D	84.82 % / 13.83 %
7	C	84.43 % / 12.3 %
8	B	80.86 % / 18.09 %
9	A	79.97 % / 10.84 %
10	C	79.38 % / 12.44 %
11	E	86.84 % / 10.98 %
12	D	87.59 % / 10.86 %
13	D	86.66 % / 12.46 %

Q.	Ans.	Correct / Skipped
14	D	80.85 % / 10.62 %
15	A	84.36 % / 11.8 %
16	A	78.67 % / 15.62 %
17	A	76.49 % / 13.58 %
18	C	80.46 % / 15.67 %
19	A	89.9 % / 10.01 %
20	C	88.44 % / 10.03 %
21	B	83.95 % / 15.43 %
22	E	81.55 % / 12.37 %
23	B	81.76 % / 12.91 %
24	B	89.17 % / 10.05 %
25	C	88.64 % / 10.31 %
26	B	88.04 % / 10.95 %

Q.	Ans.	Correct / Skipped
27	B	83.02 % / 16.59 %
28	C	88.88 % / 10.09 %
29	D	85.35 % / 10.33 %
30	A	77.03 % / 13.17 %
31	D	82.5 % / 13.0 %
32	D	88.51 % / 10.09 %
33	A	87.58 % / 10.18 %
34	C	80.73 % / 13.12 %
35	B	83.04 % / 13.34 %
36	B	88.37 % / 10.88 %
37	C	83.68 % / 11.97 %
38	D	82.29 % / 12.27 %
39	B	84.39 % / 11.26 %

Q.	Ans.	Correct / Skipped
40	E	82.88 % / 14.81 %
41	A	86.63 % / 11.42 %
42	D	88.43 % / 10.3 %
43	C	84.95 % / 14.04 %
44	C	83.91 % / 12.55 %
45	A	81.25 % / 14.21 %
46	C	80.83 % / 15.89 %
47	A	89.2 % / 10.7 %
48	C	81.98 % / 16.52 %
49	A	83.58 % / 12.96 %
50	B	82.88 % / 15.08 %
51	C	81.11 % / 13.49 %
52	B	88.6 % / 11.18 %

Q.	Ans.	Correct / Skipped
53	C	81.44 % / 14.15 %
54	A	78.31 % / 18.08 %
55	C	81.35 % / 10.24 %
56	C	79.28 % / 10.72 %
57	B	86.53 % / 12.82 %
58	C	81.98 % / 14.26 %
59	C	81.18 % / 16.86 %
60	B	85.96 % / 12.97 %
61	C	84.77 % / 10.23 %
62	B	85.76 % / 10.36 %
63	A	77.91 % / 21.1 %
64	D	89.39 % / 10.54 %
65	A	82.61 % / 16.79 %

Performance Analysis

Avg. Score (%)	36.0%
Toppers Score (%)	58.0%
Your Score	

//Hints and Solutions//

1. The Karnataka government launched the Janasevaka scheme in a few municipal corporation wards.

It will ensure home delivery of various services like ration cards, senior citizen identity and health cards.

A toll-free helpline has been set up for this scheme which will work from 8 am to 8 pm.

A sum of Rs 115 will be charged to provide the home delivery services.

Karnataka: State Animal - Indian elephant

State Bird - Indian roller

2. Tripura CM Biplab Kumar Deb announced that around 1,100 Gram Sevaks will be recruited in the state soon.

He made the announcement while commencing of Police Week Parade at Manoranjan Debbarman Stadium at Agartala on 9 Jan 2020.

He inaugurated the Police Gallery at Tripura State Museum which has been set up by Tripura Police.

It has been set up to showcase the sacrifice of police martyrs.

Tripura: State Animal - Phayre's leaf monkey

State Bird - Green imperial pigeon

3. Among the Padma Shri award recipients for 2020 are two women from Sri Lanka for their pioneering contributions in their individual fields and for strengthening India-Sri Lanka ties.

The awards have been conferred on Dr Vajira Chitrasena for her contribution to dance and Late Prof. Indra Dassanayake for her contribution to Hindi literature.

Previously, in 2002, Government of India had honoured the legendary Sri Lankan musician and Magsaysay award winner WD Amaradeva with Padma Shri for his contribution to strengthening India-Sri Lanka musical ties.

4. The RBI appointed its Executive Director Janak Raj as member of the Monetary Policy Committee (MPC), the highest interest rate-setting body.

The Monetary Policy Committee takes decisions based on majority vote.

Each member has one vote but the RBI Governor gets a casting vote in case of a tie.

Raj will replace M D Patra, who was recently elevated as Deputy Governor of the RBI.

5. The Indian embassy has started free Hindi classes for Americans and foreign nationals having a keen interest to learn the language and enhance their understanding of India's culture.

The free Hindi classes would be imparted by Moxraj, a teacher of Indian Culture at the embassy, from 16 Jan 2020.

Moxraj is the first cultural diplomat appointed by India at the Indian embassy in Washington DC.

6. Harsh Vardhan Shringla took charge as new foreign secretary succeeding Vijay Gokhale, on 29 Jan 2020.

In the headquarters of the Ministry of External Affairs, Shringla served as Joint Secretary.

He has also headed the United Nations Political and SAARC divisions in the ministry.

Earlier, he served as director of the northern division dealing with Nepal and Bhutan.

7. To help violence affected women, the centre sets up One Stop Centres (OSC). The scheme is operated by the Women and Child Development Ministry since 2015 having 189 branches across the country. The sole purpose of these OSCs is to facilitate integrated services to those women's by providing them services like police assistance; medical aid, psycho-social counselling and all these can now be available under one roof.

8. A consumer price index (CPI) measures changes in the price level of market basket of consumer goods and services purchased by households. It is a statistical estimate constructed using the prices of a sample of representative items whose prices are collected periodically. Consumer Price index for Industrial Workers (CPI-IW) is released by Labour Bureau.

9. Consumer price index(CPI) measures changes in the price level of a market basket of consumer goods and services purchased by households. The CPI is a statistical estimate constructed using the prices of a sample of representative items whose prices are collected periodically.

10. There are four series of consumer price index:-

- CPI UNME (urban non-manual employee)

- CPI AL (agricultural labourer)

- CPI RL (rural labourer)

- CPI IW (industrial worker)

11. Sikkim has lowest rural population according to census 2011.

12. According to census 2011 the total literacy of India is 74.04%

13.

- Difference in the value of exports and imports of visible items is called Balance of Trade.
- When Export values are more than the import Values, then the balance of trade becomes surplus and is considered as positive.
- When Import values are more than Export values, then the balance of trade becomes deficit, and is considered as negative

14. The correct answer is All of the above.

- India's foreign trade occurs through oceanic routes predominantly. Around 68% of trade is oceanic.
- The foreign trade is biased towards increasing imports than exports, which has resulted in deficit in balance of trade.

- Post-Independence, the agricultural goods were major exports but present scenario reflects the shift from agricultural goods to manufactured goods like fertilizers, chemicals, petroleum products etc.

15. The term ' Laissez Faire' is used in order to denote the capitalist type of economy.

It means that the economy is market-based and there is no role of the government in this kind of economy.

In case of a socialist economy, all the means of production and distribution are controlled by the government.

In the mixed economy, there are characteristics of both the capitalist economy and the socialist economy.

India is an example of mixed economy whereas US and China are the examples of capitalist and socialist economies respectively.

16. The SEZ Act – Special Economic Zone Act was passed in May, 2005. The act envisages that the SEZs would attract a large flow of foreign and domestic investment in infrastructure and productive capacity leading to generation of additional economic activity and creation of employment opportunities.

17. The Employees Provident Fund Organisation (EPFO) aims to cover all the workers in the country under provident fund (PF), pension and life insurance by 2030. The retirement fund body has set itself this ambitious target in its vision document. The vision also talks about online services for all EPFO benefits with state-of-the-art technology.

18. The Fees & Allowances of the members of the ESI Corporation is prescribed by the Central Government.

According to the Employee State Insurance Act 1948, Chapter 2, Section 15:

Members of the ESI Corporation, the Standing Committee and the Medical Benefit Council shall receive such fees and allowances as may from time to time be prescribed by the Central Government.

19. The Drought-Prone Area Programme was launched in the year 1973 with an aim to undertake various development activities in order to improve the economy of the drought-prone areas of the country.

The Nehru Rozgar Yojana was launched in the year 1989 and it was later revised in 1990. It focused on micro enterprises development, urban wage employment etc.

The Swarna Jayanti Shahari Rozgar Yojana was launched in 1997 in order to alleviate poverty from the urban areas.

The Economic liberalization in India refers to the reforms and changes which were initiated in 1991, with an aim to make the economy more service- and market-oriented.

20. The Employees' State Insurance Corporation (ESIC) has approved a new scheme- 'Atal Bimit Vyakti Kalyan Yojna' for Insured Persons covered under the Employees' State Insurance Act. This scheme is a relief payable in cash directly to their Bank Account in case of unemployment and while they search for new engagement. The ESIC also approved the proposal for increasing the funeral expenses.

21. SAKSHAM comes under the centrally sponsored Rajiv Gandhi scheme to empower adolescent boys by the Ministry of Women and Child Development.

The aim of this scheme is the holistic development of adolescent boys aged between 11-18 years, based on the similar pattern of SABLA, which is a centrally sponsored scheme to empower adolescent girls.

UJJWALA is a comprehensive scheme which aims at preventing trafficking of women and children.

22. Sakhi provide an integrated range of services to women affected by violence. These services include medical aid, police assistance, legal aid/case management, psychosocial counselling and temporary support services. Women in distress can reach the Centres physcially or over the phone. One Sakhi Centre is to be set up in every district of India.

23. The Union Ministry of Women and Child Development (WCD) has launched online portal NARI (nari.nic.in) for the empowerment of women. It has been developed by the Ministry to provide easy access to information on government schemes and initiatives for women.

24. The RBI announced a Digital Payments Index (DPI) to assess and capture the extent of digitalisation of payments effectively.

The DPI would be based on multiple parameters and shall reflect accurately the penetration and deepening of various digital payment modes.

The DPI will be made available from July 2020 onwards.

25. The West Bengal Finance Minister, Dr Amit Mitra proposed Rs 2,55,677 cr Budget for the next fiscal in the state assembly.

Dr. Mitra proposed Revenue Receipts of Rs 1,79,398 cr while receipts from public debt and loans around Rs 80,000 crore.

The Budget puts emphasis on employment generation and economic development besides launching of several social sector schemes.

West Bengal: State Animal - Fishing cat

State Bird - White-throated kingfisher

National Parks - Buxa Tiger Reserve, Gorumara National Park, Jaldapara National Park, Neora Valley National Park, Singalila National Park, Sundarbans National Park

26. WhatsApp has received permission from the National Payments Corporation of India (NPCI) to expand its pilot UPI services to 10 million users.

Its payment feature, called WhatsApp Pay, allows users to pay others or do business transactions through their bank accounts.

WhatsApp has been running a pilot for one million users and has struggled to get a full-fledged licence since 2018.

National Payments Corporation of India (NPCI) is an umbrella organization for all retail payments in India.

It was set up with the guidance and support of the Reserve Bank of India (RBI) and Indian Banks Association (IBA).

NPCI: Headquarters - Mumbai

27. The Income-Tax Department has launched an e-calculator for individuals to estimate their tax liability.

The calculator, with a comparative table to compare taxes in the old and the new tax regime, has been hosted on the official e-filing website of the dept.

The web portal is used for filing of electronic income tax returns (ITRs) by individuals and various other categories of taxpayers.

28. The RBI announced its sixth bi-monthly monetary policy statement for 2019-20 on 6 Feb 2020 in which the repo rate was left unchanged.

The Monetary Policy Committee (MPC), led by Governor Shaktikanta Das, said it has decided to keep the policy repo rate unchanged at 5.15%.

RBI has increased the real GDP growth for the fiscal year 2020-21 from 5% to 6%.

29. Option 4 is correct:

Ahead of Union Budget 2020, Finance Minister **Nirmala Sitharaman** unveiled Economic Survey 2019-20.

This year's Economic Survey is **lavender** in colour, symbolizing the integration of old and new.

The colour lavender, also used in the new ₹100 note.

Reserve Bank of India (RBI) issued lavender-coloured ₹100 currency notes in 2018.

The theme of this year's Economic Survey was **"wealth creation"**.

The cover of the Economic Survey is printed in different colours every year. The colour represents the government's focus areas for that year's economic planning.

Current Chief Economic Advisor is **Krishnamurthy V Subramanian**.

30. Paytm launched its Android POS device for merchant partners and small businesses in India.

This device helps merchants to accept payments through Paytm Wallet, all UPI-based apps, debit and credit cards, as well as cash.

Besides accepting payments, merchants will also be able to generate GST compliant bills and manage all transactions and settlements through their 'Paytm for Business' app.

31. IRDAI has imposed a penalty of Rs. 1 cr each on ICICI Lombard GIC and Tata AIG General Insurance Company for violation of various norms.

It has slapped the penalty on ICICI Lombard for violation of certain provisions related to health insurance policies.

IRDAI imposed the penalty on Tata AIG General Insurance Company for violation of provisions for the protection of policyholders' interests.

IRDAI is an autonomous, statutory body tasked with regulating and promoting the insurance and re-insurance industries in India.

IRDAI Headquarters: Hyderabad

32. Burger King India Ltd has received Sebi's approval to float its initial public offering (IPO).

The company, which had filed its draft IPO papers with the markets watchdog in Nov 2019, obtained its final observations on January 24, 2020.

The regulator's observations are necessary for any company to launch public issues such as initial public offer, follow-on public offer and rights issue.

33. The government has announced the sale of 100% stake in debt-laden Air India.

As part of the strategic disinvestment, Air India would also sell 100 per cent stake in low-cost airline Air India Express and 50 per cent shareholding in joint venture AISATS.

Management control of the airline would also be transferred to the successful bidder.

34. Reliance Jio has launched UPI-powered payments service and has started offering the feature to its subscribers.

The company has become the first telecom operator to enter the UPI payments space.

Currently, Reliance Jio is India's largest telecom operator with over 370 million subscribers. Jio's UPI payments feature is only available for select users now.

35. The RBI has cancelled the Certificate of Authorisation (CoA) of digital payment wallet Vodafone m-pesa Limited.

The central bank announced the cancellation after the company voluntarily surrendered its CoA.

Following the cancellation of the CoA, the company cannot transact the business of issuance and operation of Prepaid Payment Instruments (PPI).

36. GAIL India Ltd plans to invest over Rs 45,000 crore over the next five years to expand the National Gas Pipeline Grid and city gas distribution network.

GAIL currently operates 12,160-km of pipeline network and markets two-thirds of all-natural gas sold in the country.

It is currently executing more than 5,500 kilometres of pipeline projects and a similar length is at the planning stage.

GAIL is looking to put up 400 CNG stations and give out a record 10 lakh piped natural gas (PNG) connections to household kitchens in the next 3-5 years

37. 0.75% is the employee's contribution rate of wages under Employees' State Insurance Scheme with effect from 01.07.2019 and 3.25% is the employer's contribution rate of wages.

Employees in receipt of a daily average wage up to Rs.137/- are exempted from payment of contribution.

The Employees' State Insurance Scheme applies to factories and other establishments wherein 10 or more persons are employed. However, in some States threshold limit for coverage of establishments is still 20.

The promulgation of Employees' State Insurance Act, 1948 (ESI Act), by the Parliament was the first major legislation on social Security for workers in independent India.

38. The reason to keep buffer stock of food grains by the Government of India are-

To meet requirements in natural calamities, Prize stabilisation in case of crop failures and to provide grains under public distribution system.

The maximum stock of wheat and rice are held by the government.

Food Corporation of India has the prime responsibility to procure the food grains and it is done at minimum support price and stored in various warehouses and then it is supplied to the state government.

The Targeted Public Distribution System was introduced effectively from June 1997 that envisaged subsidized distribution of food grains to poor families.

39. Ministry of Statistics and Program Implementation is responsible for macroeconomic data gathering and statistical record-keeping in order to calculate GDP.

The Central Statistics Office that comes under this Ministry actually keeps and analysis all the record.

The Office conducts an annual survey of industries and compilation of various indexes like the Index of Industrial Production (IIP), Consumer Price Index (CPI), etc.

The GDP in India is calculated using two different methods-at factor cost and at market prices.

GDP at factor cost is the most commonly followed figure and reported in the media.

40. The following eight industry sectors - Agriculture, forestry, and fishing Mining and quarrying Manufacturing Electricity, gas and water supply Construction Trade, hotels, transport, and communication Financing, insurance, real estate, and business services Community, social and personal services.

It is calculated by collecting data for the net change in value for each sector during a particular time period.

GDP at Factor Cost = total value of goods & services produced at factor cost in a geographic boundary of a country.

GDP at factor cost plus indirect taxes less(-) subsidies on products = "GDP at producer price".

41. The Department of Telecom (DoT) has approved raising of foreign direct investment in Bharti Airtel to 100 per cent from 49 per cent allowed earlier.

The company also has the approval of the Reserve Bank of India (RBI) that allowed foreign investors to hold up to 74 per cent stake in the company.

The approval comes a few days before the company has to clear the statutory liabilities of up to nearly Rs 35,586 crore, of which Rs 21,682 crore is licence fee and another Rs 13,904.01 crore is spectrum dues.

42. BSNL has secured a Rs. 3,000-crore loan from State Bank of India, which will enable it to clear some vendor dues and salaries.

The loan was sanctioned a couple of weeks ago and Rs. 2,500 crore has been utilised so far, of which Rs. 1,700 crore went towards clearing dues of some of the vendors.

The remaining Rs. 500 crore can be used for paying salaries for December.

43. Millions of users can pay up to ₹10 lakh per transaction instantly from their Paytm App using NEFT powered by Paytm Payments Bank.

IMPS (Immediate Payment Service) facility allowed 24x7 fund transfers online but it had a limit of ₹2 lakhs.

Now, transfers greater than Rs 2 lakhs and up to Rs 10 lakhs to other Bank Accounts can be done through NEFT (National Electronic Funds Transfer).

The Receiving Bank can take up to 2 hours to credit the money in the receiver's account.

NEFT is now available 24*7.

Transfers up to Rs 2 lakhs to Other Bank Accounts are done through IMPS (Immediate Payment Service) which is real-time and available 24×7 including Sundays and bank holidays.

44. Finance Minister Smt. Nirmala Sitharaman, in her Budget speech, proposed 100% tax exemption to the sovereign wealth funds on investment in infrastructure projects.

This proposal will give a boost to the infrastructure investments in India.

She has announced the abolition of dividend distribution tax (DDT) which is beneficial for the global yield-seeking infrastructure investors in India.

The National Investment and Infrastructure Fund (NIIF) is India's first sovereign wealth fund that was established by the Government of India in February 2015.

Its headquarters is in Mumbai.

Shree Sujoy Bose is currently Managing Director & CEO of the National Investment and Infrastructure Fund of India (NIIF).

45. The Finance Minister Nirmala Sitharaman, in her Budget speech proposed to provide about Rs 3,000 crore for skill development.

Shree Mahendra Nath Pandey is a Union Minister for Skill Development and Entrepreneurship.

He laid the foundation stone of Indian Institute of Skills (IIS) at Mumbai in the campus of National Skill Training Institute (NSTI) in copartnership with the Tata Education Development Trust (TEDT).

Union Cabinet also wants to establish the Indian Institute of Skills (IISs) in 3 cities namely Mumbai, Ahmedabad and Kanpur to give support to the Skill India Mission.

The Pradhan Mantri Kaushal Vikas Yojana (PMKVY) is one of the flagship programmes of the government and was launched by PM Shree Narendra Modi on July 15, 2015.

Bollywood stars Varun Dhawan and Anushka Sharma have been signed on to promote the Skill India Mission."Skill India" logo is shown below

46. Bidar airport is all set to begin operations on February 7, taking the number of airports in Karnataka to eight.

Located in the north-eastern part of the state, Bidar houses several religious shrines and monuments, including Guru Nanak Jhira Sahib, one of the holiest sites for the Sikhs.

The city is also renowned for Bidriware metal handicraft products that have been recognised with the Geographical Indication (GI) tag.

Developed under the Centre's regional connectivity scheme UDAN, the airport will be commissioned, operated and maintained by GMR Hyderabad International Airport Ltd (GHIAL).

The state of Karnataka was formed in 1956 and renamed it as Karnataka in 1973.

The capital of Karnataka is Bengaluru.

47. RBI Governor Shaktikhanta Das has been chosen as the Central Banker of the Year 2020 for the Asia Pacific Region by The Banker magazine.

The Banker is a London-based international financial affairs publication owned by The Financial Times.

It is known for its annual rankings of the world's top banks.

The 2020 list"celebrates the officials that have best managed to stimulate growth and stabilise their economy".

Shaktikanta Das is the 25th governor of the Reserve Bank of India (central bank of India).

48. January 26, 2023, has been set as the deadline for the Delhi-Mumbai expressway.

With its construction, one would be able to drive from Delhi to Mumbai in just 12 hours.

The expressway will have eight lanes, and provision has been made for its expansion to 12 lanes to meet future traffic growth.

Those driving from Delhi to Jaipur on the expressway will save nearly 1.6 hours.

49. Option 1 is correct:

After helping the Tamil Nadu police beat stress, the National Institute of Mental Health and Neurosciences (NIMHANS) is planning to train IndoTibetan Border Police (ITBP) staff in combating stress and other psychological issues.

The National Institute of Mental Health and Neuro Sciences (Nimhans) will train as many as 450 personnel of the Indo-Tibetan Border Police (ITBP) to cope with stress and other psychological issues.

A batch of 90 education and counselling staff, which is part of the ITBP, has already been trained at the Nimhans. They will, in turn, go back and work in the north-eastern regions to help the personnel in the force manage stress.

There are about 90,000 personnel in the ITBP.

S.S. Deswal is the current Director-General of ITBP.

50. External Affairs Minister S Jaishankar co-chaired the 19th Joint Commission meeting with Foreign Minister of Iran in Tehran on 22 Dec 2019.

The meeting was very productive and reviewed the entire gamut of the cooperation.

Both the nations agreed on accelerating the Chabahar project. India and Iran will work together closely on their shared interests.

51. Deepak Punia has been named 'Junior Wrestler of the Year' by United World Wrestling (UWW).

Deepak had bagged the 86kg freestyle crown in Tallinn, Estonia, in August 2018 to become India's first World junior champion in 18 years.

He became the first Indian wrestler and second from the country to get the international federation honour.

52. CBI officer BP Raju has won the 'India Cyber Cop of the Year 2019' award by NASSCOM-DSCI.

He won it for cracking a fraud case in an online entrance exam conducted by an engineering college in Rajasthan.

The award was given to Raju by Secretary, Ministry of Electronics and Information Technology, Ajay Prakash Sawhney, during the annual Information Security Summit held at Gurgaon.

53. India has become the world's third largest publisher of science and engineering articles, according to a US government agency data.

The data has been topped by China.

As per the statistics compiled by the US National Science Foundation (NSF), the number of scientific papers published worldwide increased from 1,755,850 in 2008 to 2,555,959 in 2018.

54. The Goods and Services Tax or GST Council has fixed a uniform tax rate of 28% on both state-run and private lottery.

It also decided to rationalise the GST rate on woven and non-woven bags to 18%.

It also decided to exempt upfront amount payable for long term lease of industrial and financial infrastructure plots by an entity having 20% or more ownership of Central or State Government.

55. Indian Railways has decided to grant 50% concession for the youth participating in the "Ek Bharat Shrestha Bharat" programme.

The concession will be given in basic fares of Second and Sleeper Class to youths with emoluments of not more than 5000 rupees per month for travelling from one State to another State to take part in the programme.

56. In Madhya Pradesh, a two-day National Conference on 'Uniformed Women in Prisons Administration' begins at Central Academy for Police Training in Bhopal began on 19 Dec 2019.

For the first time, the conference is being held in Madhya Pradesh, outside Delhi.

At present, there are more than 900 uniformed women government servants working in the state jail department.

57. Bollywood actress Deepika Padukone has been honoured with the World Economic Forum's 26th Annual Crystal Award for raising mental health awareness.

She is the only Indian actress to feature in Davos 2020 winners list which includes a total four winners.

The winners will be honoured at the opening session of the World Economic Forum Annual Meeting 2020 on 20 January 2020.

58. The Govt is setting up over 1000 fast track special courts for expeditious trial and disposal of rape cases, including that of minors.

The scheme will cost 767.25 crore rupees to the Centre and States.

A fast-track court in Telangana's Warangal district in August 2019 sentenced a 28-year-old man to death for committing the heinous act.

59. Social Justice and Empowerment Minister Thawarchand Gehlot launched Braille version of the book Exam Warriors written by PM Narendra Modi.

The braille version in English and Hindi has been printed by Rajasthan Netraheen Kalyan Sangh in Jaipur.

The book contains animated pictures and various yoga asanas which will let students imagine the pictorial graphics with ease.

60. Ministry of Commerce and Industry appointed Rohan Shah as India's Representative and Governor on board of Economic Research Institute for ASEAN and East Asia (ERIA).

He is a practising counsel at the Supreme Court.

The appointment is for a period of three years.

The Board of ERIA meets once in every six months in Jakarta and then in Japan.

61. Niranjan Hiranandani has taken over as the new President of The Associated Chambers of Commerce & Industry of India (Assocham), the country's apex organisation of industry and trade.

He succeeded Balkrishan Goenka, the Welspun Group Chairman.

Niranjan Hiranandani is the Co-Founder and Managing Director of the Hiranandani Group of Companies.

62. HDFC Bank has become the 3rd Indian firm to cross $100 billion mark in market capitalisation on 19 Dec 2019.

It has joined the league of Reliance Industries Ltd, which has a market cap of $140.74 billion, and TCS with a market cap of $114.60 billion.

Among the world's most valued banks and financial companies which have a market cap of over $100 billion, HDFC Bank is ranked at 26th position.

63. Privatisation means transfer of ownership, management and control of public sector enterprises to the private sector.

It is aimed to strong momentum to the inflow of FDI.

In 1991, the primary objectives of privatization in India -a) To raise the revenue in the market because of the fiscal crunch.b) Improve the profitability and efficiency of public enterprises.

Dr Manmohan Singh, then Finance Minister of India introduced major economic reforms- liberalization of the Indian Economy and the LPG reforms.

64. P V Narsimha Rao was the Prime Minister of India when Economy Policy-1991 was launched.

It aimed at rapid industrialisation and the abolition of industrial licensing.

It also allowed foreign investment and steps for the coexistence of public sector and private sector were also taken by the government.

The Monopolies & Restrictive Trade Practices (MRTP) Act was also repealed to eliminate the requirement for prior approval to be taken by big companies for expansion or diversification.

65. The Mixed Economy exists in India which means both capitalism and socialism exist together.

Mixed Economy- It allows a level of economic freedom to the companies in using the capital, but it also allows governments to interfere in economic activities of the companies in order to achieve social aims.

Socialist Economy- The economy of a country is controlled and regulated by the government in order to ensure the welfare and equal opportunity to the people in a society.

Capitalist Economy - Private individuals or businesses own capital goods. They make independent decisions about prices, production, and distribution of goods and the government does not interfere.

Q.1 The Surcharge to be levied on individuals with income between Rs. 50 lakh to Rs. 1 crore is –

A. 5%   B. 10%   C. 12%   D. 15%

E. 11%

Q.2 Which of the following is not correct.

A. Domestic production is the production activity irrespective of whether performed by citizens of India or not.

B. National income is defined as Net National product at factor cost

C. National product includes the production activities of resident with respect of where it is performed within the economic territory or outside of it.

D. According to expenditure method, national income is obtained by adding all the expenditure made on goods and services during a year.

E. All are correct

Q.3 Who headed the committee which recommended to avail Public distribution benefits to the migrants in country?

A. Sanjay Mitra

B. Partha Mukhopadhyay

C. Subir gokaran

D. H R Khan

E. A K Shah

Q.4 According to economic survey 2016-17, The current account deficit has declined to reach about what percent of GDP in the first half of 2016-17?

A. 1%   B. 0.3%   C. 1.2%   D. 0.9%

E. 0.7%

Q.5 'India vision 2020' is prepared by –

A. Arvind Panagriya   B. M. Subramaniam

C. A.P. Shah   D. S.P. Gupta

E. RBI

Q.6 Measure of the total inflation within an economy, including commodities such as food and energy prices (e.g., oil and gas) is

A. Core inflation

B. Underlying inflation

C. Headline inflation

D. Skewflation

E. Stagflation

Q.7 First masala bond is issued by -

A. IFC   B. HDFC

C. NHAI   D. ICICI

E. None of the above

Q.8 Who headed the committee which examined the existing framework related to virtual currencies?

A. Suresh Baijal   B. Ashok Lavasa

C. Dinesh Sharma   D. S.Christopher

E. A k Shah

Q.9 What is the India's rank in Economic Freedom Index 2017?

A. 141st   B. 142th   C. 140th   D. 145th

E. 143rd

Q.10 World economic situation and prospects report is published by –

A. WEF   B. IMF

C. United Nation   D. World Bank

E. IBRD

Q.11 In IIP index, which sector accounts for maximum weightage?

A. Crude oil production

B. Petroleum refinery

C. Steel

D. Fertilizer production

E. Electricity

Q.12 In terms of % of GDP which of the following deficits is minimum in Budget estimates of 2017-18?

A. Fiscal deficit

B. Primary deficit

C. Revenue deficit

D. Effective revenue deficit

E. None of these

Q.13 According to Fitch's review rating, India's sovereign rating is –

A. AAA   B. AA

C. BBBD. BBB   D. BB

E. None of the above

Q.14 Who regulates Asset reconstruction companies?

A. SEBI   B. RBI

C. Ministry of Finance   D. Special committee

E. IBA

Q.15 The situation when taxpayer uses fiscal incentives like tax concession given by government to lower the tax burden is termed as –

A. Tax advantage   B. Tax avoidance

C. Tax planning   D. Tax mitigation

E. None of these

Q.16 The audit limit of business entities opting presumptive scheme to be increased from Rs. 1 crore to?

A. 1.25 crores   B. 1.5 crores

C. 1.75 crores   D. 2 crores

E. 2.5 crores

Q.17 The first index price number for Wholesale prices commenced in India in the year

A. 1950   B. 1952   C. 1947   D. 1942

E. 1949

Q.18 From 16 June 2017 Petrol and diesel prices are being fixed on daily basis matching with fluctuation in international oil market. Till now the prices were revised on –
A. 1st and 15th of every month
B. 15 of every month
C. Weekly
D. After every 14 days
E. 1st and 16th of every month

Q.19 In union budget 2017-18, the limit of cash donation to political parties is set to –
A. 5,000   **B.** 10,000   **C.** 15,000   **D.** 2,000
E. 20,000

Q.20 What is the full form of UNESCAP?
A. UN Economical and social conference on Asia and Pacific
B. UN Economic standards conference for Asia and Pacific
C. UN Economic and social commission for Asia and Pacific
D. UN Economic sustainability committee on Asia and Pacific
E. UN economical standards commission for Asia and Pacific

Q.21 Inflationary gap is defined as –
A. The shortfall in total spending of the government (i.e., fiscal surplus) over the national income
B. This inflation takes place when the supply falls drastically and the demand remains at the same level
C. The excess of total government spending above the national income
D. An inflationary situation in an economy which results out of a process of wage and price interaction
E. The bonus brought by inflation to the borrowers

Q.22 India's growth rate projected for 2017-18 in regional economic outlook of IMF –
A. 7%   **B.** 7.1%   **C.** 7.5%   **D.** 7.7%
E. 7.2%

Q.23 which asset is termed as doubtful asset?
A. If sub-standard asset remains so for a period of 12 more months.
B. If standard asset remains so for a period of 12 more months
C. If loan remains SMA for a period less than or equal to 12 months
D. If loan remains SMA for a period less than or equal to 6 months
E. If loan remains SMA for a period less than or equal to 2 years

Q.24 Which of the following is not correct?
A. Revenue Deficit = Revenue expenses- Revenue receipts
B. Gross fiscal deficit = Total expenditure – (revenue receipts + Non debt creating capital receipts)
C. Fiscal Deficit = revenue deficit + Capital expenditure – Non debt creating capital receipts)
D. Effective revenue Deficit-= Revenue Deficit – grants for the creation of capital assets
E. All are correct

Q.25 Which committee was set up to recommend GAAR provisions?
A. Parathsarthi Shome Committee
B. Arvind Mayaram committee
C. Kasturirangan Committee
D. Jha committee
E. Rangrajan committee

Q.26 Which state becomes the first state to change its financial year to January – December?
A. Assam   **B.** Jharkhand
C. Madhya Pradesh   **D.** Gujrat
E. Maharashtra

Q.27 Custom Duty on LNG to be reduced from 5 per cent to __per cent.
A. 4%   **B.** 3.5%   **C.** 2.5%   **D.** 3%
E. 2.75%

Q.28 What does I' stands for in STRIVE?
A. Institute   **B.** Institutional
C. Industrial   **D.** Internet
E. Indian

Q.29 Philip curve shows relationship between –
A. Indirect tax and inflation
B. Tax and income
C. GDP and per capita income
D. GDP and Employment
E. Inflation and unemployment

Q.30 Which of the following is incorrect about Unicorns?
A. India is home to 20 unicorn companies
B. Flipkart, snapdeal and PAytm are Unicorn companies
C. Unicorns are startups with more than a billion dollar valuation
D. US tops the list with 144 unicorn companies
E. All are correct

Q.31 Which is the first small finance bank in India?
A. Ujjivan finance service pvt limited
B. Suryodaya Finance pvt limited
C. Au Financiers limited
D. Capital local area bank
E. Catholic finance bank

Q.32 The period of availment of MAT credit to be increased from 10 years to
A. 12 years   **B.** 18 years   **C.** 20 years   **D.** 14 years
E. 15 years

Q.33 Dearness allowance to employees in India is determined on the basis of –
A. WPI   **B.** CPI
C. WPI-Urban   **D.** IIP
E. Both WPI and CPI

Q.34 What is India's rank in Global FDI confidence index?
A. 3rd   **B.** 5th   **C.** 7th   **D.** 9th
E. 8th

Q.35 National Bank for Agriculture & Rural Development (NABARD) will make short term borrowings at prevailing market rate of interest for approx. Rs.20,000 crore for on-lending to Cooperative Banks at what rate of interest?

A. 4% **B.** 3.5% **C.** 6% **D.** 4.5%
E. 5%

Q.36 In which year did India initiate privatisation and economic liberalisation?

A. 1991 **B.** 1995 **C.** 1987 **D.** 1990
E. 1985

Q.37 What is the current economic rank of India in terms of GDP?

A. First **B.** Tenth **C.** Seventh **D.** Third
E. Second

Q.38 On what date does India's financial year begin?

A. 1st May **B.** 31st March
C. 1st February **D.** 28th February
E. 1st April

Q.39 Who is the current Managing Director of International Monetary Fund?

A. Dominique Strauss-Kahn
B. Christine Lagarde
C. Jim Yong Kim
D. Robert Zoellick
E. Frederick Musiiwa Makamure Shava

Q.40 'Multiculturalism' refers to the social phenomenon where:

A. Multiple people follow the same culture
B. One person follows multiple culture
C. Multiple people follow various cultures in one society
D. Multiple cultures are used to govern the society
E. None of the above

Q.41 The process where coins or banknotes cease to be legal tenders is called:

A. Demonetisation
B. Economic conservatism
C. Subsidization
D. Monetisation
E. Nationalisation

Q.42 The positive discrimination used to help the historically discriminated and marginalized groups is known as:

A. Preventive Action **B.** Curative Action
C. Affirmative Action **D.** Aided Action
E. Democratisation

Q.43 Free and compulsory education is a fundamental right for children between the age of:

A. 10 and 18 **B.** 6 and 14
C. 6 and 21 **D.** 3 and 18
E. 10 and 21

Q.44 Who is the current Governor of Reserve Bank of India:

A. Raghuram Rajan **B.** Arun Jaitley

C. Viral Acharya **D.** Urjit Patel
E. Shaktikanta Das

Q.45 Which is the institution that reviews, monitors and gives direction for implementation of population policy in India?

A. National Commission on Population
B. Indian Population Control Agency
C. Family Planning Commission of India
D. National Population Agency
E. Indian Commission of Population Analysis

Q.46 In 2015, BJP Government opened up the insurance sector by allowing what percent of FDI?

A. 6% **B.** 52% **C.** 49% **D.** 30%
E. 10%

Q.47 Every election party in India must register itself with:

A. Democratic Institutions of Indian Politics
B. Election Commission of India
C. Electoral Politics Organisation of Indian Republic
D. Electoral Commission of India
E. Political Party Registration Commission

Q.48 The formation of World Trade Organisation was done on:

A. 1st January 1997 **B.** 1st December 1996
C. 7th January 1995 **D.** 1st January 1995
E. 1st March 1995

Q.49 The anti-insurgency militia started by Mahendra Karma to tackle Naxalism in India was known as:

A. Salwa Muram **B.** Mao Judum
C. Bari Judum **D.** Salwa Judum
E. Bari Muram

Q.50 The founder of the social organization called 'Dalit Panthers' is:

A. Keshav Baliram Hedgewar
B. Narendra Dabholkar
C. Balasaheb Deoras
D. Ram Vilas Paswan
E. Namdeo Dhasal

Q.51 What term did Mahatma Gandhi use to describe Dalits in India?

A. Bahujan **B.** Harijan **C.** Swajan **D.** Divyang
E. Shrijan

Q.52 What is the literacy rate of India, according to the 2011 Census of India?

A. 74.04% **B.** 71.10% **C.** 77.11% **D.** 69.04%
E. 72.00%

Q.53 What is the name of the current Chief Minister of Telangana?

A. Nara Chandrababu Naidu
B. Ekkadu Srinivasan Lakshmi Narasimhan
C. Kalvakuntla Chandrashekar Rao
D. Narayan Dutt Tiwari
E. A. P. Jithender Reddy

Q.54 The Indian system involving Rajya Sabha and Lok Sabha is known as:
A. Bilateralism
B. Dual-power
C. Governmental Distribution
D. Bicameralism
E. Duomeralism

Q.55 The most populous state in India is:
A. Rajasthan
B. Bihar
C. Maharashtra
D. Madhya Pradesh
E. Uttar Pradesh

Q.56 What is a gilt-edged market?
A. Market where only two producers compete
B. Market of government securities
C. Bullion market
D. Market run on Keynesian principles
E. None of these

Q.57 In which year did paper currency first start in India?
A. 1880   B. 1950   C. 1861   D. 1542
E. 1861

Q.58 Who started the Operation Flood in India?
A. Verghese Kurien
B. William Gande
C. M. S. Swaminathan
D. Norman Borlaug
E. Radha Mohan Singh

Q.59 The emigration of highly trained or qualified people from a particular country is called:
A. Meritomigration
B. Relative Deprivation
C. Buffer Theory
D. Brain Drain
E. Qualitative Migration Phenomenon

Q.60 The farming in which the farmers focus on growing enough food to feed themselves and their families is called:
A. Organic Farming
B. Industrial Farming
C. Ley Farming
D. Individual Farming
E. Subsistence Agriculture

Q.61 Pradhan Mantri Jan-Dhan Yojana was launched on?
A. 25 August 2014
B. 28 August 2014
C. 15 August 2015
D. 1 August 2016
E. 28 August 2015

Q.62 Who is current Minister of Agriculture in India?
A. Radha Mohan Singh
B. Narendra Singh Tomar
C. Ram Vilas Paswan
D. Shripad Yasso Naik
E. Manoj Sinha

Q.63 The full form of RRB is:
A. Reserve Rural Bank
B. Regional Reserve Bank
C. Regional Rural Bank
D. Reserve Regional Bank
E. Rescheduled Region's Bank

Q.64 Which of the following industries was deserved in 1993
A. Railways
B. Atopic Minerals
C. Atomic Energy
D. Mining of Copper and Zinc
E. None of the above

Q.65 The term 'black money' is primarily used to describe that money which is:
A. Counterfeit
B. Earned from chit funds
C. Earned through underhand deals
D. Not currently in use
E. Income on which tax is evaded

// Smart Answer Sheet //

Correct — Indicates percentage of students who answered questions correctly.

Skipped — Indicates percentage of students who skipped questions.

Q.	Ans.	Correct / Skipped
1	B	82.34 % / 13.98 %
2	C	78.67 % / 14.56 %
3	B	77.16 % / 18.39 %
4	B	89.47 % / 10.26 %
5	D	76.12 % / 10.11 %
6	C	78.63 % / 17.07 %
7	B	86.86 % / 11.03 %
8	C	82.07 % / 12.34 %
9	E	88.11 % / 11.08 %
10	C	78.55 % / 13.27 %
11	E	83.34 % / 11.73 %
12	B	83.12 % / 16.51 %
13	C	84.2 % / 10.49 %
14	B	86.56 % / 12.38 %
15	D	87.01 % / 10.81 %
16	C	76.19 % / 11.1 %
17	D	81.11 % / 10.32 %
18	E	81.66 % / 14.93 %
19	D	84.0 % / 10.73 %
20	C	78.24 % / 16.83 %
21	D	79.32 % / 19.6 %
22	E	86.58 % / 12.55 %
23	A	87.97 % / 10.03 %
24	E	82.42 % / 16.78 %
25	A	82.9 % / 13.62 %
26	C	87.11 % / 10.44 %
27	C	86.99 % / 10.52 %
28	C	89.95 % / 10.02 %
29	E	79.56 % / 19.51 %
30	A	87.15 % / 10.94 %
31	D	88.26 % / 11.65 %
32	E	79.65 % / 18.66 %
33	B	89.5 % / 10.43 %
34	E	77.63 % / 11.43 %
35	D	85.9 % / 10.17 %
36	A	77.59 % / 21.48 %
37	D	80.21 % / 13.35 %
38	A	88.02 % / 11.44 %
39	B	76.64 % / 14.74 %
40	C	79.18 % / 19.89 %
41	A	88.85 % / 10.94 %
42	C	76.56 % / 22.66 %
43	B	88.34 % / 11.24 %
44	E	81.48 % / 10.36 %
45	A	81.88 % / 10.13 %
46	C	86.95 % / 11.14 %
47	B	88.25 % / 10.82 %
48	D	88.28 % / 11.49 %
49	D	85.22 % / 14.23 %
50	E	84.34 % / 10.32 %
51	B	80.3 % / 17.02 %
52	A	77.48 % / 17.29 %
53	C	79.62 % / 17.18 %
54	D	87.06 % / 12.07 %
55	E	88.95 % / 10.39 %
56	B	81.25 % / 12.68 %
57	C	81.9 % / 12.58 %
58	A	85.38 % / 14.54 %
59	D	79.1 % / 16.72 %
60	E	88.23 % / 10.79 %
61	B	79.26 % / 16.73 %
62	A	83.92 % / 11.92 %
63	C	89.15 % / 10.78 %
64	D	85.61 % / 13.36 %
65	E	89.69 % / 10.1 %

Performance Analysis

Avg. Score (%)	53.0%
Toppers Score (%)	75.0%
Your Score	

//Hints and Solutions//

1. Surcharge is a tax on tax. It is levied on the tax payable, and not on the income generated. In India, a surcharge of 10% is levied if an individual's income is more than Rs. 50 Lakhs and a surcharge of 15% is levied if the individual's income is more than Rs 1 crore.

2. National product includes the production activities of resident irrespective of where it is performed within the economic territory or outside of it.

3. The 'Working Group on Migration' headed by Partha Mukhopadhay suggested that migrants should be enabled to avail benefits of public distribution system (PDS) in the destined state by providing interstate operability of PDS.

4. According to economic survey 2016-17, The current account deficit has declined to reach about 0.3 percent of GDP in the first half of 2016-17.

5. The Planning Commission constituted a Committee on Vision 2020 for India in June 2000 under the chairmanship of Dr. S.P. Gupta, Member, Planning Commission. This initiative brought together over 30 experts from different fields.

6. Headline Inflation in India is measured in terms of Wholesale Price Index and the Office of Economic Advisor, Department of Industrial Policy and Promotion is entrusted with the task of releasing this index.

7. Masala bonds are bonds that are issued outside India but are denominated in Indian Rupee, rather than the local currency.

8. Dinesh Sharma headed the committee which examined the existing framework related to virtual currencies.

9. India ranks 143rd in 2017 Economic Freedom Index. India was ranked 143rd out of 186 economies in the annual Index of Economic Freedom 2017 that measures the degree of economic freedom in the countries of the world.

10. The WESP is the United Nations' flagship publication on expected trends in the global economy, produced annually by the UN Department of Economic and Social Affairs (DESA), the UN Conference on Trade and Development (UNCTAD) and the five UN regional commissions.

11. IIP measures variations in the production volume of a basket of industrial goods during one month period. The eight core sectors in which electricity has maximum weightage and fertilizer production has lowest weightage

12. In terms of % of GDP Primary deficit is minimum in Budget estimates of 2017-18.

13. It is the lowest investment grade rating.

14. Assets reconstruction companies are recognized by RBI as NBFC whose main objective is to handle NPA of the banks. They are specialised agencies with the main role of resolving the stressed assets issue of the Indian Banking system.

15. Tax mitigation is a situation where the taxpayer uses a fiscal incentive available to him in the tax legislation and thus availing a tax benefit.

16. The audit limit of business entities opting presumptive scheme to be increased from Rs. 1 crore to 1.75 crores.

17. The Office of the Economic Adviser to the Government of India undertook to publish for the first time, WPI with base week ended August 19, 1939, from the week commencing January 10, 1942.

18. The everyday change in fuel prices is because of a dynamic pricing system that reflects fluctuations in global oil market. Earlier petrol prices were revised every fortnight, meaning that unlike now, the prices were changed on the 1st and 16th of every month.

19. In union budget 2017-18 , the limit of cash donation to political parties is set to 2000. This is aimed at ushering in transparency in political funding, as several parties oppose sharing details of cash donations they receive.

20. The United Nations Economic and Social Commission for Asia and the Pacific (UNESCAP) is one of the five regional commissions under the jurisdiction of the United Nations Economic and Social Council. It was established in order to increase economic activity in Asia and the Far East, as well as to foster economic relations between the region and other areas of the world.

21. This is intended to increase the production level which ultimately pushes the prices up due to extra creation of money during the process.

22. India's growth rate projected for 2017-18 in regional economic outlook of IMF was 7.2% and 7.7% for 2018-19.

23. NPA is classified in three categories - Standard asset, substandard asset and loss asset.

24. All are correct

25. The Parthasarathy Shome panel was formed by PM of India in 2012, for drawing up the final guidelines on GAAR and mainly to bring about tax clarity and address the concerns of foreign investors.

26. A panel set up by the NITI Aayog in July 2016, recommended starting the nextfiscal year from 1 January to 31 December after the end of the current five-yearplan. On 4 May 2017, Madhya Pradesh announced that it would move to January–December financial year, becoming the first Indian state to do so.

27. Union Minister of Petroleum & Natural Gas, Shri Dharmendra Pradhan has said that in order to promote gas usage and to increase use of cleaner fuel and making Liquefied Natural Gas (LNG) more affordable to end users in the industries, Government reduced the basic customs duty on LNG from 5 per cent to 2.5 percent.

28. Skill Strengthening for Industrial Value Enhancement - STRIVE

29. The Phillips curve is an economic concept developed by A. W. Phillips stating that inflation and unemployment have a stable and inverse relationship.

30. In the venture capital industry, a unicorn refers to any tech startup company that reaches a $1 billion dollar market value as determined by private or public investment.

31. It is among the 10 entities that were given the in-principle approval by the Reserve Bank of India (RBI) to set up small finance banks.

32. The MAT credit can be carried forward only for a period of 15 years after which it will lapse. In other words, if MAT credit cannot be utilised by the company within a period of 15 years, immediately succeeding the assessment year in which such credit was generated, then such credit will lapse.

33. CPI – Consumer Price Index

34. The index is an annual analysis of how political, economic and regulatory changes will likely effect FDI flows into countries in coming years.

35. National Bank for Agriculture & Rural Development (NABARD) will make short term borrowings at prevailing market rate of interest for approx. Rs.20,000 crore for on-lending to Cooperative Banks at 4.5% rate of interest.

36. Privatisation is the process of transferring ownership of a business, enterprise, agency, public service or public property from government to a private sector. In 1991, India initiated privatisation and economic liberalisation.

37. India is poised to become the fifth-largest economy overtaking the United Kingdom by 2019 as per the IMF projection. The country ranks third when GDP is compared in terms of purchasing power parity at $9.45 trillion.

38. In India, Financial Year is taken as per the Income Tax Act 1961. It starts from 1st April every year and ends on 31st March of the next year.

39. On 28th June 2011, Christine Lagarde was confirmed as managing director of the International Monetary Firm (IMF) since 5th July 2011.

40. Multiculturalism is the presence of or support for the presence of several distinct cultural or ethnic groups within a society.

41. Demonetization is the act of stripping a currency unit of its status as legal tender. It occurs whenever there is a change of national currency. The current form or forms of money is pulled from circulation and retired, often to be replaced with new notes or coins.

42. Positive discrimination is an action favouring those who suffer from discrimination.

43. The Right of Children to Free and Compulsory Education Act or Right to Education Act also known as RTE is an act of the Parliament of India enacted on 4th August 2009which describes the modalities of the importance of free and compulsory education for children between 6 and 14 in India under article 21A.

44. Reserve Bank of India (RBI) governor Shaktikanta Das took charge after government selected him to replace Urjit Patel as the head of India's monetary authority.

45. National Population Commission is a commission of the Indian government. It was established in 11 May 2000. It is chaired by the prime minister with the Deputy Chairman Planning Commission (now NITI Aayog) as vice chairman.

46. In 2015, BJP Government opened up the insurance sector by allowing 49% percent of FDI.

47. The Election Commission of India is an autonomous constitutional authority responsible for administering election processes in India.

48. The World Trade Organization (WTO) is an intergovernmental organization that is concerned with the regulation of international trade between nations. The WTO officially commenced on 1 January 1995 under the Marrakesh Agreement, signed by 124 nations on 15 April 1994, replacing the General Agreement on Tariffs and Trade (GATT), which commenced in 1948.

49. Salwa Judum (meaning "Peace March" or "Purification Hunt" in Gondi language) was a militia that was mobilised and deployed as part of anti-insurgency operations in Chhattisgarh, India, aimed at countering Naxalite violence in the region.

50. Dalit Panthers is a social organisation that seeks to combat caste discrimination. It was founded by Namdeo Dhasal and J.V. Pawar on on 29th May 1972 in the Indian state of Maharashtra.

51. Harijan was the name given to the Dalit community in India by Mahatma Gandhi.

52. 74.04% is the literacy rate of India, according to the 2011 Census of India.

53. Telangana's first CM, K Chandrashekhar Rao, of Telangana Rashtra Samiti, is also the current incumbent. He has held office since the day Telangana was formed, 2nd June 2014.

54. A bicameral legislature divides the legislators into two separate assemblies, chambers, or houses. Bicameralism is distinguished from unicameralism, in which all members deliberate and vote as a single group, and from some legislatures that have three or more separate assemblies, chambers, or houses.

55. Uttar Pradesh tops the chart in most densely populated state in India. According to recent estimates, there are more than 210 million people living in the state of Uttar Pradesh.

56. The gilt-edged market is the market in government securities or the securities guaranteed by the government.

57. With the Paper Currency Act of 1861, the British colonial government got serious with the business of bank note making in India. Since then, banks lost their right to issue currency, leaving only the state in-charge of it. These notes came along to be the firstofficial paper notes by a government in India.

58. Operation Flood, launched in 1970, was a project of National Dairy Development Board (NDDB), which was the biggest dairy development program.

59. Brain drain is a situation in which large numbers of educated and skilled people leave their own country or area to live and work in another one where they can earn more money or conditions are better.

60. Subsistence agriculture is self-sufficiency farming in which the farmers focus on growing enough food to feed themselves and their families. The output is mostly for local requirements with little or no surplus trade.

61. Pradhan Mantri Jan Dhan Yojana, is financial inclusion program of Government of India which is applicable to 20 to 65 years age group, that aims to expand and make affordable access to financial services such as bank accounts, remittances, credit, insurance and pensions.

62. The three broad areas of scope for the Ministry are agriculture, food processing and co-operation. The agriculture ministry is headed by Minister of Agriculture Radha Mohan Singh. Abhishek Singh Chauhan, Krishna Raj and Parsottambhai Rupala are the Ministers of State.

63. Regional Rural Banks (RRBs) are Indian Scheduled Commercial Banks (Government Banks) operating at regional level in different States of India. They have been created with a view of serving primarily the rural areas of India with basic banking and financial services.

64. Mining of Copper and Zinc was dereserved in 1939. Railways, atomic energy and atomic minerals continued to be under the public sector.

65. Black money is basically a term that refers to money/funds earned by individuals, which they have not declared for tax purposes.

Q.1 The full form of PPP in India is:
A. Purchasing Power Parity
B. Product Purchasing Parity
C. Promotion Per Product
D. Personal Pension Plan
E. Preservation Power Product

Q.2 Which Act grants special powers to the Indian Armed Forces in "disturbed areas"?
A. Armed Forces Tribunal Act
B. Armed Forces (Special Powers) Act
C. The Disturbed Areas (Special Courts) Act
D. Army Act
E. Special Power for Indian Force Act

Q.3 The national initiative is run by:
A. Ministry of Women and Child Development
B. Ministry of Human Resource Development
C. Ministry of Health and Family Welfare
D. The first two
E. The first three

Q.4 According to Index of Economic Freedom, 2016 , what is the rank of India on the list of countries based on economic freedom?
A. 100th   B. 7th   C. 128th   D. 15th
E. 54th

Q.5 The Supreme Court of India re-criminalized homosexual behaviour among other things in the year:
A. 2009   B. 2012   C. 2016   D. 2010
E. 2013

Q.6 The Department of Health belonging to Ministry of Health and Family Welfare has programmes related to the following problems in the country:
A. Tobacco   B. Leprosy
C. AIDS   D. Iodine Deficiency
E. All of the above

Q.7 Approximately what percentage of people are Below Poverty Line in India?
A. 35%   B. 22%   C. 19%   D. 10%
E. 25%

Q.8 What does the term 'devaluation' mean?
A. Increase in the official value of a currency in relation to other currencies
B. Decrease in the availability of currency in an economy
C. Decrease in the official value of a currency in relation to other currencies
D. Cessation of the printing of a previous available currency
E. Decrease in the GDP

Q.9 The inflation rate of 2015 in India was:

A. 3.78%   B. 9.6%   C. 15.33%   D. 1.2%
E. 7.62%

Q.10 After how long does the Department of Economic Affairs present Economic Survey of India?
A. Every 10 years   B. Every 2 years
C. Every 5 years   D. Every year
E. Every 3 years

Q.11 Which of the following institutions are part of Maharatna PSUs?
A. Coal India Limited
B. Bharat Heavy Electricals Limited
C. Bharat Petroleum Corporation Limited
D. First two
E. First three

Q.12 Which of the following are not a part of the international forum G20?
A. Indonesia   B. European Union
C. Mexico   D. Italy
E. Pakistan

Q.13 Uniform Civil Code in India is opposed by which of the following groups?
A. Indian National Congress
B. Bharatiya Janta Party
C. All India Muslim Personal Law Board
D. All of the above three
E. Only Indian National Congress and All India Muslim Personal Law Board

Q.14 In 2015, how much was the agricultural output in Nominal GDP of India, according to IMF?
A. 1088   B. 413   C. 41   D. 290
E. 106

Q.15 The income tax in India is?
A. Direct and proportional
B. Indirect and progressive
C. Direct and progressive
D. Indirect and proportional
E. None of the above

Q.16 The first attempt to start economic planning in India was made by:
A. Balwantrai Mehta   B. Vallabhai Patel
C. Manmohan Singh   D. M. Visvesvaraya
E. Jawaharlal Nehru

Q.17 The process by which businesses or other organizations develop international influence or start operating on an international scale is known as?
A. Globalization
B. Multiculturalism

C. Nationalisation
D. Economic Conservatism
E. Liberalism

Q.18 The Indian movement devoted toward universalization of elementary education is known as:
A. Sarva Gyan Yojna
B. Gyan Dhan Yojna
C. Sarva Shiksha Abhiyan
D. Shikshan Bharatiya Yojna
E. Gyan Abhiyan

Q.19 Which is the current apex financing agency for the institutions providing investment and production credit for promoting the various developmental activities in rural areas?
A. Reserve Bank of India
B. National Bank for Agriculture and Rural Development
C. Agriculture Credit Department
D. Rural Planning and Credit Cell
E. Agricultural Bank of India

Q.20 Which institution was replaced by the formation of World Trade Organization?
A. International Monetary Fund
B. United League of Nations
C. Economic Council of Global Development
D. General Agreement on Trade Policy Regulation
E. General Agreement on Tariffs and Trade

Q.21 Who is the managing director of Patanjali Ayurveda?
A. Acharya Balkrishna
B. Acharya Balarama
C. Ramakrishna Shridhar
D. Baba Ramdev
E. Acharya Shiv Shankara

Q.22 Which political party did rationalist Govind Pansare belong to?
A. Bharatiya Janta Party
B. Indian National Congress
C. Bahujan Samaj Party
D. Communist Party of India
E. Shiv Sena

Q.23 The Draft of Five Years Plan is approved by:
A. Ministry of Finance
B. National Productivity Council
C. Planning Commission
D. National Development Council
E. Department of Economic Affairs

Q.24 The headquarters of International Monetary Fund is in the city of:
A. New York
B. Amsterdam
C. Massachusetts
D. Geneva
E. Washington D.C

Q.25 What was considered to be the ideology of Rashtriya Swayamsevak Sangh?

A. Hindutva
B. Manuvada
C. Sanatana Bharatwada
D. Swatantratva
E. Swarajyavada

Q.26 In which year was the Swachh Bharat Abhiyaan launched by Prime Minister Modi?
A. 2013   **B.** 2014   **C.** 2015   **D.** 2016
E. 2017

Q.27 Which initiative aims to improve farm productivity and ensure better utilization of the resources in the country?
A. Kisan Sahayak Yojana
B. Kisan Sinchai Yojana
C. Krishi Sinchai Yojana
D. Krishi Sahayak Yojana
E. None of the above

Q.28 When economic planning of a country is defined by the pressure of national economic development, it is known as?
A. Spatial Planning
B. Sectoral Planning
C. Normative Planning
D. Approach Planning
E. None of the above

Q.29 Planning Commission has been replaced by NITI Ayog. Which among the following was true regarding the Planning Commission?
A. Planning Commission was a non-statutory body
B. Planning Commission was an advisory body to the government of India
C. Planning Commission was chaired by the Deputy Chairman of the Commission appointed by the Government of India
D. Both A and B
E. All the above

Q.30 National Development Council was established in the year
A. 1950   **B.** 1951   **C.** 1952   **D.** 1953
E. 1969

Q.31 In recent years, it has been recognized increasingly that a large section of the rural population is out of the reach of the formal banking services. Which of the following is the name of the concept being floated around to bring most of the people in the net of formal banking and financial sector?
A. Corporate Governance
B. Financial Inclusion
C. Credit Management
D. Wealth Creation
E. Risk Management

Q.32 The phenomenon of the decline, however initiated, occurring in some measures of aggregate economic activity and causing declines in GDP and other key measures of Economic activity is called-
A. Recession
B. Deflation
C. Terminal Growth
D. Business Cycle

E. Domino Effect

Q.33 Who among the following holds the majority share in NABARD?

A. Reserve Bank of India
B. Government of India
C. Life Insurance Corporation of India
D. Government of Maharashtra
E. None of the above

Q.34 Which is the highest finance body for small scale industries?

A. IDBI   **B.** SIDBI
C. IFCI   **D.** NABARD
E. SFC

Q.35 The concept of MSP is very prevalent in the agricultural sector of the economy. The full form of MSP is -

A. Minimum Support Price
B. Maximum Stability Price
C. Minimum Static Price
D. Minimum Stability Price
E. None of the above

Q.36 If you are not able to pay your premium for the insurance policy, your policy gets terminated. This is known as –

A. Lapse   **B.** Liquidity
C. Liquidity Trap   **D.** Nullification
E. Void

Q.37 Which of the following Five Year Plans aimed at reducing the annual birth rate to 32 by the end of its duration?

A. Third Five Year Plan
B. Fourth Five Year Plan
C. Fifth Five Year Plan
D. Second Five Year Plan
E. None of the above

Q.38 The first blueprint of Indian planning was developed by –

A. The Congress Plan   **B.** FICCI Proposal
C. M Visvesvaraya   **D.** The Bombay Plan
E. First Five Year Plan

Q.39 Parampargat Krishi Vikas Yojana has been announced in order to promote which among the following?

A. Use of technology in agriculture
B. Sustainable irrigation practices
C. Organic Farming
D. Sustainable agricultural practice
E. None of the above

Q.40 The first channel completely dedicated to farmers in India was launched in May 2015. The name of the channel is -

A. DD Bharat   **B.** DD Krishi
C. DD Kisan   **D.** DD Uttaran
E. DD Khet

Q.41 National Statistical Commission was established in the year 2006 on the recommendations of the commission headed by –

A. Raghuram Rajan   **B.** YV Reddy
C. C Ventak Reddy   **D.** C Rangrajan
E. Bimal Jalan

Q.42 Which among the following is the regulator of the capital market in India?

A. Reserve Bank of India
B. NABARD
C. SEBI
D. SIDBI
E. IRDA

Q.43 The famous Beti Bachao Beti Padhao Scheme was launched in January 2015 in which among the following states in India?

A. West Bengal   **B.** Punjab
C. Haryana   **D.** Tamil Nadu
E. None of the above

Q.44 The Tendulkar committee report is associated with which among the following?

A. Measurement of poverty in India
B. Measurement of illiteracy in India
C. Reform of judicial sector in India
D. Reform of Panchayati Raj institutions in India
E. Reform of vigilance mechanism in the government departments in India

Q.45 Which of the following are the mandates of Krishi Vigyan Kendras?

(I) Conducting on-farm testing to identify the location specificity of agricultural technologies under

various farming systems.

(II) Organizing frontline demonstrations to establish production potential of various crops and

enterprises on the farmers' fields.

(III) Creating awareness about improved agricultural technologies among various clienteles through

an appropriate extension programmes

(IV) Construction of back end infrastructure and food processing zones in all districts 1. I, II and III

only

A. II, III and IV only `   **B.** I, III and IV only
C. I, II and IV only   **D.** I and III only
E. none of these

Q.46 Which of the following are possible causes for methane emissions that amount to global warming?

(I) Extensive rice agriculture

(II) Raising of livestock

(III) Wetlands

A. I only   **B.** I and II only
C. II and III only   **D.** I and III only
E. All I, II and III

Q.47 Which of the following is not a mission under India's National Action Plan on Climate Change?

A. National Mission for Enhanced Energy Efficiency

B. National Mission on Sustainable Habitats
C. National Mission on Tidal Energy
D. National Mission for a Green India
E. National Mission for Sustainable Agriculture

Q.48 The Indian Institute of Forest Management is located in which of the following places?
A. Deheradun
B. Mussorie
C. Bhopal
D. Tawang
E. Dispur

Q.49 Which of the following is rated the poorest region of the world?
A. The Middle East
B. Asia
C. Sub Saharan Africa
D. Latin America
E. None of the above

Q.50 Bharatnet project is related to?
A. Free wifi to students in rural area
B. High speed internet to farmers
C. Broadband connectivity to gram panchayats
D. A project connecting rural area with Urban areas
E. None of the above

Q.51 What amount has been allocated for MGNREGA in budget 2017-18?
A. 50,000 crores
B. 68,000 crores
C. 1000 crores
D. 48,000 crores
E. 23,000 crores

Q.52 Govt. of India recently announced its action plan on Sachchar Committee Report. What actions are being taken on the report ?
1. Govt. to bear all expenses of poor students who get into top institutions on merit basis.
2. Revision of Madarsa Modernization programme.
3. Special Rural Employment Guarantee Scheme for minority population.
A. Only 1 is correct
B. Only 2 is correct
C. Both 1 and 2 are correct
D. Only 3 is correct
E. All 1, 2 and 3 are correct

Q.53 Which of the following committees has been constituted to prepare a blueprint for doubling the farmers income by 2022?
A. Mihir Shah Committee
B. Ashok Dalwai Committee
C. Ashok Gulati Committee
D. Sarada Kumari Committee
E. Priyanka Singh Committee

Q.54 Which of the following departments of India is associated with the National Mission on BioDiesel
A. Department of New and Renewable Energy
B. Department of Land Resources
C. Department of Energy
D. Department of Rural Development

E. None of the above

Q.55 The Vanabandhu Kalyan Yojana has been launched by the government for the holistic development of which of following sections of people?
A. Minorities
B. Scheduled Castes
C. Scheduled Tribes
D. Poor people
E. None of the above

Q.56 The first forest survey of India was conducted in which year?
A. 1981
B. 1977
C. 1987
D. 1985
E. None of these

Q.57 COP 22 was held at?
A. Paris
B. Bali
C. Marrakech
D. Bonn
E. New York

Q.58 What is the minimum age of eligibility for entry into the skill program of Deen Dayal Upadhay Grammen Kaushalya Yojana?
A. 18 years
B. 12 years
C. 15 years
D. 14 years
E. 20 years

Q.59 Environmental protection act is also known as?
A. Central law of Environment
B. The umbrella Legislation
C. Law of Environment
D. None of these
E. All of these

Q.60 Out of the total population of the world, about 80% of it lives in ___?
A. Developed Countries
B. BRIC Countries
C. Latin America
D. Developing Countries
E. None of the above

Q.61 What is the full form of ASEAN?
A. Association of South East Agro Nations
B. Association of South East Asian Nations
C. Alliance of South East Asian Nations
D. Alliance of South East Asian Neighbours
E. None of the above

Q.62 How is dual economy distinguished from other economies? It is a mixture of __?
A. Industrial sector and manufacturing sector
B. Traditional agricultural sector and modern industrial secto
C. state ownership of the means of production in cooperation of foreign organisations
D. industrial sector and trading of goods obtained through imports
E. None of the above

Q.63 First separate department of agriculture is established in which year?

A. 1800   B. 1878   C. 1881   D. 1890
E. 1875

Q.64 The Scheduled Castes and Tribes (Prevention of Atrocities) Act was enacted in the year:
A. 1965   B. 1997   C. 1982   D. 1989
E. 1977

Q.65 Who introduced the Anti-Discrimination and Equality Bill, 2016?
A. Rajiv Gandhi   B. Shashi Tharoor
C. Irom Sharmila   D. Arvind Kejriwal
E. Sushma Swaraj

// Smart Answer Sheet //

Correct Indicates percentage of students who answered questions correctly.

Skipped Indicates percentage of students who skipped questions.

Q.	Ans.	Correct / Skipped
1	A	76.24 % / 12.58 %
2	B	84.71 % / 12.87 %
3	E	78.17 % / 20.46 %
4	C	80.27 % / 14.17 %
5	E	80.3 % / 12.51 %
6	E	86.55 % / 13.04 %
7	B	86.93 % / 11.88 %
8	C	79.53 % / 12.47 %
9	A	80.01 % / 13.06 %
10	D	76.54 % / 18.01 %
11	D	84.25 % / 11.15 %
12	D	80.83 % / 11.76 %
13	E	87.1 % / 11.55 %

Q.	Ans.	Correct / Skipped
14	B	79.61 % / 11.9 %
15	C	85.42 % / 13.57 %
16	D	78.68 % / 10.38 %
17	A	80.85 % / 14.91 %
18	C	78.74 % / 18.34 %
19	B	86.34 % / 13.21 %
20	E	88.96 % / 10.62 %
21	A	84.86 % / 14.56 %
22	D	85.71 % / 11.39 %
23	D	83.56 % / 14.29 %
24	E	88.2 % / 11.07 %
25	A	82.4 % / 15.22 %
26	B	84.02 % / 12.3 %

Q.	Ans.	Correct / Skipped
27	C	84.52 % / 10.78 %
28	A	77.78 % / 15.33 %
29	D	79.11 % / 17.79 %
30	C	81.77 % / 17.46 %
31	B	80.5 % / 10.08 %
32	A	82.22 % / 13.93 %
33	B	88.41 % / 10.88 %
34	B	78.25 % / 20.79 %
35	B	79.54 % / 11.29 %
36	A	87.77 % / 12.01 %
37	B	89.23 % / 10.75 %
38	C	87.67 % / 11.54 %
39	C	86.81 % / 10.27 %

Q.	Ans.	Correct / Skipped
40	C	81.0 % / 13.31 %
41	D	86.73 % / 11.08 %
42	C	79.8 % / 15.86 %
43	C	89.16 % / 10.33 %
44	A	78.92 % / 18.29 %
45	A	78.61 % / 15.66 %
46	E	88.25 % / 10.73 %
47	C	83.83 % / 12.14 %
48	C	84.61 % / 12.99 %
49	C	78.64 % / 15.98 %
50	C	81.82 % / 12.5 %
51	D	82.35 % / 11.87 %
52	C	77.3 % / 15.11 %

Q.	Ans.	Correct / Skipped
53	B	84.24 % / 14.34 %
54	B	76.64 % / 17.96 %
55	C	88.94 % / 10.99 %
56	D	89.82 % / 10.0 %
57	C	84.59 % / 12.96 %
58	C	86.11 % / 12.29 %
59	B	77.27 % / 13.95 %
60	D	89.13 % / 10.79 %
61	B	88.07 % / 10.27 %
62	B	86.84 % / 10.84 %
63	C	79.71 % / 15.88 %
64	D	89.84 % / 10.03 %
65	B	82.48 % / 13.96 %

Performance Analysis

Avg. Score (%)	71.0%
Toppers Score (%)	72.0%
Your Score	

//Hints and Solutions//

1. Purchasing power parity (PPP) is an economic theory that compares different countries' currencies through a "basket of goods" approach.

2. Armed Forces (Special Powers) Acts (AFSPA), are Acts of the Parliament of India that grant special powers to the Indian Armed Forces in which each act terms "disturbed areas".

3. The national initiative is run by The first three.

4. Index of freedom measures economic freedom of 186 countries based on trade freedom, business freedom, investment freedom and property rights.

5. The Supreme Court of India re-criminalized homosexual behaviour among other things in the year 2013.

6. The Department of Health belonging to Ministry of Health and Family Welfare has programmes related to the tobacco, leprosy, AIDS are the following problems in the country .

7. In 2012, the Indian government stated 22% of its population is below its official poverty limit. The World Bank, in 2011 based on 2005's PPPs International Comparison Program, estimated 23.6% of Indian population, or about 276 million people, and lived below \$1.25 per day on purchasing power parity.

8. In modern monetary policy, a devaluation is an official lowering of the value of a country's currency within a fixed exchange rate system, by which the monetary authority formally sets a new fixed rate.

9. The inflation rate of 2015 in India was 3.78%.

10. The Department of Economic Affairs, Finance Ministry of India presents the Economic Survey in the parliament every year, just before the Union Budget. It is prepared under the guidance of the Chief Economic Adviser, Finance Ministry.

11. Maharatna is the status given to top public sector enterprises where the companies have the authority to make foreign investments of upto Rs 5,000 crores without taking any government approval. At present the companies which have Maharatna status are: SAIL, ONGC, NTPC, CIL, IOCL, BHEL and GAIL.

12. The International forum G20 is a forum for the governments and central bank governors of 20 major economies of the world.

13. Uniform Civil Code is the constitutional mandate to replace the personal laws based on the scriptures and customs of each major religious community in India with a common set governing every citizen.

14. In 2015, 413 was the agricultural output in Nominal GDP of India, according to IMF.

15. Income tax is the most important of all direct taxes and with the application of progressive rate schedule, provision of exemption limit and incorporation of a number of incentive provisions.

16. The first attempt to start economic planning in India was made by M. Visvesvaraya.

17. Globalization is defined as an increase in economic integration among nations. It is the process of interaction and integration among people, companies, and governments worldwide.

18. Sarva Shiksha Abhiyan, or SSA, is an Indian Government programme aimed at the universalisation of elementary education in a time bound manner.

19. NABARD or National Bank for Agriculture and Rural Development is an apex development bank in India. It is headquartered in Mumbai and has branches all over India.

20. WTO replaced the GATT or General Agreement on Trade and Tariffs as the cry for globalization in world economy grew louder day by day. The replacement was pushed by developed countries of the world. India became one of the founding members of the organization.

21. Patanjali Ayurveda is an Indian FMCG company. The company manufactures mineral and herbal products.

22. Govind Pasare was a left-wing Indian politician and belonged to the Communist Party of India.

23. The National Development Council or Rashtriya Vikas Parishad is the apex body for decision creating and deliberations on development matters in India, presided over by the Prime Minister.

24. The International Monetary Fund (IMF) is an international organization headquartered in Washington, D.C., consisting of 189 countries working to foster global monetary cooperation secure financial stability, facilitate international trade, promote high employment and sustainable economic growth, and reduce poverty.

25. Rashtriya Swayamsevak Sangh, abbreviated as RSS, is an Indian right-wing, Hindu nationalist, paramilitary volunteer organisation that is widely regarded as the parent organisation of the ruling party of India, the Bharatiya Janata Party.

26. The Swacch Bharat Abhiyaan, launched in 2014 by Prime Minister Narendra Modi, is the most significant and one of the largest cleanliness drives launched by the Government of India.

27. Pradhan Mantri Krishi Sinchai Yojana is a national mission to improve farm productivity and ensure better utilization of the resources in the country.

28. Economic Planning may be divided into two types - Sectoral and Spatial. In Spatial planning, development is seen in the spatial framework. The spatial dimensions of development might be defined by the pressure and requirements of national economic development.

29. The Planning Commission was established in the year 1950 with a view to develop national planning for India. Important details about the now-defunct organization are as under: • It was an extra-constitutional and non-statutory body

• It was an advisory body to the Government of India on issues pertaining to national development

• It had the PM as the ex-officio chairman and a Deputy Chairman appointed by the Government. The main function of

the Deputy Chairman was to coordinate the work of
the commission

• It had an open provision for the total number of members other
than six cabinet ministers and a Member Secretary. Minister of
Planning was already an ex-officio member of the Commission

• It was an autonomous body entitled to form its own views on
important issues and place them before the governments

• It was a technical body with experts and professionals coming
from an array of specific areas as per the need of the planning of
the concerned period • The Commission had executive powers

30. The National Development Council was established on
August 6, 1952 by a resolution of the Union Cabinet. The sole
objective of the council was to create a platform where the centre
and the states can come together and discuss their issues
regarding implementation of planning programmes.

31. Financial inclusion is the pursuit of making financial services
accessible at affordable costs to all individuals and businesses.

32. A recession is a term that refers to a significant decline in
general economic activity in a region, country, or the entire world
leading to a decline in GDP and other economic indicators.

33. NABARD is the apex financial institution for rural and
agricultural credit in India. It was established in 1982 by RBI.
Later, RBI transferred its shares to the Government of India and
at present, Government of India holds the majority shares in the
organization with 99.60%.

34. The government established SIDBI under a special Parliament
Act as a subsidiary of the IDBI. Now the SIDBI is an independent
body of its own that focuses mainly on the financing of the
Small, Micro and Medium Enterprise (MSME) Sectors of the
economy.

35. Minimum Support Price is defined as the minimum rate at
which government buys the crops grown by farmers in a season.
It is the minimum price that a farmer is supposed to get for his
production.

36. If somebody stops paying the premium for his or her
insurance policy, the policy gets terminated. A lapse notice is sent
in writing to the policy holder when the policy is lapsed.

37. In 1952, the Family Planning Programme was launched, in the
Fourth Five Year Plan (1969-1974) a target was set to reduce the
birth rate to 32 by 1974 and Family Planning was given high
priority.

38. The first blueprint of Indian Planning was proposed by the
popular civil engineer and the ex-Dewan of Mysore state, M
Visvesvaraya- in his book The Planned Economy of India
published in 1934.

39. Parampargat Krishi Vikas Yojana was launched by the Union
Government in order to promote organic farming in the country
in cluster based model. Under this scheme, a group of farmers
will form a cluster having 50 acres of land to take up organic
farming under the scheme.

40. DD Kisan is the first ever channel launched by the Union
Government to dedicate to the cause of the farmers. This 24 ✕7

channel telecasts updated information on agriculture and related
subjects for the benefit of its target audience including cattle
rearers, bee keepers, poultry owners, mechanics and craftsmen.

41. National Statistical Commission was established in the year
2006 on the recommendations of the Rangrajan Commission that
reviewed the Indian statistical system in 2001.

42. Securities and Exchange Board of India is the regulator of the
capital market in India. It was created by an act of Parliament in
1992.

43. The Union Government has launched the famous Beti Bachao
Beti Padhao scheme in January 2015 amid fanfare in Haryana
(Panipat), a state that is noted for one of the lowest sex ratios in
the country according to the census by the union government in
2011.

44. The poverty estimates in India are done on the basis of
household per capita expenditure on a monthly basis. It is done
based on the recommendations of a committee headed by Prof
Suresh D Tendulkar who suggested the method in his report in
2009.

45. The Indian Council of Agricultural Research (ICAR), New Delhi
has started the Krishi Vigyan Kendras (KVKs) in all the districts of
the country with the following Mandates:

Conducting on-farm testing to identify the location specificity of
agricultural technologies under various farming systems.

Organizing frontline demonstrations to establish production
potential of various crops and enterprises on the farmers' fields.

Organizing need based training for farmers to update their
knowledge and skills in modern agricultural technologies related
to technology assessment, refinement and demonstration,
and training of extension personnel to orient them in the frontier
areas of technology development

Creating awareness about improved agricultural technologies
among various clienteles through an appropriate extension
programmes

Production of quality seeds, planting materials, livestock breeds,
animal products, bioproducts etc., as per the demand and supply
the same to different clienteles

Work as resource and knowledge centre of Agricultural
Technology to support the initiatives of public, private and
voluntary sectors for improving the agricultural economy of the
district

46. Methane is emitted by natural sources such as wetlands, as
well as human activities such as leakage from natural gas
systems, raising of livestock and extensive rice agriculture.
Natural processes in soil and chemical reactions in the
atmosphere help remove CH_4 from the atmosphere.

47. National Action Plan on Climate Change (NAPCC) is a
comprehensive action plan which outlines measures on climate
change related adaptation and mitigation while simultaneously
advancing development. The 8 Missions form the core of the
Plan, representing multi-pronged, long termed and integrated
strategies for achieving goals in the context of climate change.
The Eight Missions are: National Solar Mission, National Mission

on Enhanced Energy Efficiency, National Mission on Sustainable Habitat, National Water Mission, National Mission for Sustaining the Himalayan Ecosystem, National Mission for a Green India, National Mission for Sustainable Agriculture and National Mission on Strategic Knowledge for Climate Change.

48. The Indian Institute of Forest Management (IIFM) (founded 1982) is an autonomous institution at Bhopal in Madhya Pradesh, India, established by the Ministry of Environment and Forests, Government of India with financial assistance from the Swedish International Development Cooperation Agency (SIDA) and course assistance from the Indian Institute of Management Ahmedabad. The institute's objective is to fulfill the growing need for managerial human resource in forest and allied sectors.

49. The continents along the equator, Africa and countries like India, are the poorest. Even within Africa this effect can be seen, as the nations farthest from the equator are wealthier. In Africa, the wealthiest nations are the three on the southern tip of the continent, South Africa, Botswana, and Namibia, and the countries of North Africa.

50. Bharatnet project is a new name of National optical fibre network. It aims to provide broadband connectivity to gram panchayats. Phase – II of the project targets to 1,50,000-gram panchayats. Universal Service obligation fund is funding this project.

51. In the fiscal year, 2017-18, the allocation for MGNREGA went up to Rs 48,000 crore. The Finance Ministry allotted an additional Rs 7,000 crore when the states demanded more funds. The NDA government continued to increase the funding. For fiscal year 2018-19, NREGS was allocated Rs 55,000 crore.

52. A High Level committee under the Chairmanship of Justice (Retired) Rajinder Sachar was constituted by the Prime Minister's Office for preparation of a comprehensive report on the social, economic and educational status of the Muslim community of India.

53. The Union Government has recently constituted 8-member inter-ministerial committee to prepare a blueprint for doubling farmers' income by 2022. The committee will be headed by Ashok Dalwai, Additional secretary at the Union Agriculture Ministry and is expected to submit the report in two months. Its members will include officials from Agriculture and Food Ministries, experts from the Delhi-based National Council of Applied Economic Research and National Institute of Agricultural Economics and Policy Research.

54. Department of Land Resources under the Ministry of Rural Development is the implementing agency of the National Mission on Bio-Diesel. The objectives of the programmes is to bring unutilzed wasteland in to productive use by promotion of Jatropha and Pongamia Plantation for 20% blending with HSD and also generating a renewable source of Bio-fuel, thereby reduce country's dependence on imported petroleum diesel.

55. Vanbandhu Kalyan Yojana has been launched by Central Government of India for holistic development and welfare of tribal population of India. The scheme as outlined by the Ministry of Tribal Affairs is launched on a pilot basis and will be implemented in only 1 block in each of the 10 states being selected for the scheme. The states which have been picked are Andhra Pradesh, Madhya Pradesh, Himachal Pradesh, Telangana, Orissa, Jharkhand, Chattisgarh, Rajasthan, Maharashtra and Gujarat. The areas in the states have been selected based on recommendations of the respective state governments.

56. State of Forests Report is published by the Forest Survey of India (FSI) on a biennial basis since 1987. It is published on a biennial basis since 1987.

57. Conference of Parties 22 was held at Marrakech, Morocco

58. Union government on 25 September 2014 launched Deen Dayal Upadhyaya Grameen Kaushalya Yojana. The Yojana was launched by Nitin Gadkari, Union Minister for Rural Development during the National Convention on Skills for Rural and Urban Poor held in New Delhi.

59. Environment Protection Act,1986 is an Act of the Parliament of India. They relate to the protection and improvement of the human environment and the prevention of hazards to human beings, other living creatures, plants and property.

60. Out of the total population of the world, about 80% of it lives in Developing Countries.

61. The Association of Southeast Asian Nations is a regional intergovernmental organization comprising ten countries in Southeast Asia, which promotes intergovernmental cooperation and facilitates economic, political, security, military, educational, and sociocultural integration among its members and other countries in Asia. It also regularly engages other countries in the Asia Pacific region and beyond.

62. A dual economy is the existence of two separate economic sectors within one country, divided by different levels of development, technology, and different patterns of demand. Dual economies are common in less developed countries, where one sector is geared to local needs and another to the global export market.

63. In 1881, Department of Revenue & Agriculture was set up to deal with combined portfolios of education, health, agriculture, revenue. However, in 1947, Department of Agriculture was redesignated as Ministry of Agriculture. And now it is redesignated as Ministry of agriculture and farmers welfare.

64. The Scheduled Castes and Tribes (Prevention of Atrocities) Act, 1989 is an Act of Parliament of India enacted to prevent atrocities against scheduled castes and scheduled tribes.

65. Shashi Tharoor, MP, introduced the Anti-Discrimination and Equality Bill, 2016 in Lok Sabha on March 10th.

Q.1 In the case of a straight-line demand curve meeting the two axes, the price-elasticity of demand at the mid-point of the line would be

A. 0   **B.** 1

C. 1.5   **D.** 2

E. None of these

Q.2 Which is the first-order condition for the profit of a firm to be maximum?

A. AC=MR   **B.** MC=MR

C. MR=AR   **D.** AC=AR

E. None of these

Q.3 Which of the following is one of the assumptions of perfect competition?

A. Few buyers and few sellers

B. Many buyers and few sellers

C. Many buyers and many sellers

D. All sellers and buyers are honest

E. None of these

Q.4 Price and demand are positively correlated in case of

A. Normal goods   **B.** Comforts

C. Giffen goods   **D.** Luxuries

E. None of these

Q.5 Identify the coefficient of price-elasticity of demand when the percentage increase in the quantity of a commodity demanded is smaller than the percentage fall in its price

A. Equal to one   **B.** Greater than one

C. Small than one   **D.** Zero

E. None of these

Q.6 In which form of the market structure is the degree of control over the price of its product by a firm very large?

A. Monopoly   **B.** Imperfect condition

C. Oligopoly   **D.** Perfect competition

E. None of these

Q.7 A firm under perfect competition is

A. Price maker   **B.** Price breaker

C. Price taker   **D.** Price shaker

E. None of the above

Q.8 The elasticity of demand of durable goods is

A. Less than unity   **B.** Greater than unity

C. Equal to unity   **D.** Zero

E. None of these

Q.9 In the case of an inferior good, the income elasticity of demand is

A. Positive   **B.** Zero

C. Negative   **D.** Infinite

E. none of these

Q.10 Which is the other name that is given to the average revenue curve?

A. Profit curve   **B.** Demand curve

C. Average cost curve   **D.** Indifference curve

E. None of these

Q.11 In this technique, personnel specialists and operating managers prepare lists of statements of very effective and very ineffective behavior for an employee.

A. Critical incident technique

B. Forced choice

C. Essay evaluation

D. Management by Objective

E. None of these

Q.12 Which of the following issues is related to microeconomics?

A. The impact of oil prices on car production

B. The impact of money on inflation

C. The impact of technology on economic growth

D. The impact of the deficit on saving

E. None of these

Q.13 The word economy comes from the Greek word for

A. "Environment."

B. "One who participates in a market."

C. "One who manages a household."

D. "Conservation."

E. None of these

Q.14 Economics deals primarily with the concept of

A. Poverty   **B.** Scarcity

C. Change   **D.** Power

E. None of these

Q.15 The opportunity cost of an item is

A. The number of hours needed to earn money to buy it.

B. What you give up to get that item

C. Always less than the dollar value of the item

D. Always equal to the dollar value of the item.

E. None of these

Q.16 Factors of production are :

A. Inputs into the production process

B. Weather, social, and political conditions that affect production.

C. The physical relationships between economic inputs and outputs

D. The mathematical calculations firms make to determine production.

E. None of these

Q.17 In the circular-flow diagram,

A. Firms are sellers in the resource market and the product market.

B. Households are sellers in the resource market.

C. Firms are buyers in the product market.

D. Spending on goods and services flow from firms to households

E. None of these

Q.18 In the circular-flow diagram,

A. Spending on goods and services flow from firms to households.

B. Goods and services flow from households to firms.

C. Factors of production flow from firms to households

D. Income from factors of production flows from firms to households

E. None of these

Q.19 Scarcity is a condition that exists when

A. There is a fixed supply of resources.

B. There is a large demand for a product.

C. Resources are not able to meet the entire demand for a product.

D. Either A or B

E. None of the above

Q.20 Company goals that are concerned with creating employee and customer satisfaction and maintaining a high degree of social responsibility are called __________ objectives.

A. Social

B. Noneconomic

C. Welfare

D. Public Relations

E. None of these

Q.21 Discuss the roles of the HR Manager

A. Administrator / evaluator / career development advisor / instructor or facilitator

B. marketing programmes and services / instructor material producer

C. Needs analyst /organisational changer / researcher + (a) above

D. Both (B) + (C)

E. None of these

Q.22 The objectives of HR audit are –

A. To determine the effectiveness of management programmes

B. Analyse the factors and recommend for correcting deviations + (A)

C. extent to which line managers have complied with HRD polices + (B)

D. To study future manpower inventory and identify shortfalls

E. None of these

Q.23 Employee accountability is strengthens in

A. HR Audit

B. HR Training

C. Succession Planning

D. HR functions

E. None of these

Q.24 The main barriers of communications are –

A. Organisational + Semantic

B. Personal + psychological + resistance to new ideas

C. Both (A) + (B)

D. Organisational / psychological

E. None of these

Q.25 Manpower planning consists of –

A. Determining the jobs to be done / identifying the skills / estimating the exists likely / filling up the requirements

B. Identifying the skills / filling up the requirements

C. Estimating the turnover likely to happen in near future

D. Determining the jobs to be done

E. None of the above

Q.26 Promotion is basically a reward for –

A. Efficiency

B. Seniority

C. Physical fitness

D. Retention

E. None of these

Q.27 What is 360° appraisal?

A. A process that provides an employee opportunity in decision making

B. A process that provides an officer opportunity of feedback about own performance

C. A process that provides an employee with feedback about his / her workplace performance

D. Both (A) + (B)

E. None of these

Q.28 Role of performance management is to accomplish –

A. Performance needs of the organisation

B. Guide the development of individuals for skill and knowledge

C. Motivate individuals / provide data adopt condition of human capital + (B)

D. Motivate individuals / provide data adopt condition of human capital + (A)

E. All above

Q.29 Competency Mapping is possible through approaches like –

A. Job analysis / workforce skills analysis / supply and demand analysis

B. Job analysis / Gap analysis / solution analysis

C. Gap analysis / solution analysis + (A)

D. Both (A) + (B)

E. None of these

Q.30 Which out of the following is not a function of management?

A. Planning

B. Staffing

C. Controlling

D. Co-operating

E. None of these

Q.31 The degree to which jobs are standardized and guided by rules and procedures is called:-

A. Formalization

B. Decentralization

C. Centralization

D. Work Specialization

E. None of these

Q.32 The following system is simple, less expensive and less time consuming-

A. Checklist Method
B. Ranking
C. Confidential report system
D. Paired comparison
E. None of the above.

Q.33 ....is the simple act of comparison and learning for organisational improvement?
A. Job Evaluation
B. Ranking
C. Benchmarking
D. (i), (ii) and (iii)
E. None of these

Q.34 What approach towards the followers dominates in the leader member exchange theory?
A. Solitary
B. Unitary
C. Dyadic
D. Task oriented
E. None of these

Q.35 The following technique is used to evaluate an employee individually.
A. Paired Comparison
B. Ranking
C. Graphic Rating Scale
D. Forced Distribution
E. None of these

Q.36 The probability of bankrupt is higher.
A. for a levered firm than an unlevered firm
B. for an unlevered firm than a levered firm
C. only levered firm
D. only unlevered firm
E. none of these

Q.37 Which of the following statement is true if the Net Present Value (NPV) of a positive?
A. The IRR must be greater than 0
B. The discount rate exceeds the cost of capital.
C. The profitability index equals 1
D. Accepting the project has an indeterminate effect on shareholders
E. none of these

Q.38 All of the following influence capital budgeting cash flows EXCEPT.
A. accelerated depreciation
B. salvage value
C. tax rate changes
D. method of project financing used
E. none of these

Q.39 If interest rates rose, you would expect to also rise.
A. business risk
B. financial risk
C. liquidity risk
D. inflation risk
E. none of these

Q.40 Financial management is indispensable in any organization as it helps in__________
A. taking sound financial decisions
B. proper use and allocation

C. improving the profitability of funds
D. all the above
E. none of these

Q.41 This type of risk is avoidable through proper diversification.
A. portfolio risk
B. systematic risk
C. unsystematic risk
D. total risk
E. none of these

Q.42 Financial analysts, working capital means the same thing as
A. total assets
B. fixed assets
C. current assets
D. current assets minus current Liabilities
E. none of these

Q.43 Which of the following is a basic principle of finance as it relates to the management of working capital?
A. Profitability varies inversely with risk
B. Liquidity moves together with risk
C. Profitability moves together with risk
D. Profitability moves together with liquidity
E. none of these

Q.44 The return relative solves the problem of
A. inflation
B. negative returns
C. interest rates
D. tax differences
E. none of these

Q.45 If the Dow Jones Industrials had a price appreciation of 6 percent one year and yet Total return for the year was 11 percent; the difference would be due to_____.
A. the tax treatment of capital gains
B. the cumulative wealth effect
C. dividends
D. profits
E. none of these

Q.46 Shareholder wealth in a firm is represented by
A. the number of people employed in the firm
B. the book value of the firm's assets less the book value of its liabilities
C. the amount of salary paid to its employees
D. the market price per share of the firms common stock
E. none of these

Q.47 In order to determine the compound growth rate of an investment over some period, an investor would calculate the
A. arithmetic mean
B. geometric mean
C. calculus mean
D. arithmetic median
E. none of these

Q.48 Net present value is a popular method which falls
A. With in non- discount cash flow method
B. With in discount cash flow method
C. Equal With in non- discount cash flow method
D. No discount cash flow

E. none of these

Q.49 A major difference between real and nominal returns is that

A. real returns adjust for inflation and nominal returns do not

B. real returns use actual cash flows and nominal returns use expected cash flows

C. real returns adjust for commissions and nominal returns do not

D. real returns show the highest possible return and nominal returns show the lowest possible return

E. none of these

Q.50 When most people refer to the mean, they are referring to the

A. median
B. arithmetic mean
C. geometric mean
D. cumulative mean
E. none of these

Q.51 The gross working capital is a

A. Going concern
B. money measurement
C. revenue concept
D. cost concept
E. none of these

Q.52 __________ is concerned with the interrelationships between security returns.

A. random diversification
B. correlating diversification
C. Friedman diversification
D. Markowitz diversification
E. none of these

Q.53 The rate of return on investment

A. falls
B. going
C. constant
D. change
E. none of these

Q.54 Portfolio weights are found by

A. dividing standard deviation by expected value

B. calculating the percentage each asset is to the total portfolio value

C. calculating the return of each asset to total portfolio return

D. dividing expected value by the standard deviation

E. none of these

Q.55 Greater the size of a business unit working capital.

A. larger
B. lower
C. no change
D. fixed
E. none of these

Q.56 The four unique elements to services include:

A. Independence, intangibility, inventory, and inception
B. Independence, increase, inventory, and intangibility
C. Intangibility, inconsistency, inseparability, and inventory
D. Intangibility, independence, inseparability, and inventory
E. none of these

Q.57 A change in an individual's behavior prompted by information and experience refers to which one of the following concept?

A. Learning
B. Role selection
C. Perception
D. Motivation
E. none of these

Q.58 While buying milk which kind of behavior is displayed by a person?

A. Extensive problem solving behavior
B. Routinized buying behavior
C. Variety seeking behavior
D. None of the above
E. All of the above

Q.59 Whether to sell via intermediaries or directly to consumers, how many outlets to sell through, and whether to control or cooperate with other channel members are examples of decisions marketers must make about

A. Promotion
B. Price
C. Distribution
D. Product
E. none of these

Q.60 The extended Ps of service marketing mix is:

A. People, Product, Place
B. Price Physical Evidence, Promotion
C. Physical Evidence, Process, People
D. Product, Process, Physical Environment
E. none of these

Q.61 A social and managerial process by which individuals and organizations obtain what they need and want through value creation refers to which one of the following concepts?

A. Selling
B. Advertising
C. Barter
D. Marketing
E. none of these

Q.62 What is the basic property of a service which makes it different from a product?

A. Shape
B. Size
C. Very expensive
D. Intangibility
E. none of these

Q.63 Which one of the following phrases reflects the marketing concept?

A. The supplier is a king in the market
B. Marketing should be viewed as hunting not gardening
C. This is what I make, won't you please buy it
D. This is what I want, won't you please make it
E. none of these

Q.64 The solution to price competition is to develop a differentiated:

A. Product, price, and promotion
B. Offer, delivery, and image
C. Package and label
D. International Web site
E. none of these

Q.65 You purchase cleaning supplies for your custodial help regularly. It is showing which buying situation?

A. Modified rebuy
B. Straight rebuy
C. Modified straight rebuy
D. Consumer buy
E. none of these

// Smart Answer Sheet //

Correct Indicates percentage of students who answered questions correctly.

Skipped Indicates percentage of students who skipped questions.

Q.	Ans.	Correct / Skipped
1	B	89.32 % / 10.04 %
2	B	76.78 % / 19.03 %
3	C	87.5 % / 10.81 %
4	C	86.6 % / 11.93 %
5	C	85.34 % / 12.88 %
6	A	83.32 % / 10.76 %
7	C	87.01 % / 10.23 %
8	B	89.03 % / 10.12 %
9	C	88.95 % / 10.89 %
10	B	85.16 % / 10.69 %
11	A	77.85 % / 17.27 %
12	A	78.17 % / 20.39 %
13	C	78.43 % / 10.95 %

Q.	Ans.	Correct / Skipped
14	B	81.22 % / 13.0 %
15	B	88.57 % / 10.6 %
16	A	83.55 % / 14.14 %
17	B	89.96 % / 10.01 %
18	A	89.16 % / 10.35 %
19	C	80.85 % / 10.4 %
20	B	85.89 % / 13.14 %
21	D	80.45 % / 14.34 %
22	C	79.03 % / 15.65 %
23	A	81.6 % / 17.59 %
24	C	76.41 % / 17.14 %
25	A	76.3 % / 19.13 %
26	A	83.02 % / 10.0 %

Q.	Ans.	Correct / Skipped
27	C	84.71 % / 13.37 %
28	E	85.99 % / 10.7 %
29	C	83.64 % / 14.17 %
30	B	89.95 % / 10.04 %
31	A	82.23 % / 12.71 %
32	A	86.61 % / 11.14 %
33	C	89.22 % / 10.09 %
34	C	80.07 % / 12.65 %
35	C	87.56 % / 10.73 %
36	C	87.68 % / 11.67 %
37	C	78.11 % / 12.26 %
38	D	85.37 % / 12.5 %
39	C	79.12 % / 13.6 %

Q.	Ans.	Correct / Skipped
40	D	88.02 % / 10.2 %
41	C	78.29 % / 18.45 %
42	D	85.22 % / 14.74 %
43	C	83.82 % / 10.67 %
44	B	88.44 % / 10.95 %
45	C	80.75 % / 10.0 %
46	D	83.45 % / 15.33 %
47	B	89.84 % / 10.04 %
48	B	87.97 % / 10.49 %
49	A	79.27 % / 15.0 %
50	B	84.13 % / 14.42 %
51	A	83.53 % / 10.49 %
52	D	86.86 % / 11.85 %

Q.	Ans.	Correct / Skipped
53	A	84.03 % / 11.26 %
54	B	77.07 % / 10.33 %
55	A	87.36 % / 10.91 %
56	C	77.6 % / 10.66 %
57	A	84.24 % / 14.5 %
58	B	84.25 % / 12.67 %
59	C	79.99 % / 14.5 %
60	C	81.02 % / 18.48 %
61	D	84.82 % / 14.8 %
62	D	85.56 % / 11.95 %
63	D	81.76 % / 16.3 %
64	B	87.38 % / 10.72 %
65	B	82.92 % / 11.92 %

Performance Analysis	
Avg. Score (%)	33.0%
Toppers Score (%)	56.0%
Your Score	

//Hints and Solutions//

1. In the case of a straight-line demand curve meeting the two axes, the price-elasticity of demand at the mid-point of the line would be 1.

2. MC=MR is the first-order condition for the profit of a firm to be maximum. The Profit Maximization Rule states that if a firm chooses to maximize its profits, it must choose that level of output where Marginal Cost (MC) is equal to Marginal Revenue (MR) and the Marginal Cost curve is rising. In other words, it must produce at a level where MC = MR.

3. Many buyers and many sellers is one of the assumptions of perfect competition. Yes, in a perfectly competitive market, there are many buyers and many sellers. As a consequence, they have no market power and cannot influence the market price. This is an assumption of the model of perfect competition

4. Price and demand are positively correlated in case of Giffen goods. A Giffen good is a product for which demand increases as the price increases and falls when the price decreases.

5. The coefficient of price-elasticity of demand is smaller than one when the percentage increase in the quantity of a commodity demanded is smaller than the percentage fall in its price.

6. In Monopoly market structure the degree of control over the price of its product by a firm very large. In a monopoly type of market structure, there is only one seller, so a single firm will control the entire market. It can set any price it wishes since it has all the market power.

7. A firm under perfect competition is Price taker. In perfect market conditions (also called perfect competition) a firm is a price taker because other firms can enter the market easily and produce a product that is indistinguishable from every other firm's product. This makes it impossible for any firm to set its own prices.

8. The elasticity of demand of durable goods is greater than unity. Price elasticity of demand for durable goods is generally more elastic in short run than in long run. That is, quantity demanded is more sensitive to price changes of such durable goods in short run and not so much in the long run.

9. In the case of an inferior good, the income elasticity of demand is Negative. A negative income elasticity of demand is associated with inferior goods; an increase in income will lead to a fall in the demand and may lead to changes to more luxurious substitutes.

10. Demand curve is the other name that is given to the average revenue curve. Average revenue curve is often called the demand curve due to its representation of the product's demand in the market.

11. In Critical incident technique, personnel specialists and operating managers prepare lists of statements of very effective and very ineffective behavior for an employee. Critical incident method or critical incident technique is a performance appraisal tool in which analyses the behavior of employee in certain events in which either he performed very well and the ones in which he could have done better.

12. The impact of oil prices on car production

13. The English term 'Economics' is derived from the Greek word 'Oikonomia'. Its meaning is 'household management'. Economics was first read in ancient Greece. Aristotle, the Greek Philosopher termed Economics as a science of 'household management'

14. Economics deals primarily with the concept of Scarcity and choice. Scarcity is the limited availability of a commodity, which may be in demand in the market. Scarcity also includes an individual's lack of resources to buy commodities.

15. Economists use the term opportunity cost to indicate what must be given up to obtain something that's desired. ... The idea behind opportunity cost is that the cost of one item is the lost opportunity to do or consume something else; in short, opportunity cost is the value of the next best alternative.

16. Factors of production are inputs used to produce an output, or goods and services. They are resources a company requires to attempt to generate a profit by producing goods and services. Factors of production are divided into four categories: land, labor, capital and entrepreneurship.

17. Households are sellers in the resource market.

Households are sellers in the market for resources. Households sell land, labor, capital, and entrepreneurial activity in exchange for money, which in this case is called income. Households are buyers in the market for goods and services. Households exchange income for goods and services.

18. Spending on goods and services flow from firms to households.

The diagram suggests that the economy can reproduce itself. The idea is that as households spend money of goods and services from firms, the firms have the means to purchase labor from the households, which the households to then purchase goods and services.

19. Resources are not able to meet the entire demand for a product.

20. Company goals that are concerned with creating employee and customer satisfaction and maintaining a high degree of social responsibility are called Noneconomic objectives.

21. B. marketing programmes and services / instructor material producer.

C. Needs analyst /organisational changer / researcher + (a) above

Human resources managers plan, direct, and coordinate the administrative functions of an organization. They oversee the recruiting, interviewing, and hiring of new staff; consult with top executives on strategic planning; and serve as a link between an organization's management and its employees.

22. HR audits may accomplish a variety of objectives, such as ensuring legal compliance; helping maintain or improve a competitive advantage; establishing efficient documentation and technology practices; and identifying strengths and weaknesses in training, communications and other employment practices.

23. HR Audit

Regardless of organization or industry, accountability in the workplace is critical to the success of your employees and your business. ... As a leader, it's your job to understand what makes each of your employees tick, then use that information to position them for success.

24. Although the barriers to effective communication may be different for different situations, the following are some of the main barriers:

- Linguistic Barriers.
- Psychological Barriers.
- Emotional Barriers.
- Physical Barriers.
- Cultural Barriers.
- Organisational Structure Barriers.
- Attitude Barriers.
- Perception Barriers.

25. Determining the jobs to be done / identifying the skills / estimating the exists likely / filling up the requirements

Manpower Planning which is also called as Human Resource Planning consists of putting right number of people, right kind of people at the right place, right time, doing the right things for which they are suited for the achievement of goals of the organization.

26. Promotion may be an employee's reward for good performance, i.e., positive appraisal. ... A promotion can involve advancement in terms of designation, salary and benefits, and in some organizations the type of job activities may change a great deal. The opposite of a promotion is a demotion.

27. a process that provides an employee with feedback about his / her workplace performance

28. Performance Management Helps to Create Employee Development Strategies. Continuous performance management means you are proactively developing employees by covering their development needs. ... Use strategies that not only play to employees' strengths but also reflect the direction the business is heading.

29. Gap analysis / solution analysis + (A)

Having a competency map makes it easier for firms to identify qualified candidates, assess performance, focus training efforts and enhance overall productivity. Common competency mapping approaches include assessment center, critical incidents technique, interviewing, questionnaires and psychometric tests.

30. There are four functions of management that span across all industries. They include: planning,organizing, leading, and controlling.Staffing forms a part of the human resource planning function.

31. Formalization in organizational structure is a process in which managers specify (in writing), procedures, rules and responsibilities for the individual   employees,organizational units,   groups,   teams   and   the organization as a whole,

which leads to the development of processes, relationships, and operating procedures Work specialization, sometimes called a division of labor, refers to the degree to which an organization divides individual tasks into separate jobs. The advantages of work specialization include: Employees can be an expert to some degree in their specific task an higher levels of productivity.

32. The following system is simple, less expensive and less time consuming Checklist Method.

33. Bench marking is a process of measuring the performance of a company's products, services, or processes against those of another business considered to be the best in the industry.The point of benchmarking is to identify internal opportunities for improvement. By studying companies with superior performance, breaking down what makes such superior performance possible, and then comparing those processes to how your business operates, you can implement changes that will yield significant improvements.

34. The leader–member exchange (LMX) theory is a relationship-based approach to leadership that focuses on the two-way (dyadic) relationship between leaders and followers. It suggests that leaders develop an exchange with each of their subordinates, and that the quality of these leader–member exchange relationships influences subordinates' responsibility, decisions, and access to resources and performance. Relationships are based on trust and respect and are often emotional relationships that extend beyond the scope of employment. Leader– member exchange may promote positive employment experiences and augment organizational effectiveness. It is widely used by many managers and is replacing many of its predecessors.

35. Graphic Rating Scale is a type of performance appraisal method in which traits or behaviours that are important for effective performance are listed out and each employee is rated against these traits. The rating scale method offers a high degree of structure for appraisals. Each employee trait or characteristic is rated on a bipolar scale that usually has several points ranging from "poor" to "excellent" (or some similar arrangement).

36. The probability of bankrupt is higher only levered firm.

37. If interest rates rises, you would expect liquidity risk to also rise. Liquidity is the ability of a firm, company, or even an individual to pay its debts without suffering catastrophic losses.

38. All of the following influence capital budgeting cash flows except method of project financing used. Capital budgeting is the process a business undertakes to evaluate potential major projects or investments.

39. If interest rates rises, you would expect liquidity risk to also rise. Liquidity is the ability of a firm, company, or even an individual to pay its debts without suffering catastrophic losses.

40. Financial management is dispensable in any organization as it helps in taking sound financial decisions, proper use and allocation and improving the profitability of funds.

41. Unsystematic type of risk is avoidable through proper diversification. Unsystematic risk, also known as specific risk or idiosyncratic risk, is a category of risk that only affects an industry or a particular company. Unsystematic risk is the risk of losing an investment due to company or industry-specific hazard.

42. Financial analysts, working capital means the same thing as current assets minus current Liabilities. Financial analyst is one of the most coveted roles in the financial services industry.

43. Profitability moves together with risk is a basic principle of finance as it relates to the management of working capital. Profitability is ability of a company to use its resources to generate revenues in excess of its expenses.

44. The return relative solves the problem of negative returns. A negative return occurs when a company or business has a financial loss or lackluster returns on an investment during a specific period of time.

45. If the Dow Jones Industrials had a price appreciation of 6 percent one year and yet Total return for the year was 11 percent; the difference would be due to dividends. A dividend is the distribution of reward from a portion of the company's earnings and is paid to a class of its shareholders.

46. Shareholder wealth in a firm is represented by the market price per share of the firms common stock. Shareholder wealth is defined as the present value of the expected future returns to the owners (that is, shareholders) of the firm.

47. In order to determine the compound growth rate of an investment over some period, an investor would calculate the geometric mean. The geometric mean is the average of a set of products, the calculation of which is commonly used to determine the performance results of an investment or portfolio.

48. Net present value is a popular method which falls with in discount cash flow method. Discounted cash flow (DCF) is a valuation method used to estimate the value of an investment based on its future cash flows.

49. A major difference between real and nominal returns is that real returns adjust for inflation and nominal returns do not.

50. When most people refer to the mean, they are referring to the arithmetic mean. The arithmetic mean is the simplest and most widely used measure of a mean, or average.

51. Gross working capital is also known as going concern concept since finance manager is highly concerned with the management of these assets with a view of bringing about productivity from other assets.

52. Markowitz diversification is concerned with the interrelationships between security returns. A strategy that seeks to combine in a portfolio assets with returns that are less than perfectly positively correlated, in an effort to lower portfolio risk (variance) without sacrificing return.

53. The rate of return on investment falls with the shortage of working capital. Return on Investment (ROI) is a performance measure used to evaluate the efficiency of an investment or compare the efficiency of a number of different investments.

54. Portfolio weights are found by calculating the percentage each asset is to the total portfolio value. A portfolio is a grouping of financial assets such as stocks, bonds, commodities, currencies and cash equivalents, as well as their fund counterparts, including mutual, exchange-traded and closed funds.

55. Greater the size of a business unit larger will be the requirements of working capital. Working capital, also known as net working capital (NWC), is the difference between a company's current assets, such as cash, accounts receivable (customers' unpaid bills) and inventories of raw materials and finished goods, and its current liabilities, such as accounts payable.

56. The four unique elements to services include Intangibility, inconsistency, inseparability and inventory. Intangibility refers to the tendency of services to be a performance that cannot be held or touched, rather than an object. Inconsistency is a characteristic of services because they depend on people to deliver them, and people vary in their capabilities and in their day-to-day performance. Inseparability refers to the difficulty of separating the deliverer of the service (hair stylist) from the service itself (hair salon). Inventory refers to the need to have service production capability when there is service demand.

57. A change in an individual's behavior prompted by information and experience refers to Learning. Learning is the process of acquiring new, or modifying existing, knowledge, behaviors, skills, values, or preferences.

58. While buying milk Routinized buying behavior kind of behavior is displayed by a person. Buying Behavior is the decision processes and acts of people involved in buying and using products.

59. Whether to sell via intermediaries or directly to consumers, how many outlets to sell through, and whether to control or cooperate with other channel members are examples of decisions marketers must make about Distribution. Distribution means the process by which we make the goods or the service available to the end consumer. Generally, the place of production is not the same as the place of consumption. So the goods have to be distributed to overcome the barrier of place.

60. The extended Ps of service marketing mix is Physical Evidence, Process, People. The physical evidence within the service marketing mix refers to an environment in which a service comes about from an interaction between an employee and a customer which is combined with a tangible commodity. The element 'Process' of the service marketing mix represents the activities, procedures, protocols and more by which the service in question is eventually delivered to the customer. As services are results of actions for or with customers, a process involves a sequence of steps and activities to get there. In Booms and Bitner's service marketing mix, 'people' include people who are directly or indirectly involved in the trade of the product or service. These are mainly customer contact employees (contact centre employees, representatives, account managers, etc.), customers, personnel and management.

61. A social and managerial process by which individuals and organizations obtain what they need and want through value creation refers to Marketing. "Marketing is a social and managerial process by which individuals and groups obtain what they need and want through creating and exchanging products and value with others."

62. Intangibility is the basic property of a service which makes it different from a product. Products have tangible qualities that provide information to consumers so they can easily compare one product to another. Services, on the other hand, are intangible. Most services cannot be experienced or consumed until the purchase is made.

63. This is what I want, won't you please make it phrases reflects the marketing concept.

64. The solution to price competition is to develop a differentiated Offer, delivery, and image. Price competition is one of many ways that a product or service can compete in the marketplace. In price competition, two products which are substantially similar are judged by prospective consumers on their respective pricing, with the purchase made mostly on the basis of which is cheaper.

65. If we purchase cleaning supplies for our custodial help regularly. It is showing Straight rebuy situation. A straight rebuy is the purchasing or reordering of supplies on a routine basis from a supplier who is on an approved list.

Q.1 Which among the following is not a correct match of international organisation and its headquarters?

A. International Maritime Organization – London
B. North Atlantic Treaty Organization - Brussels
C. International Olympic Committee – Lausanne
D. The Organization for the Prohibition of Chemical Weapons – The Hague
E. International Cricket Council - Wales

Q.2 Under the Ayushman Bharat programme, the government has set a target of eradicating Tuberculosis from the country by _______.

A. 2029   **B.** 2028   **C.** 2027   **D.** 2026
E. 2025

Q.3 The University Grants Commission (UGC) has released a list of how many institutes for the grant of the status of Institutions of Eminence (IoE)?

A. 20   **B.** 10   **C.** 14   **D.** 25
E. 30

Q.4 A pension scheme for _______ has been notified in the country on 22 July 2019.

A. old aged
B. retailers
C. ex-servicemen
D. retired government employees
E. None of these

Q.5 Which state has the highest rate of refilling LPG under the UJJWALA scheme?

A. Uttarakhand   **B.** West Bengal
C. Delhi   **D.** Telangana
E. Chhattisgarh

Q.6 The annual Shakambari festival at the historic _______ temple began from 3 July 2019 and will run up to July 16, 2019.

A. Konark Sun   **B.** Meenakshi
C. Brihadisvara   **D.** Bhadrakali
E. Sabarimala

Q.7 Recently, the US has designated _______ a currency manipulator.

A. Turkey   **B.** Japan
C. UAE   **D.** China
E. Indonesia

Q.8 What was the name of China's satellite to explore the dark side of moon?

A. Ranger 4   **B.** Yutu
C. Queqiao   **D.** Change'1
E. Change'2

Q.9 Who among the following was the head of the Special Investigation Team (SIT) on Black Money Committee?

A. RS Gujral   **B.** MB Shah
C. A K Khandelwal   **D.** Vipin Malik
E. AC Shah

Q.10 Employees' Provident Fund Organisation (EPFO) has introduced UAN-Aadhaar linking facility for the convenience of members using EPFO Link in _______ Mobile App.

A. UMANG   **B.** Paytm
C. BHIM   **D.** Airtel
E. None of the above

Q.11 By which Ministry of India is **Pradhan Mantri Rojgar Protsahan Yojana (PMRPY)** Scheme being implemented through the Employees' Provident Fund Organization (EPFO)?

A. Ministry of Industry and Power
B. Ministry of Labour and Employment
C. Ministry of Rural Development
D. Ministry of Human Resources and Development
E. Ministry of Commerce

Q.12 Recently, BCCI has agreed to come under the purview of NADA. What does 'D' mean in NADA?

A. Development   **B.** Divers
C. Doping   **D.** damage
E. Dichotomy

Q.13 The Supreme Court has formed a panel to frame emergency plan regarding the extinction of two Indian birds. Which of the following birds are included in this?

A. The Lesser Florican and the White bellied Heron
B. The White bellied Heron and Indian Vulture
C. The Great Indian Bustard and the Lesser Florican
D. The Great Indian Bustard and the Great Indian Hornbill
E. The Himalayan Quail and the Great Indian Bustard

Q.14 The Supreme Court (Number of Judges) Amendment Bill proposes an increase in number of judges in SC to _______ excluding the Chief Justice of India.

A. 32   **B.** 33   **C.** 34   **D.** 35
E. 36

Q.15 The Rajya Sabha passed the Motor Vehicles (Amendment) Bill, 2019. It seeks to amend the _______.

A. Motor Vehicles Act, 1962
B. Motor Vehicles Act, 171
C. Motor Vehicles Act, 1979
D. Motor Vehicles Act, 1988
E. Motor Vehicles Act, 1992

Q.16 Who was appointed as the Chief Executive Officer (CEO) of LIC Mutual Fund in May 2019?

A. Shyam Srinivasan
B. Amitabh Chaudhry
C. Chandra Shekhar Ghosh
D. Dinesh Pangtey

E. Mahesh Kumar Jain

Q.17 Who among the following is known as "The Plastic Man of India" for making roads with plastic waste?

A. M. Visvesvaraya
B. Tathagata Roy
C. Rajagopalan Vasudevan
D. Munirathna Anandakrishnan
E. None of the above

Q.18 Where did the Portuguese set up their first factory?

A. Surat
B. Masulipatnam
C. Cochin
D. Bombay
E. None of the above

Q.19 Of which state has Anandiben Patel been appointed as the Governor?

A. Gujarat
B. Madhya Pradesh
C. Uttar Pradesh
D. Tamil Nadu
E. Tripura

Q.20 Which among the following sports does Apurvi Singh Chandela associate with?

A. Cricket
B. Shooting
C. Weightlifting
D. Boxing
E. Wrestling

Q.21 Tilaiya Dam is built on _______ river.

A. Barakar
B. Kolar
C. Bokaro
D. Koyna
E. None of the above

Q.22 Balukhand Wildlife Sanctuary is located in _______.

A. Jharkhand
B. Odisha
C. Madhya Pradesh
D. Uttarakhand
E. Rajasthan

Q.23 The horizontal demand curve parallel to x-axis implies that the elasticity of demand is:

A. Equals to 1
B. Equals to -1
C. Infinite
D. Equals to 0
E. Equals to 100

Q.24 Which of the following is the official currency of Bhutan?

A. Rupiah
B. Ngultrum
C. Zaire
D. Baht
E. Rouble

Q.25 The Laffer curve shows the relationship between

A. the level of government spending and GDP growth
B. tax rates and amount of revenue collection
C. household expenditure and household income
D. rate of unemployment and rate of inflation
E. None of the above

Q.26 The rate at which RBI borrows money from commercial banks within the country is known as

A. Reverse Repo Rate
B. Base Rate
C. Savings Deposit Rate
D. Bank Rate
E. Repo Rate

Q.27 The statutory base for the depositor Education and Awareness Fund (DFAF) constituted by the Reserve Bank of India is provided by _______.

A. Section 21A of the Reserve Bank of India Act, 1935
B. Section 21A of the Banking Companies Act, 1976
C. Section 26A of the Reserve bank of India Act, 1935
D. Section 26A of the Banking Regulation Act, 1949
E. Section 21A of the Banking Regulation Act, 1949

Q.28 As per the interim budget 2019, in the event of the death of a labour during service, the amount to be paid by EPFO has been enhanced from Rs. 2.5 lakh to Rs. _______.

A. Rs 3 lakh
B. Rs 6 lakh
C. Rs 9 lakh
D. Rs 8 lakh
E. Rs 4 lakh

Q.29 Of how many beneficiaries have Pradhan Mantri Rozgar Protsahan Yojana (PMRPY) crossed the milestone in January, 2019?

A. 10 crore
B. 10 lakh
C. 1 crore
D. 5 crore
E. 1 lakh

Q.30 The alphabet 'D' in the abbreviation 'NSDL' stands for

A. Derivative
B. Debt
C. Dematerialisation
D. Depository
E. Demand

Q.31 There are different phases in the Operations Research Project. They are:

(i) Research phase

(ii) Action phase

(iii) Judgment phase

The correct sequence of these phases is:

A. (i), (ii), (iii)
B. (iii), (i), (ii)
C. (iii), (i), (ii)
D. (iii), (ii), (i)

Q.32 In economics, ___________________ are inputs to production that a firm uses closely together.

A. Market ability of products
B. Complementarity of inputs
C. Specificity of inputs
D. Substitutability of inputs
E. Market value

Q.33 The Graphical method can be used to solve:

(A) A Linear Programming Problem (LPP) with all integer data.

(B) A LPP with two decision variables.

A. Only A
B. Only B
C. Neither A nor B
D. Either A or B
E. A and B both

Q.34 In a business venture, a man can take profit of rs 3000 with a probability of0.4 or have a loss of rs 1500 with a probability of 0.6.

A. Rs. 300
B. Rs. 600
C. Rs. 800
D. Rs. 500
E. Rs. 900

Q.35 If the EOQ for an item of inventory in a firm is 4000 units, the estimated demand for the term next year gets doubled, what shall be the revised EOQ next year, all other relevant costs remaining unchanged?

A. 4000
B. 5000
C. 5656
D. 5696
E. None of the above

Q.36 Macroeconomics is concerned with______________and______ level of the economy as it is a macro aspect of the economy.

A. Industry, Trade and Commerce
B. Agriculture, Industry & Trade
C. Employment, Inflation & Growth
D. Population, Income and Economic Planning
E. only trade

Q.37 Identify the window not associated with SPSS.

A. Editor
B. Syntax
C. Output
D. Format Cells
E. Input

Q.38 Chi-square distribution has a number of applications which are enumerated below:
a) To test if the population has a specified value of the variance a^2
b) Chi-square test of goodness of fit.
c) Chi-square test for independence of attributes.

A. Either a or b
B. Only a
C. Only b
D. Both A and B
E. All of these

Q.39 It studies the functional relationship between physical inputs and physical outputs. It is expressed as Qx = ?

A. F(L,K)
B. F(L,Y)
C. F(T,K)
D. Both A and C
E. None of the above

Q.40 An Entrepreneur who is dominated more by customs, religions, traditions and past practices and he is not ready to take any risk is called as:

A. Drone Entrepreneur
B. Adoptive Entrepreneur
C. Fabian Entrepreneur
D. Financial Entrepreneur
E. None of the above

Q.41 How many types of Agriculture Business?

A. 7
B. 3
C. 4
D. 6
E. 8

Q.42 __________ is the action that governments take in the economic field.

A. Industrial policy
B. Monetary policy
C. Economic policy
D. Question does not provide sufficient data or is vague
E. Industrial policy

Q.43 Non-technical entrepreneurs are :

A. those who are mainly concerned with developing alternative marketing and distribution strategies to promote their business.
B. who are technically skill by nature in the sense of having the capability of developing new and improved quality of goods and services out of their own knowledge, skill and specialisation.
C. their profession to establish business enterprise, initially they work hard, and put maximum efforts and efficiency get a reputation with a purpose, to sell them once they are established.
D. Only A and B
E. None of the above.

Q.44 The examples of esteem needs are:
(i) Self-respect (ii) Self-recognition (iii) Self-image

A. Only (i)
B. Only (ii)
C. Only (iii)
D. Both (i) and (iii)
E. All of these

Q.45 On which factors, the Survival and success of a business depend upon?

A. External factors
B. Internal factors
C. Both a. and b. are correct
D. Only A
E. Question does not provide sufficient data or is vague

Q.46 ________________ is the study of human use of space and the effects that population density has on behaviour, communication, and social interaction.

A. Semantics
B. Proxemics
C. Kinesics
D. Gemantics
E. None of the above

Q.47 It is an additional output produced by the use of an additional unit of the variable factor, fixed factor remaining constant.

A. $AP = TP + L$
B. $MP = \frac{\Delta TP}{\Delta L}$
C. $AP = TP \times L$
D. Only 1
E. None of these

Q.48 Average Revenue always equal to price:

A. $AR = 0$
B. $AR = \frac{TR}{Q}$
C. $AR = P$
D. $AR = Q$
E. None of the above

Q.49 ______________related professional knowledge, tools or techniques that allow us to work within our professions.

A. Conceptual Skills
B. Soft Skills
C. Political Skills
D. Hard Skills
E. Personality development

Q.50 The specific actions selected for implementation that are intended to bring about the envisioned change is called______

A. Reinforcement
B. Intervention
C. Ability for self-renewal

D. Evaluation
E. Reinvent

Q.51 The correct combination is:
A. Theory of Associates – Marshall
B. Operant Conditioning Theory – B F Skinner
C. Theory of Conditioning – Bernara
D. Stimulus Response Theory – Hoodman
E. None of the above

Q.52 _____ means identifying and imitating the best in the world at specific tasks and functions.
A. Quality circle
B. Benchmarking
C. Outsourcing
D. Constraints
E. None of the above

Q.53 _____________is to lead others whereas monitors are the one who monitors everything and take cares of each and every thing.
A. Monitors
B. Leaders
C. Distribution handlers
D. Resource allocators
E. Prefect

Q.54 As per Rorsach value survey, which of the following is not an instrumental value?
A. Ambitious
B. Wise
C. Imagination
D. Capable
E. Leadership

Q.55 _____________is the kind of perception taken based on past performances or results.
A. Contrast effect
B. Stereotyping
C. Selective Perceptive
D. Objective prespective
E. Halo effect

Q.56 For 'make or buy decision', which cost is to be considered?
(A) Marginal cost
(B) Total cost
A. Only A
B. Only B
C. Either A or B
D. Both A and B
E. None of these

Q.57 Which of the following project appraisal method is not based on time value of money?
A. Payback method
B. Net present value method
C. Internal rate of return method
D. Discounted payback method
E. None of the above

Q.58 Selection is the process in which candidates for employment are divided into two classes – those who are to be offered employment and those who are not." This is stated by:
A. Dale Yoder
B. Milton M. Mandell

C. R.D. Agarwal
D. Edwin Flippo
E. None of the above

Q.59 The exchange rate between the currencies of two countries will be equal to the ratio of the price indices in these countries is explained by:
A. Inflation adjustment
B. Interest rate parity
C. Purchase power parity
D. Both A and C
E. None of the above

Q.60 _________________is based on the assumption that both support each other harmoniously to achieve organisational objectives.
A. Non zero-sum conflict
B. Zero-sum conflict
C. Line-staff conflict
D. Formal-informal conflict
E. None of the above

Q.61 Theory of cognitive dissonance was given by:
A. Maslow
B. Pavlov
C. Hofstede
D. Festinger
E. None of the above

Q.62 A_______________ is a collection of people that we use as a standard of comparison for ourselves regardless of whether we are part of that group.
A. Formal group
B. Informal group
C. Secondary group
D. Reference group
E. None of the above

Q.63 The ultimate mission or purpose is to relate human resources to future enterprise needs, so as to maximize the future return on investment in human resources. It is referred to:
A. Demand and Supply
B. Forecasting
C. Human Resource Planning
D. Demand
E. None of the above

Q.64 Who gave the concept of transactional and transformation leadership?
A. James Burns
B. Likert
C. Simon
D. Question does not provide sufficient data or is vague
E. None of these

Q.65 Principles by which the process of perceptual organization works was first identified by Max Wertheimer in the Year:
A. 1933
B. 1981
C. 1923
D. 1924
E. 1928

// Smart Answer Sheet //

Correct — Indicates percentage of students who answered questions correctly.

Skipped — Indicates percentage of students who skipped questions.

Q.	Ans.	Correct / Skipped	Q.	Ans.	Correct / Skipped	Q.	Ans.	Correct / Skipped	Q.	Ans.	Correct / Skipped	Q.	Ans.	Correct / Skipped
1	E	77.97 % / 12.53 %	14	B	77.76 % / 21.05 %	27	D	89.15 % / 10.14 %	40	C	80.41 % / 12.76 %	53	B	82.18 % / 11.02 %
2	E	85.81 % / 13.55 %	15	D	84.73 % / 11.4 %	28	B	79.44 % / 16.69 %	41	C	81.93 % / 10.28 %	54	B	77.4 % / 17.37 %
3	A	87.74 % / 10.18 %	16	D	83.57 % / 13.18 %	29	C	89.07 % / 10.48 %	42	C	84.97 % / 11.56 %	55	A	81.48 % / 14.77 %
4	B	76.2 % / 18.42 %	17	C	77.37 % / 13.49 %	30	D	78.76 % / 16.75 %	43	A	88.58 % / 11.11 %	56	A	78.38 % / 14.99 %
5	C	86.02 % / 11.26 %	18	C	89.36 % / 10.29 %	31	B	84.76 % / 12.32 %	44	E	78.53 % / 17.56 %	57	A	80.31 % / 13.04 %
6	D	89.88 % / 10.06 %	19	C	80.18 % / 13.87 %	32	B	77.81 % / 15.93 %	45	C	87.89 % / 10.04 %	58	A	76.15 % / 11.81 %
7	D	89.35 % / 10.09 %	20	B	78.33 % / 19.3 %	33	B	89.88 % / 10.04 %	46	B	84.49 % / 10.38 %	59	C	89.24 % / 10.26 %
8	C	84.1 % / 12.89 %	21	A	81.49 % / 16.5 %	34	A	86.74 % / 10.76 %	47	B	80.9 % / 10.85 %	60	C	76.16 % / 12.18 %
9	B	87.9 % / 11.17 %	22	B	76.86 % / 20.86 %	35	C	79.01 % / 14.46 %	48	C	80.04 % / 19.32 %	61	D	86.71 % / 10.55 %
10	A	78.78 % / 18.02 %	23	C	87.75 % / 11.84 %	36	C	82.66 % / 12.71 %	49	D	87.69 % / 11.78 %	62	D	89.93 % / 10.0 %
11	B	82.31 % / 15.96 %	24	B	79.84 % / 11.27 %	37	D	89.89 % / 10.03 %	50	B	81.17 % / 11.26 %	63	C	81.88 % / 12.38 %
12	C	88.78 % / 11.02 %	25	B	87.41 % / 11.66 %	38	E	82.73 % / 12.58 %	51	B	80.72 % / 13.68 %	64	A	87.57 % / 11.09 %
13	C	77.92 % / 18.56 %	26	A	84.82 % / 11.33 %	39	A	89.0 % / 10.89 %	52	B	78.13 % / 10.07 %	65	C	84.02 % / 14.95 %

Performance Analysis

Avg. Score (%)	31.0%
Toppers Score (%)	58.0%
Your Score	

//Hints and Solutions//

1.

- International Cricket Council - Dubai, UAE
- International Maritime Organization , Secretary General - Kitack Lim.
- North Atlantic Treaty Organization , Secretary General - Jens Stoltenberg.
- International Olympic Committee, President - Thomas Bach.
- Organization for the Prohibition of Chemical Weapons , Director General - Fernando Arias.

Hence the correct answer is option (E).

2.

- 20,000 wellness centres will be completed by the end of the current year under Ayushman Bharat programme.
- A total of 1.5 lakh wellness centres are to be established in the country under this programme.
- The government has set a target of eradicating Tuberculosis from the country by **2025**.
- Ayushman Bharat programme as a successful model in implementing universal health.

Hence the correct answer is option (E).

3.

- The University Grants Commission (UGC) has released a list of 20 institutes - 10 public and 10 private for the grant of the status of Institutions of Eminence (IoE).
- The Institute of Eminence scheme aimed at developing 20 world-class institutions which would put India on the global education map.
- Those selected will be given greater autonomy and freedom to decide fees, course durations and governance structures.
- The public institutions will also receive a government grant of ₹1,000 crore.

Hence the correct answer is option (A).

4.

- Santosh Kumar Gangwar-led labour ministry has notified the pension scheme for **retailers and traders** benefitting over three crore self-employed workers in the country on 22 July 2019.
- The scheme, which is an extension of the PM Shram Yogi Maan-Dhan Yojana, will make all beneficiaries eligible for a monthly pension of Rs 3000 after the age of 60 at a minuscule monthly contribution.

Hence the correct answer is option (B).

5.

- The government's flagship pro-poor scheme **Pradhan Mantri Ujjwala Yojana** (PMUY) has found maximum success in **Delhi, Goa, Haryana, Uttarakhand** and **Puducherry**. Delhi topped the list of states with maximum percentage of PMUY beneficiaries availing at least **four refills**.
- **Telangana, Chhattisgarh** and **Tripura** were in the **bottom** of the list.

Hence the correct answer is option (C).

6.

- The annual Shakambari festival at the historic Bhadrakali temple began from 3 July 2019 and will run up to July 16, 2019.
- It is believed that by worshipping Goddess Shakambari, people can live in peace.
- The temple will be closed at 6 p.m. on July 16 and reopen at 10 a.m. the next day after conducting samprokshana.
- The temple is in Warangal, Telangana.

Hence the correct answer is option (D).

7.

- The US has designated **China** a currency manipulator.
- China is intent on continuing to receive the hundreds of Billions of Dollars they have been taking from the US with unfair trade practices and currency manipulation.
- China has a long history of facilitating an undervalued currency through protracted, large-scale intervention in the foreign exchange market.

Hence the correct answer is option (D).

8.

- **China** is the **first country** to launch a satellite to **explore the dark side of moon.**
- It launched the satellite named **Queqiao (Magpie Bridge)** that was carried by a **Long March-4C rocket.**
- It is a **400 kg relay satellite** to enable a rover to communicate with the Earth from the Moon's dark side.
- It will be the world's first communication satellite operating in the halo orbit around the **second Lagrangian (L2) point of the Earth-Moon system,** about **455,000 kms from the Earth.**
- The **dark side of the moon is the far side of the moon that always faces away from the Earth.**
- **China's National Space Agency-China National Space Administration.**
- **China Capital-Beijing.**
- **China Currency-Renminbi.**
- **China President-Xi Jinping.**

Hence the correct answer is option (C).

9.

- **Justice MB Shah** was the **head of the Special Investigation Team (SIT)** on **Black Money Committee.**

- The SIT was formed by the central government in **2014 on directions of Supreme Court.** The panel has been continuously **suggesting anti-black money measures to the government.**

- It recommendations are as following:

1. The central government should **cap the cash holding limit** at **Rs 1 crore instead of its earlier suggestion of Rs 20 lakh.**

2. The entire amount found in **seizures** crossing that limit should go to the **government treasuries.**

Hence the correct answer is option (B).

10. Employees' Provident Fund Organisation (EPFO) has introduced UAN-Aadhaar linking facility for the convenience of members using EPFO Link in UMANG Mobile App. The facility on e-KYC Portal has further added a new feature to link UAN with Aadhaar online using biometric credentials. For using this facility with UMANG APP, member will have to provide his/her UAN.

Hence the correct answer is option (A).

11.

- PMRPY is being implemented by **Ministry of Labour and Employment** through the Employees' Provident Fund Organization (EPFO).

- Under the scheme, Government is paying full employers' contribution of 12% (towards Employees' Provident Fund and Employees' Pension Scheme both), for a period of 3 years in respect of new employees who have been registered with the EPFO on or after 1st April 2016, with salary up to Rs. 15,000 per month.

- The entire system is online and AADHAR based with no human interface in the implementation of the scheme.

- Pradhan Mantri Rozgar Protsahan Yojana (PMRPY) had crossed the milestone of one crore beneficiaries as on January 14, 2019.

Hence the correct answer is option (B).

12. The BCCI agreed to come under the purview of the National Anti Doping Agency (NADA).

This decision makes it a sports federation according to government norms, despite being financially autonomous.

This development is expected to have major consequences as the BCCI has now become a designated National Sports Federation and will face more pressure to come under the government's Right to Information Act.

NADA is the national organization responsible for promoting, coordinating and monitoring the doping control program in sports in all its forms in India.

13.

- The **Supreme Court** constituted a **high powered committee** to urgently **frame and implement an**

emergency response plan for the **protection of the Great Indian Bustard and the Lesser Florican.**

- A **three member panel** comprising **Director of Bombay Natural History Society; Dr Asad R Rahmani** former Director of Bombay Natural History Society and member of governing body of Wetlands International South Asia and **Dr Dhananjai Mohan, Chief Conservator of Forests of Uttarakhand.**

- Both the birds are protected under the **Wild Life (Protection) Act, 1972** but despite being accorded the highest level of protection under national law, the birds face the **threat of imminent extinction.**

- The different reasons for extinction of the birds are: **mortality by collision with infrastructure, particularly powerlines and wind turbines, depletion of grasslands, hunting, development of mines and human habitation in and around their habitats and ingestion of pesticides.**

- Under the emergency steps taken should include- **urgent dismantling and undergrounding of powerlines and wind turbines, immediate embargo on any upcoming wind, solar power projects, and powerlines in and around critical habitats.**

- **CJI(Chief Justice of India)**--Ranjan Gogoi

- **Union Environment Minister-Prakash Javedkar.**

Hence the correct answer is option (C).

14.

- The Supreme Court (Number of Judges) Amendment Bill was passed in the Lok Sabha.

- It proposes an increase in number of judges in SC from 30 to **33** excluding the Chief Justice of India.

- The bill will amend the Supreme Court (Number of Judges) Act, 1956.

Hence the correct answer is option (B).

15.

- The Rajya Sabha passed the Motor Vehicles (Amendment) Bill, 2019 with some amendments.

- The bill seeks to amend the **Motor Vehicles Act, 1988** to provide for road safety.

- Provisions related to increasing penalties of traffic violations, addressing issues on third-party insurance, regulation of cab aggregators and road safety are proposed in the amendment.

Hence the correct answer is option (D).

16.

- LIC Mutual Fund appointed Dinesh Pangtey as the company's Chief Executive Officer (CEO).

- He joined LIC as a direct recruit officer in 1984.

- He has also served as Regional Manager Marketing channel in Western Zone spanning the states of Maharashtra, Gujarat and Goa.

Hence the correct answer is option (D).

17. Rajagopalan Vasudevan is known as "The Plastic Man of India". He developed the technique to use waste plastic, along with bituminous mixes, for road construction. He was awarded the Padma Shri in 2018.

Hence the correct answer is option (C).

18. Vasco da Gama was the first Portuguese to penetrate into India. He was welcomed by the Zamorin of Calicut. They established their first factory in Cochin (now called Kochi) in Kerala.

Hence the correct answer is option (C).

19.

- Madhya Pradesh Governor and former Chief Minister of Gujarat Anandiben Patel replaced Ram Naik as the Governor of Uttar Pradesh.

- The Centre appointed 10 new Governors for the following states. The list is given below

State	Governor
Madhya Pradesh	Lal Ji Tandon
Gujarat	Acharya Dev Vrat
Bihar	Phagu Chauhan
Uttar Pradesh	Anandiben Patel
West Bengal	Jagdeep Dhankar
Tripura	Ramesh Bais
Himachal Pradesh	KalRaj Mishra
Chhattisgarh	Anandiben Patel(Till 28th july) Anusuiya Uikey(From 29th July)
Andhra Pradesh	BB Harichandan
Nagaland	R.N.Ravi

Hence the correct answer is option (C).

20.

- Apurvi Singh Chandela is associated with the shooting.

- She is an Indian shooter from Jaipur, Rajasthan.

- She is among five Indian shooters who have already secured 2020 Olympics quotas for India.

- She has been a gold medallist at Commonwealth Game 2014, Glasgow, UK and a bronze medal winner in next edition of Commonwealth at Gold Coast.

Hence the correct answer is option (B).

21.

- Tilaiya Dam was constructed across the **Barakar River in Koderma district of Jharkhand.**

- The Barakar River is the main tributary of the **Damodar river** in eastern India.

- It is a concrete gravity dam.

- The dam is owned by **Damodar Valley Corporation.**

Hence the correct answer is option (A).

22.

- **Balukhand Wildlife Sanctuary** is located along the Bay of Bengal coast in **Odisha.**

- **Olive Ridley Sea Turtles** nests along its coast.

- It is famous for the occurrence of a large number of **blackbucks and spotted deer.**

- This sanctuary was badly affected by cyclone **Fani** and it damaged nearly 55 lakh trees in the sanctuary.

Hence the correct answer is option (B).

23.

- The horizontal demand curve parallel to x-axis implies that the elasticity of demand is infinite.

- The demand curve illustrates the relationship between price and quantity demanded of a particular good or service.

- The elasticity measures the extent to which a change in price affects the quantity demanded of that particular good or service.

- In the case of a product with a horizontal demand curve, elasticity is said to be perfectly elastic.

- A perfectly elastic demand is a demand where any price increase would cause the quantity demanded to fall to zero, and reducing the price of a good or service will not increase sales.

- Luxury goods are often very elastic – if the price increases a little, then people will move over to something else.

Hence the correct answer is option (C).

24. Bhutan - Ngultrum, Congo - Zaire, Russia - Rouble, Thailand - Baht, Indonesia - Rupiah.

Hence the correct answer is option (B).

25. The Laffer Curve is a theory developed by Arthur Laffer to show the relationship between tax rates and the amount of tax revenue collected by governments. The curve is used to illustrate the premise that the more an activity, such as production, is taxed, the less of it is generated.

Hence the correct answer is option (B).

26. Reverse Repo rate is the short term borrowing rate at which RBI borrows money from banks. The Reserve bank uses this tool when it feels there is too much money floating in the banking system.

Hence the correct answer is option (A).

27. The statutory base for the Depositor Education and Awareness Fund (DEAF) constituted by the Reserve Bank of India is provided by Section 26 A of the Banking Regulation Act, 1949. In March 2014, section 26A was inserted in the Banking Regulation Act, 1949, empowering the central bank to establish the Fund under the Depositor Education and Awareness Fund Scheme, 2014. Under this fund, all the banks are required to transfer money lying in accounts that have been inoperative for at least 10 years to the Fund according to specific guidelines. Banks will also have to list out inoperative accounts every month and transfer funds lying in these, along with interest accrued, by the end of the subsequent month.

Hence the correct answer is option (D).

28.

- As per the interim budget 2019, in the event of the death of a labour during service, the amount to be paid by EPFO has been enhanced from Rs. 2.5 lakh to Rs. 6 lakh.

- Minimum pension for every labourer has been fixed at Rs 1,000 per month.

- Employment opportunities are expanded and EPFO membership increased by 2 crore.

Hence the correct answer is option (B).

29.

- Pradhan Mantri Rozgar Protsahan Yojana (PMRPY) had crossed the milestone of **one crore** beneficiaries as on January 14, 2019.

- Under the scheme, Government is paying full employers' contribution of 12% (towards Employees' Provident Fund and Employees' Pension Scheme both), for a period of 3 years in respect of new employees who have been registered with the EPFO on or after 1st April 2016, with salary up to Rs. 15,000 per month.

- The entire system is online and AADHAR based with no human interface in the implementation of the scheme.

- PMPRY is being implemented by **Ministry of Labour and Employmen**t through the Employees' Provident Fund Organization (EPFO).

Hence the correct answer is option (C).

30. The alphabet 'D' in 'NSDL' stands for Depository. National Securities Depository Limited (NSDL) is an Indian central securities depository based in Mumbai. It was established in 1996 as the first electronic securities depository in India with national coverage based on a suggestion by a national institution responsible for the economic development of India. NSDL is promoted by Industrial Development Bank of India Limited, UTI and National Stock Exchange of India Limited.

Hence the correct answer is option (D).

31. There are different phases in the Operations Research Project. They are:

Judgment phase

Research phase

 Action phase

Above these are the correct sequences.

Hence the correct answer is option (B).

32. In economics, complementary inputs are inputs to production that a firm uses closely together.

The economic effect of their complementary nature is that when the price of one of the inputs increases, then the firm will use both inputs less even at constant output.

Hence the correct answer is option (B).

33. The Graphical method can be used to solve an LPP with two decision variables.

Hence the correct answer is option (B).

34. Given In a business venture a man can take profit of Rs 3000 with a probability of 0.4 or have a loss of Rs 1500 with a probability of 0.6. His expected profit will be

We know that P = 0.4, and profit = 3000

Given P = 0.6 and loss = 1500

When P(x) = 0.4, x = 3000

When P(x) = 0.6, x = 1500

We get 0.4 3000 = 1200

and 0.6 1500 = 900

E(x) = $\sum$ x P(x)

= 1200 – 900

= 300

Hence the correct answer is option (A).

35. EOQ is abbreviation of Economic Order Quantity and formulae to find EOQ is $EOQ = \sqrt{2DK/h}$ Whereas $D =$ annual demand Quantity $K =$ Fixed cost and $h =$ holding cost Here, $EOQ = 4000$ unit and we have to find EOQ for the next year. In the next year, only demand for quantity is doubled everything else remained constant. Thus, putting values in a formula we have given two equations.

$$4000 = \sqrt{d}$$
$$x = \sqrt{2d}$$
$$= 1.414 \times 4000$$
$$= 5656$$

Hence the correct answer is option (C).

36. Macroeconomics deals with aggregate level of output, income and spending for all goods and services. It concerns with whole economy and its sectors and not any individual sector. Therefore, Choice A & B is not correct option as, it just focused on Industrial sectors only.

Choice D also focuses on the population and income area only. Therefore, it is also not correct answer. Macroeconomics is concerned with Inflation & growth and employment level of the economy as it is a macro aspects of economy.

Hence the correct answer is option (C).

37. The format cell is not associated with SPSS. Hence the correct answer is option (D).

38. Applications of the χ2–distribution

- Chi-square distribution has a number of applications which are enumerated below:

- To test if the population has a specified value of the variance σ2.

- Chi-square test of goodness of fit.

- Chi-square test for independence of attributes.

Hence the correct answer is option (D).

39. It studies the functional relationship between physical inputs and physical outputs. It is expressed as $Q_x = F(L, K)$

Where, Q_x = Quantity of output, F = Function, L = Labour, K = Capital.

Hence the correct answer is option (A).

40. Fabian Entrepreneur:

He is dominated more by customs, religions, and past practices and he is not ready to take any risk at all.

Hence the correct answer is option (C).

41. Types of Agriculture Business:

- Crop production: The businesses are engaged in the production and selling of crops like fruits, vegetables, coffee, cotton, maize, tea, flowers, tobacco, etc.

- Livestock production: The businesses are engaged in the rearing and selling of different animals for their meat and other products like milk and skins, etc.

- Poultry keeping: The businesses concentrate on rearing and selling different types of birds for their meat, eggs, skins and feathers.

- Agricultural support businesses: Such businesses provide extension services, inputs like fertilizers, drugs, etc.

Hence the correct answer is option (C).

42.

- Economic policy refers to the action that governments takes in the economic field is called economic policy.

- It covers the systems for setting levels of taxation, government budgets, money supply and interest rates.

- It also related to labour market, national ownership and many other areas of government interventions into the economy.

- Many factors of economic policy can be divided into either fiscal policy which deals with government actions regarding taxation or spending or monetary policy.

Hence the correct answer is option (C).

43. Non-technical Entrepreneur: Non-technical entrepreneurs are those who are mainly concerned with developing alternative marketing and distribution strategies to promote their business. They are not concerned with the technical aspects of the product and services they are dealing with.
Hence the correct answer is option (A).

44. Higher esteem needs might include the desire for physical strength, knowledge, competence, independence, and freedom. Lower esteem needs might include status, recognition, fame, celebrity, prestige, and any form of attention. Self-respect, Self-recognition, Self-image are examples of esteem needs.

Hence the correct answer is option (D).

45.

- Business environment consists of all those factors that have a bearing on the business.

- The survival and success of business depends upon both internal factors and external factors.

- Internal factors- Internal environment.

- External factors- External environment.

Hence the correct answer is option (C).

46. Proxemics is the study of human use of space and the effects that population density has on behaviour, communication, and social interaction. Proxemics is one among several subcategories in the study of nonverbal communication, including haptics, kinesics, vocalics, and chronemics.
Hence the correct answer is option (B).

47. Marginal Product (MP) It is an additional output produced by the use of an additional unit of the variable factor, fixed factor remaining constant.

$$MP_{nth} = TP_n - TP_{n-1} \text{ or } MP = \frac{\Delta TP}{\Delta L}$$

Where, ATP = Change in Total Product AL = Change in labour (variable factor).
Hence the correct answer is option (A).

48. Ans.Average Revenue is the per unit revenue (price) received from the sale of one unit of a commodity.

As we know, $\quad AR = \frac{TR}{Q} \quad TR = P \times Q$

(Here, P = Price, Q = Quantity or Output sold) Thus,

$$AR = \frac{P \times Q}{Q}$$

Hence, it is proved AR = Price. Hence the correct answer is option (c).

49.

- Hard skills are related professional knowledge, tools or techniques that allow us to work within our professions whereas.

- Soft skills are the collection of our social, communication and self-management behavior. It is the ability to understand, communicate with, motivate and support other people, both individually and group.

- Conceptual skills are the skills that allow people to visualize the entire thing and work with ideas and the relationships between abstract concepts. It is not related to the question and therefore it is not correct answer.

- Political skills are about using politics at workplace and to motivate or support other people. Therefore it is also incorrect answer.

Hence the correct answer is option (D).

50.

- Organizational development (OD) is deliberately planned, organization-wide effort to increase an organization's effectiveness and health through planned interventions in in the organizations processes, using behavioral science knowledge.

- Intervention means the specific actions selected for implementation that are intended to bring about the envisioned change.

Hence the correct answer is option (B).

51.

- There are 3 theory of conditioning, out of them operant conditioning theory is given by B. F. Skinner.

- Ivan Pavlov has given theory of Stimulus response through experiments with dogs. Theory of associates is also not given by Marshall

- Thus, Operant Conditioning Theory given by B. F. Skinner is correct answer.

Hence the correct answer is option (B).

52. Benchmarking is the process through which a company measures its products, services, and practices against its toughest competitors, or those companies recognized as leaders in its industry. Benchmarking is one of a manager's best tools for determining whether the company is performing particular functions and activities efficiently, whether its costs are in line with those of competitors, and whether its internal activities and business processes need improvement. The idea behind benchmarking is to measure internal processes against an external standard. It is a way of learning which companies are best at performing certain activities and functions and then imitating—or better still, improving on—their techniques.

Hence the correct answer is option (B).

53.

- Leaders work is to lead others whereas monitors are the one who monitors everything and take cares of each and every thing. Distribution handlers do the work related to the distribution activity whereas resource allocators are the one who allocates all the resources.

- All from the option have the work related to specific area except monitors. Monitors are the one who have to take care of every department and connect all of them through providing information just like managers, who receive a wide variety of information and serve as the nerve centres of internal and external information of the organization.

Hence the correct answer is option (B).

54. Rorsach value survey is a classification system of values consisting two sets of values.

- Terminal values
- Instrumental values

Each one has 18 individual value items in it. Out of them the Instrumental Values are:

- Cheerfulness
- Ambition
- Love
- Cleanliness
- Self-Control
- Capability
- Courage
- Politeness
- Honesty
- Imagination
- Independence
- Intellect
- Broad-Mindedness
- Logic
- Obedience
- Helpfulness
- Responsibility
- Forgiveness

Thus, from this list we can say that wise is not included in this.

Hence the correct answer is option (B).

55.

- Selective perception is a type of bias related to how a person's expectations or degree to which stand out can affect observations. One perceives what they want to perceive is called selective perception. In case of Halo effect, one perceives other on the basis of their first impression. How one's first impression is in the minds of perceivers reflects in Halo Effect.

- Contrast effect is the kind of perception taken based on past performances or results.

- Stereotyping is a kind of bias or shortcut used in perception theory while judging other. In this, one judges others on the basis of one's perception towards the group to which one belongs.

Hence the correct answer is option (A).

56. The cost to buy an item should include -purchase price of the item or component, transportation cost, sales tax and octopi, procurement cost, carrying cost, receiving and incoming inspection costs. The analysis of these two costs helps take decision whether to make or buy(Marginal cost).

Hence the correct answer is option (A).

57. Payback Method

This method is relatively easy since the cash flow doesn't need to be discounted. Its major weakness is that it ignores the cash inflows after the payback period, and does not consider the timing of cash flows.

Hence the correct answer is option (A).

58. Selection is the process in which candidates for employment are divided into two classes – those who are to be offered employment and those who are not." This is stated by Dale Yoder.

Hence the correct answer is option (A).

59. Purchasing power parity (PPP) is a measurement of prices in different countries that uses the prices of specific goods to compare the absolute purchasing power of the countries' currencies.

Hence the correct answer is option (C).

60. Line and staff relationship is based on the assumption that both support each other harmoniously to achieve organisational objectives. However, there are frequent instance of conflict between line and staff in the organisation. This generates lots of friction loss of time and consequently organisational effectiveness. Therefore, there is a need for analysing the sources of line and staff conflict and then to take actions to overcome the problem of conflict.

Hence the correct answer is option (C).

61. Leon Festinger gave cognitive dissonance theory.

According to theory, there is a tendency for individuals to seek consistency among their cognitions (i. e. , beliefs, opinions). When there is an inconsistency between attitudes or behaviors (dissonance), something must change to eliminate the dissonance. it is a condition in which two attitudes or a behaviour and an attitude conflicts with each other.

Festinger argued that any kind of inconsistency or dissonance is uncomfortable and the individual attempts to reduce dissonance.

Hence the correct answer is option (D).

62. A reference group is a collection of people that we use as a standard of comparison for ourselves regardless of whether we are part of that group. We rely on reference groups to understand social norms, which then shape our values, ideas, behavior, and appearance.

Hence the correct answer is option (D).

63. The ultimate mission or purpose is to relate human resources to future enterprise needs, so as to maximize the future return on investment in human resources. It is referred to Human Resource Planning.

Hence the correct answer is option (C).

64.

- James MacGregor Burns was best known for his contributions to the transactional, transformational, aspirational, and visionary schools of leadership theory.

- According to James Burns, there are two types of leader-first transformational leaders they provide a sense of vision and feeling of pride, faith and respect to the employees.

- They recognize and satisfy the needs of his followers while elevating them.

- Transactional leaders clarify subordinates role, job requirement and rewards to subordinates. His focus is on achieving organizational goal and emphasizes impersonal and unemotional aspects.

Hence the correct answer is option (A).

65.

- The principle of perceptual organization was first identified by Max Wertheimer in the year 1923.

- According to this principle closed areas of similar properties such as lightning, chromatic color, texture likely to be perceived initially a single unit.

Hence the correct answer is option (C).

Q.1 India signed Rs. 200 crore Strum Ataka anti-tank missile deal with which of the following countries?

A. Australia   **B.** Israel   **C.** China   **D.** Japan

E. Russia

Q.2 Recently, India's Veer Chotrani has won the Squash title in the Under 19 category at the Asian Junior Championship in __________.

A. China   **B.** Russia

C. Vietnam   **D.** Japan

E. Indonesia

Q.3 Who became the first woman fighter pilot to fly Hawk jet in IAF?

A. Kriti Rathore   **B.** Aarti Singh

C. Neha Bansal   **D.** Mohana Singh

E. Joshna Desai

Q.4 In economics, _____________ occurs when people are willing to work, but the people searching for work are not qualified for the job.

A. Frictional Unemployment

B. Structural Unemployment

C. Creeping Unemployment

D. Static Unemployment

E. Cyclical Unemployment

Q.5 Government recently changed the name for 'Department of Industrial Policy and Promotion' to _____________________

A. Department of Internal Trade policies

B. Department for Promotion of Industry and Internal Trade

C. Department for Industries Development

D. Department of Trade & Regulations

E. Department for Industries & Trade policy

Q.6 ADB &__________ have decided to Expand Development Finance in Asia and Pacific.

A. AIIB   **B.** RBI

C. NABARD   **D.** MIGA

E. NDB

Q.7 SENSEX is the index of Bombay Stock Exchange which is created on the basis of average price movement of how many stocks listed on BSE?

A. 100 companies/stocks

B. 500 companies/stocks

C. 50 companies/stocks

D. 150 companies/stocks

E. 200 companies/stocks

Q.8 Chit funds have been in news due to the Saradha scam in West Bengal. These funds are regulated by which among the following?

A. Union Government

B. State Governments

C. Reserve Bank of India

D. Securities and Exchange Board of India

E. Cabinet Committee of Economic Affairs

Q.9 P.K. Purwar has assumed the additional charge of Chairman & Managing Director of ________.

A. Vodafone   **B.** Airtel

C. BSNL   **D.** Jio

E. None of the above

Q.10 Which committee has submitted a new draft education policy to the HRD Ministry?

A. Bhurelal Committee

B. Bimal Jalan Committee

C. Kasturirangan Committee

D. Chandrashekhar Committee

E. Dave Committee

Q.11 Reserve Bank of India has recently revised the exposure limit under Single Limit for Domestic and Foreign Investors to how much amount in Exchange Traded Currency Derivatives Market recently?

A. USD 35 Million   **B.** USD 55 Million

C. USD 90 Million   **D.** USD 100 Million

E. USD 80 Million

Q.12 Negotiated Dealing System – Order Matching is an order driven electronic system launched by Reserve bank of India for trading government securities, NDS – OM is operated by which of the following organizations on behalf of RBI?

A. Fixed Income Money Market and Derivatives Association

B. Financial Benchmark India Pvt Ltd

C. Clearing Corporation of India Ltd

D. National Payments Corporation of India

E. State Bank of India

Q.13 What is the rank of India in IMD World Competitiveness Rankings?

A. 67th   **B.** 54th   **C.** 43rd   **D.** 18th

E. 78th

Q.14 Which of the following types of instruments are debentures which are redeemed at a premium over the face value of the debentures?

A. Redeemable Debentures

B. Zero Coupon Debentures

C. Fully Convertible Debentures

D. Floating Rate Debentures

E. Secured Premium Notes

Q.15 Which of the following is not one of the type of financial instruments which are traded in the capital markets?

A. Hybrid Instruments

B. Equity Instruments

C. Derivative Instruments

D. Debt Instruments

E. Commercial Instruments

Q.16 Which of the following ratios determines the net income generated by the total assets by comparing net income over total assets over a period of time?

A. Return on Investment Ratio

B. Debt Service Coverage Ratio

C. Gearing Ratio

D. Return on Assets Ratio

E. Operating Ratio

Q.17 Credit Rating Agencies in India are regulated by which of the following organizations?

A. Reserve Bank of India

B. Ministry of Corporate Affairs

C. Credit Regulatory Board of India

D. Securities and Exchange Board of India

E. Association of Credited Companies in India

Q.18 Chit Fund companies in India are regulated by which of the following organizations?

A. Small Industries Development Bank of India

B. Pension Fund Regulatory Development Authority

C. Reserve Bank of India

D. Respective State Governments

E. Securities and Exchange Board of India

Q.19 The aggregate lending exposure to all borrowers at any Point of time, across all Peer-to-Peer(PtoP) lenders shall be subject to a Cap of how much amount as notified by Reserve Bank of India?

A. Rs 15 Lakhs

B. Rs 25 Lakhs

C. Rs 75 Lakhs

D. Rs 100 Lakhs

E. Rs 10 Lakhs

Q.20 World Bank, Kerala government and the central government has signed a loan agreement of __________ for the first resilient Kerala Programme.

A. $ 200 million

B. $ 250 million

C. $ 150 million

D. $ 100 million

E. $ 300 million

Q.21 Which Financial Instrument is used in case an asset is held by a third party on behalf of two other parties that are in the process of completing a transaction?

A. Nodal Account

B. Escrow Account

C. Translator Account

D. Current Account

E. None of the above

Q.22 Which of the following is not a non-monetary incentive used by the manager sometimes to build up the morale of the sub-ordinate staff?

A. Job security

B. Promotion Opportunity

C. Bonus Scheme

D. Job enrichment

E. Recognition

Q.23 By the Rule of 72, how long will it take for an investment to double its value, if the interest rate is 7.5%?

A. 15.8 Years

B. 9.6 Years

C. 8 Years

D. 12.2 Year

E. 14 Years

Q.24 Fiscal Responsibility and Budget Management Act has been enacted in which of the following years, which is aimed at incorporate financial discipline, set targets for government of India from time to time to reduce fiscal deficit?

A. 2012

B. 2010

C. 2005

D. 2000

E. 2003

Q.25 Which of the following banks/ financial institutions is the largest holder of stake in Small Industries Development Bank of India, a total of 29 institutions hold stake in the bank?

A. State Bank of India

B. General Insurance Corporation of India

C. IDBI Bank

D. MUDRA Bank

E. Life Insurance Corporation of India

Q.26 National Housing Bank was setup in which of the following years under the National Housing Bank act?

A. 1997

B. 1979

C. 1988

D. 1992

E. 1991

Q.27 Which of the following types of funding belongs to Alternate Sources of Finance categorization?

A. Government Bonds

B. Investment in an immovable property

C. Equity Investments

D. Venture Capital

E. None of the above

Q.28 All transactions of International Banking Units set up at IFSC (International Financial Service Centers) Unit shall be in currencies other than which of the following currencies?

A. YUAN

B. USD

C. EURO

D. YEN

E. INR

Q.29 As per the ICDR regulations of SEBI, retail investor is defined as a persons who holds investments upto what amount in a public issue?

A. Rs 10 Lakhs

B. Rs 2 Lakhs

C. Rs 50,000

D. Rs 1 Lakh

E. Rs 5 Lakhs

Q.30 __________ refers to the process of selling off a company's inventory in order to generate cash.

A. Merger

B. Liquidation

C. Solvency

D. Arbitration

E. Mortgage

Q.31 In case a decrease in price of a commodity results in an increase in its demand on a negatively sloping demand curve, it is known as:

A. An increase in demand

B. An increase in quantity demanded

C. Law of demand

D. Law of supply
E. None of the above

Q.32 The consists of economic conditions, economic policies, industrial policies, and economic systems is called:
A. Economic environment
B. Natural environment
C. Business environment
D. Question does not provide sufficient data or is vague
E. None of the above

Q.33 Currently the bank rate is 6%, then banks rate means:-
A. RBI lends money and charges for it for long learn
B. Commercial banks lends money to RBI
C. None of the above
D. Question does not provide sufficient data or is vague
E. Both A and B

Q.34 Which of the following is not one of the types of Financial Futures Contracts?
A. Futures on Stock bearing Indices
B. Futures on Interest bearing instruments
C. Futures on Mutual Funds
D. Futures on Currencies
E. Futures on Commodities

Q.35 Which one is the type of economic system?
A. Socialism
B. Capitalism
C. Mixed economy
D. All of these
E. None of them

Q.36 What does "I" Stand for in FRDI Bill which has been in news recently?
A. Information
B. Insolvency
C. Insurance
D. Investment
E. Industrial

Q.37 According to management theorists, when diversity is not managed properly, there is a potential for:-
A. High creativity
B. Communication benefits
C. High turnover
D. Labour cost inequity
E. none of the above

Q.38 Who developed the "two-factor theory" of motivation?
A. A H Maslow
B. Hackman
C. Herzberg
D. Lawless, David J
E. none of the above

Q.39 Which one is the type of communication in small group?
A. Circular flow with feedback
B. Centralised flow with feedback
C. Chain flow with feedback
D. All a, b. and c. are correct
E. only A and B are correct

Q.40 The Practice of Management written by:-
A. Peter Drucker
B. Terry

C. Hendry Fayol
D. Frank Gehry
E. None of the above

Q.41 Which is related to the leadership theory?
A. Trait theory
B. Transactional theory
C. Behavioral theory
D. Both A and C
E. All of these

Q.42 Which leadership theory is developed by Kelly?
A. Trait Theory
B. Situational Theory
C. Great Man Theory
D. Behavioural Theories
E. Only C

Q.43 Which is the example of Centralised flow with feedback?

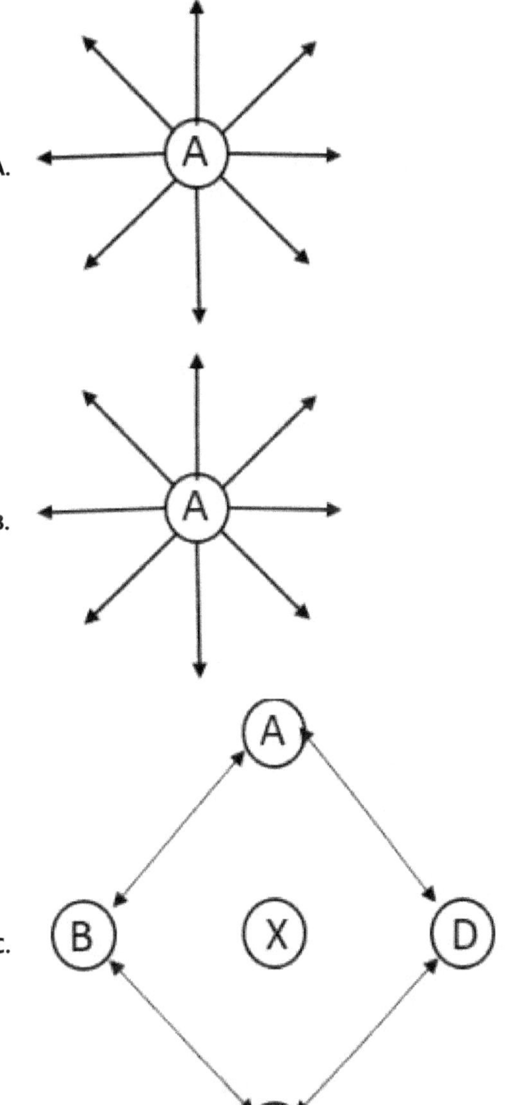

D.

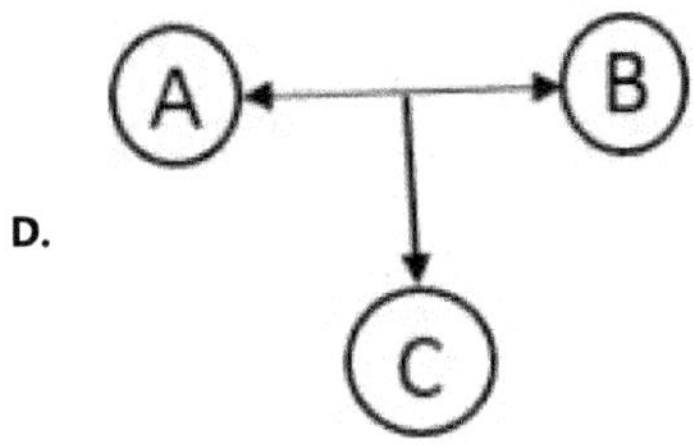

E. None of these

Q.44 Which of the following is/are a step in planning?
A. Establishing objectives
B. Developing premises
C. Determining Alternative courses
D. All of the above
E. Both A and C

Q.45 Which one of the following types of strikes is without the consent of the official of the union?
A. Jurisdictional strike
B. Slow down strike
C. Sympathy strike
D. Wild cat strike
E. General strike

Q.46 Which one of the following is a contract made through collusion between management and labour representatives and contains terms beneficial to management and unfavourable to union workers?
A. Invalid contract
B. Aleatory contract
C. Sweetheart contract
D. Unilateral contract
E. Unit price contract

Q.47 Hygiene factors Herzberg relating to the work include:-
A. Relationship with supervisor, peers and subordinates
B. Technical supervision
C. Company policy and administration
D. All a. , b. and c. are correct
E. None of these

Q.48 A ____________is your approach to directing, managing, motivating and communicating with employees.
A. Attitudinal style
B. Motivation style
C. Supervisory style
D. Power style
E. Interaction style

Q.49 The goal-setting theory was proposed by:-
A. Victor Vroom
B. Clayton Adderfer
C. Edwin Locke
D. Mc Gregor
E. none of the above

Q.50 Which one is the extrinsic motivation?
A. Margin profit
B. Pension
C. Life insurance
D. All a. , b. and c. are correct
E. Only A and B

Q.51 In which of the following, the payment of bonus is linked to the performance of specific employees or groups of employees?

(a) Profit-sharing
(b) Gainsharing plans
(c) The social system plans 4 code:
A. Only a
B. Only b
C. Only c
D. All of the above
E. Both A and B

Q.52 'Employee relations' include which of the following?
(a) Organisation's efforts to manage relationships between employer and employees.
(b) The programs to prevent and resolve problems arising from work situations.
(c) Relations between management and trade unions.
(d) Organisation's structure of managing rapport between boss and staff.
Code:
A. a and b
B. a, b and d
C. b and c
D. All of the above
E. Only A

Q.53 Theory Y is a theory of:-
A. Controlling
B. Management
C. Financial planning
D. Learning
E. Education

Q.54 Who gave the Expectancy theory of motivation?
A. Porter and lawler
B. Mc Gregor
C. Vroom
D. J. stacy Adams
E. None of the above

Q.55 Which is/are the principle of delegation?
A. Absoluteness of Responsibility
B. Integrity
C. Unity of command
D. Both A and C
E. Only B

Q.56 When employees work longer days in exchange for long weekends or other days off, it is called:
A. Flexy time
B. Compressed workweek
C. Extended timing
D. Job sharing
E. Work sharing

Q.57 Acquisition of firms is the same as:
(a) a merger
(b) an amalgamation
(c) a takeover
Select the correct code.
A. Only a
B. Only b
C. Only c
D. All of the above
E. Both A and C

Q.58 For the following two statements of Assertion (A) and Reason (R) select the correct code:
Assertion (A): Risk analysis of capital investment is the most complex and controversial area in finance.

Reason (R): Capital investment decisions are based on estimates of future cash inflows.

code:

A. (A) is correct, but (R) is incorrect.

B. (A) and (R) both are correct, but R is not the right explanation of (A).

C. (A) and (R) both are correct and (R) is the right explanation of (A).

D. (A) is incorrect, but (R) is correct.

E. None of above are correct

Q.59 In case the profitability index of an investment is equal to one (=1), the net present value of the investment will be:

A. More than one (>1) B. Equal to one (=1)

C. Less than one (<1) D. Equal to zero (=0)

E. More than zero (>0)

Q.60 A _________________ is a set of standards, qualifications and guidelines used to recognize and assess the skills and knowledge people need to perform effectively in the workplace.

A. On the job training

B. Training through correspondence course

C. Packaged training

D. All a. , b. and c. are correct

E. All of the above are incorrect

Q.61 Performance = f (m, a, e). In this expression 'e' stands for:-

A. Effectiveness B. Environment

C. Efficiency D. Entrepreneurship

E. Essential

Q.62 Which one of the following is not a factor that reduces the price sensitivity of a product?

A. The product is more distinctive.

B. Buyers are fully aware of substitutes.

C. Buyers cannot store the product.

D. The product is assumed to have more quality, prestige, or exclusiveness.

E. None of the above

Q.63 ___________ is a preplanned course of action establishing a guide to work toward acceptable outcomes and objectives.

A. Probation policy B. Review of progress

C. Employment policy D. Working policy

E. None of the above

Q.64 _____________is about giving motivation to the employees for better job performance.

A. Attrition

B. Job enrichment

C. Performance appraisal

D. Job evaluation

E. None of the above

Q.65 On-the-job training methods are based on:-

A. Informal training

B. Apprenticeship method

C. Demonstration method

D. All of the above

E. None of these

// Smart Answer Sheet //

Correct   Indicates percentage of students who answered questions correctly.

Skipped   Indicates percentage of students who skipped questions.

Q.	Ans.	Correct / Skipped		Q.	Ans.	Correct / Skipped		Q.	Ans.	Correct / Skipped		Q.	Ans.	Correct / Skipped		Q.	Ans.	Correct / Skipped
1	E	87.79 % / 10.71 %		14	E	81.14 % / 10.45 %		27	D	87.04 % / 11.71 %		40	A	86.74 % / 11.65 %		53	B	80.5 % / 12.85 %
2	A	87.87 % / 11.38 %		15	C	87.89 % / 11.13 %		28	E	77.19 % / 17.03 %		41	E	85.6 % / 11.75 %		54	C	77.51 % / 17.9 %
3	D	78.02 % / 10.64 %		16	D	88.32 % / 11.28 %		29	B	79.55 % / 19.05 %		42	A	80.79 % / 13.24 %		55	D	84.21 % / 11.03 %
4	B	78.25 % / 14.87 %		17	D	83.13 % / 13.66 %		30	B	83.94 % / 11.07 %		43	B	78.33 % / 20.49 %		56	B	84.89 % / 14.9 %
5	B	85.15 % / 11.51 %		18	D	88.03 % / 10.15 %		31	C	88.1 % / 10.7 %		44	D	87.38 % / 12.4 %		57	C	84.51 % / 13.2 %
6	D	78.98 % / 12.9 %		19	E	87.24 % / 12.07 %		32	A	78.07 % / 20.11 %		45	D	79.34 % / 13.52 %		58	C	80.81 % / 12.16 %
7	C	83.82 % / 10.36 %		20	B	87.83 % / 11.35 %		33	A	87.62 % / 10.39 %		46	C	88.52 % / 10.44 %		59	D	89.62 % / 10.34 %
8	B	83.4 % / 12.87 %		21	B	79.42 % / 17.75 %		34	C	87.7 % / 10.81 %		47	D	88.16 % / 10.29 %		60	C	81.61 % / 17.21 %
9	C	88.98 % / 10.33 %		22	C	77.84 % / 18.38 %		35	C	80.69 % / 12.6 %		48	C	76.93 % / 17.83 %		61	B	89.23 % / 10.4 %
10	C	80.26 % / 15.28 %		23	B	85.05 % / 13.89 %		36	C	80.77 % / 16.19 %		49	C	87.82 % / 11.47 %		62	B	86.87 % / 10.57 %
11	D	84.25 % / 15.47 %		24	E	89.54 % / 10.17 %		37	C	87.68 % / 10.23 %		50	D	76.84 % / 11.33 %		63	A	81.57 % / 10.3 %
12	C	84.82 % / 15.12 %		25	A	83.72 % / 12.24 %		38	C	89.59 % / 10.11 %		51	B	80.62 % / 10.97 %		64	B	82.89 % / 15.16 %
13	C	81.42 % / 11.57 %		26	C	80.62 % / 11.09 %		39	D	78.3 % / 16.54 %		52	B	77.26 % / 22.01 %		65	D	82.68 % / 10.52 %

Performance Analysis

Avg. Score (%)	36.0%
Toppers Score (%)	55.0%
Your Score	

//Hints and Solutions//

1. India signed a deal to acquire Strum Ataka anti-tank missile from Russia for its fleet of Mi-35 attack choppers. Deal for missiles is around 200 cr in order to give an added capability to the Mi-35 attack choppers to take out enemy tanks/armoured elements.

Hence the correct answer is option (e).

2.

- In Squash, India's Veer Chotrani beat Yash Fadte to win the Under-19 title at the Asian Junior Championship in Macau, China.
- He became the third Indian to win the Asian trophy after Ravi Dixit and Vela Senthilkumar.

Hence the correct answer is option (a).

3. Flight Lieutenant Mohana Singh has become the first woman fighter pilot to fly by day a Hawk advanced jet aircraft, a defence release has said. She achieved the feat at the Kalaikunda Air Force Station in West Bengal.

Hence the correct answer is option (d).

4. Structural unemployment is a type of long-term unemployment caused by shifts in the economy occurring when there is an oversupply of jobs and people are willing to work, but the people searching for work are not qualified.

One of the reasons behind structural unemployment is technological advances and decline in an industry. Technological advances can cause some types of skilled laborers to become obsolete.

Hence the correct answer is option (b).

5. The Government has changed the name of the Department of Industrial Policy and Promotion (DIPP) in the Ministry of Commerce and Industry to the **Department for Promotion of Industry and Internal Trade (DPIIT)**

It will continue to look after General Industrial Policy; Administration of the Industries (Development and Regulation) Act, 1951 (65 of 1951); Industrial Management; and Productivity in Industry.

In the list of distribution of subjects, new subjects such as Promotion of Internal Trade, including Retail Trade; Welfare of Traders and their Employees; Matters relating to facilitating "Ease of Doing Business"; and Matters relating to Start-Ups have been added under the DPIIT.

Hence the correct answer is option (b).

6. The Asian Development Bank (ADB) and the Multilateral Investment Guarantee Agency (MIGA), agreed to cooperate more closely to increase the flow of private sector investment into emerging economies in Asia and the Pacific, in line with the 2030 development goals. MIGA was created in 1988 as a member of the World Bank Group.

Hence the correct answer is option (d).

7. SENSEX is the index of Bombay Stock Exchange which is created on the basis of average price movement of 50 companies/stocks listed on BSE.

Hence the correct answer is option (C).

8. Chit funds in India are governed by the Chit Funds Act, 1982. Under this Act, the chit fund businesses can be registered and **regulated only by the respective State Governments**. Regulator of chit funds is the Registrar of Chits appointed by respective state governments under Section 61 of Chit Funds Act.

Hence the correct answer is option (b).

9. The government has appointed MTNL Chairman and Managing Director P.K. Purwar as the CMD of Bharat Sanchar Nigam Ltd for a period of three months. He is expected to follow the directions by the Department of Telecom.

Hence the correct answer is option (c).

10. Former ISRO chief Dr. Kasturirangan led Committee submitted the draft National Educational Policy (NEP) to the HRD Minister. It recommends incorporation of Indian knowledge systems in the curriculum, constituting a National Education Commission.

Hence the correct answer is option (c).

11. Reserve Bank of India has recently revised the exposure limit under Single Limit for Domestic and Foreign Investors to USD 100 Millionamount in Exchange Traded Currency Derivatives Market recently.

Hence the correct answer is option (D).

12. Negotiated Dealing System – Order Matching is an order driven electronic system launched by Reserve bank of India for trading government securities, NDS – OM is operated by Clearing Corporation of India Ltd organizations on behalf of RBI.

Hence the correct answer is option (C).

13. According to IMD World Competitiveness Rankings, Singapore has ranked as the world's most competitive economy for the first time since 2010, as the United States slipped from the top spot. India has improved its rank to one place to rank 43rd.

Hence the correct answer is option (c).

14. Secured Premium Notes ypes of instruments are debentures which are redeemed at a premium over the face value of the debentures.

Hence the correct answer is option (E).

15. Commercial Instruments is not one of the type of financial instruments which are traded in the capital markets.

Hence the correct answer is option (E).

16. Return on Assets Ratio determines the net income generated by the total assets by comparing net income over total assets over a period of time.

Hence the correct answer is option (D).

17. Credit Rating Agencies in India are regulated by Securities and Exchange Board of India.

Hence the correct answer is option (D).

18. Chit Fund companies in India are regulated by Respective State Governments.

Hence the correct answer is option (D).

19. The aggregate lending exposure to all borrowers at any Point of time, across all Peer-to-Peer(PtoP) lenders shall be subject to a Cap of Rs 10 Lakhs as notified by Reserve Bank of India.

20. GoI, Kerala govt & World Bank signed a loan agreement of $250 million for the First Resilient Kerala Programme to enhance the state resilience against the impact of natural disasters and climate change.

Hence the correct answer is option (b).

21. An **escrow account** is a temporary pass through account held by a third party during the process of a transaction between two parties.

This is a temporary account as it operates until the completion of a transaction process, which is implemented after all the conditions between the buyer and the seller are settled.

Hence the correct answer is option (b).

22. Bonus Scheme is not a non-monetary incentive used by the manager sometimes to build up the morale of the sub-ordinate staff.

Hence the correct answer is option (C).

23. By the Rule of 72, 9.6 Years will it take for an investment to double its value, if the interest rate is 7.5%?

Hence the correct answer is option (B).

24. Fiscal Responsibility and Budget Management Act has been enacted in 2003, which is aimed at incorporate financial discipline, set targets for government of India from time to time to reduce fiscal deficit?

Hence the correct answer is option (E).

25. State Bank of India banks/ financial institutions is the largest holder of stake in Small Industries Development Bank of India, a total of 29 institutions hold stake in the bank.

Hence the correct answer is option (A).

26. National Housing Bank was setup in 1988under the National Housing Bank act.

Hence the correct answer is option (C).

27. Venture Capital of funding belongs to Alternate Sources of Finance categorization.

Hence the correct answer is option (D).

28. All transactions of International Banking Units set up at IFSC (International Financial Service Centers) Unit shall be in currencies other than INR currencies.

Hence the correct answer is option (E).

29. As per the ICDR regulations of SEBI, retail investor is defined as a persons Rs 2 Lakhs holds investments upto what amount in a public issue.

Hence the correct answer is option (B).

30. Liquidation generally refers to the process of selling off a company's inventory, typically at a big discount, to generate cash.

In most cases, a liquidation sale is a precursor to a business closing. Once all the assets have been sold, the business is shut down.

In the accounting world, liquidation refers to the process of selling all of a company's assets to generate cash to pay off creditors, or anyone the company owes money to.

Hence the correct answer is option (b).

31.

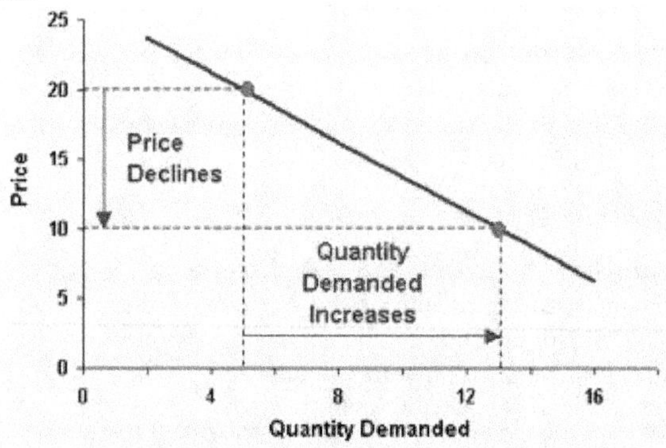

The Given Image Shows Price and Quantity of Demand

- Law of demand says that when price of a commodity will increase, demand for that commodity will decrease and if price for a commodity will decrease then demand for that commodity will increase. Thus, it shows negative relationship between price of a commodity and its demand.

- So, we can say that decrease in price of a commodity causes increase in its demand on a negatively sloping demand curve is called Law of demand.

Hence the correct answer is option (c).

32.

- Economic environment consists of economic conditions, economic policies, industrial polices, and economic systems.

- Business environment consists of internal environment and external environment.

- Natural environment consists of season raining, earth quake which occurs naturally in environment.

Hence the correct answer is option (a).

33.

- Bank rate is the interest rate at which a nation's central bank lends money to domestic banks, often in the form of very short-term loans.

- Managing the bank rate is method by which central banks affect economic activity.
- Lower bank rates can help to expand the economy by lowering the cost of funds for borrowers.
- Higher bank rates help to reign in the economy when inflation is higher than desired.
- It is the rate at which RBI lends money to other banks or financial institutes.

Hence the correct answer is option (a).

34. Futures on Mutual Funds is not one of the types of Financial Futures Contracts.

Hence the correct answer is option (C).

35. The economic system is a system of production, resource distribution, and distribution of goods and services within a society or a given geographic area.

There are three types of economic systems such as the capitalistic economic system socialistic economic system and the mixed economy system.

Hence the correct answer is option (c).

36. "I" Stand Insurance for in FRDI Bill which has been in news recently.

Hence the correct answer is option (C).

37.

- High turnover defined as the rate of change in the working staff of a concern during a definite period. It signifies the shifting of the workforce into and out of an organisation.
- It is as a measurement of labor unrest which can develops from if management work not properly.
- Turnover includes both employees who quit their job and those who are asked to leave.

Hence the correct answer is option (c).

38.

- Herzberg a behavioral scientist developed two factor theory. It also known as Herzberg's motivation-hygiene theory and dual-factor theory.
- This theory states that there are certain factors in the workplace that cause job satisfaction though a separate set of factors cause dissatisfaction. Theorized that job satisfaction and job dissatisfaction act independently of each other.

Hence the correct answer is option (c).

39.

- The process of communication is given below:

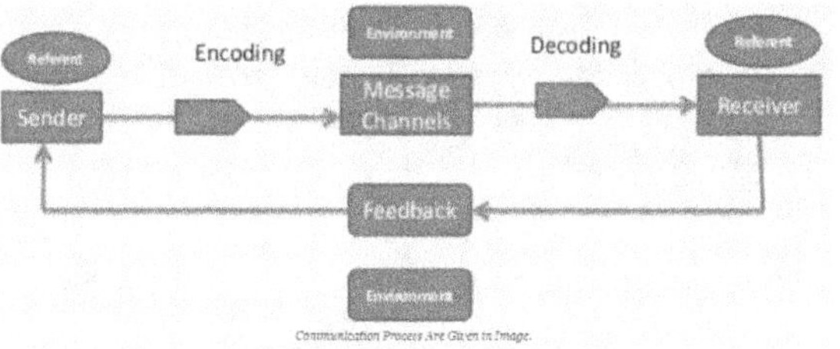

Communication Process Are Given in Image.

There are various type of communication in small group. Communication flow is slow and used in small group. Centralized flow is also known as the wheel network.

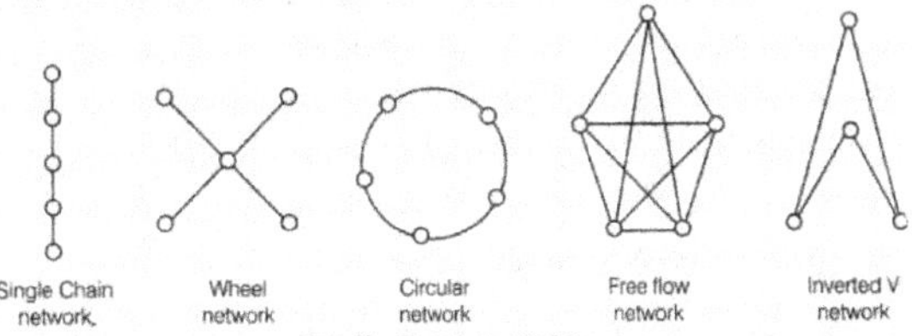

Hence the correct answer is option (d).

40. The Practice of Management is written by Peter F Drucker. Peter Drucker (1909-2005) was one of the most widely-known and influential thinkers on management, whose work continues to be used by managers worldwide.

Hence the correct answer is option (A).

41. Leadership theories are related to behaviour of followers and employees. Leadership theories includes:

- Great Man Theory
- Trait Theory
- Behavioural Theories
- Contingency Theories
- Transactional Theories
- Transformational Theories

Hence the correct answer is option (d).

42.

- Kelly developed trait leadership theory in 1974. Trait theory related with personality and the success of leadership.
- Trait theory is the great men approach based on that leaders and that is the trait-oriented and traditional approach. the leader is by born great organizers they possess certain qualities of head and heart which make him successful. their personality should be genetic which make the best leader and executive.

Hence the correct answer is option (a).

43.

- It is the example of Centralized flow with feedback. It relates with communication. Therefore, it refers to sharing of ideas, facts, opinions, information, and understanding.

- It is the transfer of some information from one person to another. two side arrow is a two -way communication ideas can be exchanged to give the answer of questions asked.

Hence the correct answer is option (b).

44. Establishing objectives, developing premises, determining alternative courses are the major steps of planning.

Planning is the first management function. For any project first planning is done. It is a long term concept.

Hence the correct answer is option (d).

45. Wild cat strikes: These strikes are conducted by workers or employees without the authority and consent of unions. In 2004, a significant number of advocated went on wildcat strike at the City Civil Court premises in Bangalore.

Hence the correct answer is option (d).

46. A sweetheart contract is a contract made through collusion between management and labor representatives which contains terms beneficial to management and unfavorable to union workers. It is also referred to as a "sweetheart agreement".

Hence the correct answer is option (c).

47. Some simple examples of hygiene factors include organizational policies and procedures, supervision, relationships with co-workers and supervisors, physical work environment, job security, and compensation. It is part of Herzberg's motivation-hygiene theory.

Hence the correct answer is option (d).

48. A supervisory style is your approach to directing, managing, motivating and communicating with employees. There are many leadership styles, each with their strengths and weaknesses. While certain supervisory styles are commonly considered superior methods, the reality is that no leadership style is one-size-fits-all.

Hence the correct answer is option (c).

49.

- Motivation and goal-setting theory given by Dr. Edwin A. Locke is widely regarded among top management theories.

- Small businesses can learn a lot from his principles of motivation and goal-setting theory. Without the most basic goals, employees would not show up for work or see a purpose in holding a job.

- Management team that helps employees set more complex and effective goals they boost performance and profits beyond their wildest expectations.

Hence the correct answer is option (c).

50.

- Definition: "Extrinsic motivation refers to our tendency to perform activities for known external rewards, whether they be tangible (e. g. , money) or psychological (e. g. , praise) in nature. "- Brown

- Extrinsic motivation is concerned with external motivators these are associated with financial rewards. such as -pay promotion, fringe benefits, retirement plans, health insurance schemes, margin profit, holidays, vacations, etc.

- So, Pension, life insurance and margin profit are the part of extrinsic motivation.

Hence the correct answer is option (d).

51. In gain sharing, the employee receives bonuses are tied to the performance of specific employees or groups whereas in profit sharing bonuses are linked to the company's overall profitability.

Hence the correct answer is option (b).

52. Organization's efforts to manage relationships between employers and employees.

The programs to prevent and resolve problems arising from work situations.

Organisation's structure of managing rapport between boss and staff. These are employee relations.

Hence the correct answer is option (b).

53. Theory X and Theory Y are theories of human work motivation and management. ... Theory X explains the importance of heightened supervision, external rewards, and penalties, while Theory Y highlights the motivating role of job satisfaction and encourages workers to approach tasks without direct supervision. In 1960, Douglas McGregor formulated Theory X and Theory Y suggesting two aspects of human behaviour at work, or in other words, two different views of individuals (employees): one of which is negative, called as Theory X and the other is positive, so called as Theory Y.

Hence the correct answer is option (b).

54. Expectancy theory of motivation was propounded by vroom. According to this theory if a person's expectations are high then he will work hard and try to achieve his goals in life. An employee's performance is based on individual's strength, skills, knowledge, personality, experience and abilities.

Hence the correct answer is option (c).

55.

- Delegation is the obligation of any responsibility or authority to another person generally from a manager to a subordinate to carry out specific activities. It is one of the basic concepts of management leadership.

- Unity of command is one of the principles of delegation. This principle states that a subordinate should report only to single superior. This will give a sense of personal responsibility. While it is possible for a subordinate to receive orders from more superiors and report to them but it creates more problems and difficulties.

- Other options are related to qualities of a successful leader and related to characteristics of leadership.

Hence the correct answer is option (c).

56. When employees work longer days in exchange for long weekends or other days off, it is called a Compressed work week.

Hence the correct answer is option (b).

57. Although technically, the words "acquisition" and "takeover" mean almost the same thing, they have different nuances on Wall Street. In general, "acquisition" describes a primarily amicable transaction, where both firms cooperate; "takeover" suggests that the target company resists or strongly opposes the purchase; the term "merger" is used when the purchasing and target companies mutually combine to form a completely new entity. However, because each acquisition, takeover, and merger is a unique case, with its own peculiarities and reasons for undertaking the transaction, use of these terms tends to overlap.

Hence the correct answer is option (c).

58. Risk analysis of capital investment is the most complex and controversial area in finance.

Capital investment decisions are based on estimates of future cash inflows.

(A) and (R) both are correct and (R) is the right explanation of (A).

Hence the correct answer is option (c).

59. In case the profitability index of an investment is equal to one (=1), the net present value of the investment will be equal to zero (=0).

Hence the correct answer is option (d).

60.

- On-the-job training (OJT) is a form of training taking place in a normal working situation. On-the-job training, sometimes called direct instruction.

- A training package is a set of standards, qualifications and guidelines used to recognize and assess the skills and knowledge people need to perform effectively in the workplace.

- Training through a correspondence course means training through distance Courses.

Hence the correct answer is option (c).

61.

- Performance is a function of Environment, Organization and leadership. Here, 'e' stands for environment.

- So, in Performance = f (m, a, e) in this expression 'e' stands for environment.

Hence the correct answer is option (b).

62. The factor that reduces the price sensitivity of a product are:

The product is assumed to have more quality, prestige, or exclusiveness.

Buyers cannot store the product.

The product is more distinctive.

Hence the correct answer is option (b).

63. Personnel policy is a preplanned course of action establishing a guide to work toward acceptable outcomes and objectives. Personnel policies are the rules that govern how to deal with human resources or personnel-related situation.

The following matters are covered in the Personnel policy:

Recruitment or hiring of employees:-

- Training programs
- Absenteeism
- Hours of work
- Conditions of employment
- Promotion, demotion and transfer etc.

Personnel policies deal all activities, which connected in firm recruitment, selection to the retirement of the employees. Therefore, Employment policy, probation policy, and review of progress are the elements of the element of ideal personnel policy.

Hence the correct answer is option (a).

64.

- Performance appraisal is a method of evaluating job performance of an employee whereas job evaluation is a systematic way of determining the value of a job compare to the other jobs in an organization.

- The objective of job evaluation is to determine which jobs should get more pay than others.

- It helps to establish a rational pay structure.

- Job enrichment is about giving motivation to the employees for better job performance.

- Attrition refers to the reduction in work force and this is also not related to the question that is asked.

Hence the correct answer is option (b).

65. On-the-job training methods include:

- Job rotation
- Coaching
- Job instruction
- Apprenticeship or
- Training through step-by-step
- Committee assignments
- It involves the person to learn the job by doing it in real work situation under the supervision of boss.

The demonstration method of teaching is a traditional classroom strategy. Apprenticeship method and Informal training are also one type of On-the-job training methods.
Hence the correct answer is option (d).

Q.1 Who among the following has received the 2020 Global Leadership Award by USIBC?
A.   Satya Narayana Nadella
B.   Ginni Rometty
C.   Indra Nooyi
D.   Natarajan Chandrasekaran
E.   None of the above

Q.2 _________ , head has been named as the new chairman of the Internet and Mobile Association of India (IAMAI)?
A. Amazon India   B. Google India
C. Microsoft India   D. Xiaomi India
E. Apple India

Q.3 What is EPF interest rate for 2020-2021?
A. 7.0%   B. 7.1%   C. 8.0%   D. 8.5%
E. 7.4%

Q.4 What edition of India's Economic Census has started recently in Tripura?
A. 6th   B. 7th   C. 8th   D. 9th
E. 5th

Q.5 _________, in May 2019 partnered with IMGC for a mortgage guarantee-backed home loan.
A. BOB   B. SBI
C. NABARD   D. HDFC
E. None of these

Q.6 _______ fall under the category of liquid assets.
A.   Banking accounts
B.   Checkable account
C.   Short-term promissory notes
D.   Treasury bills
E.   All of the above

Q.7 What was the theme for Global Innovation Index (GII), 2020?
A.   "Assessing the innovation capabilities"
B.   "Future of healthcare and its potential impact"
C.   "Who Will Finance Innovation?"
D.   "India's R&D Expenditure Ecosystem"
E.   None of these

Q.8 Jayshree Vyas has been appointed as the first independent woman director of _________.
A. BSE   B. NBSA
C. NTPC   D. None of these
E. NSE

Q.9 Who among the following has been sworn in as new Prime Minister of Greece?
A. A. U. Celestine   B. Alexis Tsipras
C. Kyriakos Mitsotakis   D. Adonis Georgiadis

E. Kostas Bakoyannis

Q.10 Recently, SIDBI has introduced a web-based application system for contribution from Funds of Funds for Start-ups. The regulator is the implementing agency of FFS with a corpus of _________ Crore.
A. ₹ 5000 Crore   B. ₹ 1000 Crore
C. ₹ 20000 Crore   D. ₹ 15000 Crore
E. ₹ 10000 Crore

Q.11 In May 2019 _______launched India's first UPI BahiKhata (Digital Ledger) for merchants.
A. PhonePe   B. BharatPe
C. Paytm   D. Mobikwik
E. Eazypay

Q.12 Former Deputy Governor of RBI Subir Gokarn passed away, recently. He was appointed as Executive Director of _________ by PM Modi government in 2015.
A.   International Monetary Forum
B.   World Economic Forum
C.   Asian Infrastructure Investment Bank
D.   World Bank
E.   Asian Development Bank

Q.13 The government has set up a working group under the chairmanship of _________ to revise the current series of Wholesale Price Index.
A. Rajiv Kumar   B. Ramesh Chand
C. Amitabh Kant   D. V.K. Saraswat
E. Dr. V.K. Paul

Q.14 As per the report by QS Quacquarelli Symonds, London has been named the World's best city for students. The number of Indians moving to the city for higher studies rose by _______ in 2017-18.
A. 24%   B. 28%   C. 32%   D. 20%
E. 18%

Q.15 Real Economic Growth Rate is the rate at which a nation's _______ changes/grows from one year to another.
A. GNP   B. GDP   C. NNP   D. GVA
E. NDP

Q.16 Under Section _______ of the Reserve Bank of India Act, the bank has the sole sight to issue bank notes of all denominations.
A. 18   B. 22
C. 24   D. 27
E. None of these

Q.17 Which among the following has launched an All- Women Police Patrol Unit 'Rani Abbakka Force' in May 2019?
A. Mangaluru Police   B. Chhattisgarh Police
C. Chennai Police   D. Delhi Police

E. Hyderabad Police

Q.18 Which of the following nation was India's largest export destination in 2018-2019?

A. China
B. Israel
C. USA
D. Pakistan
E. Sri Lanka

Q.19 The 23rd edition of National Conference on e-Governance will be held in __________.

A. Vishakhapatnam
B. Kolkata
C. Kochi
D. Mumbai
E. Chennai

Q.20 What is the maximum maturity for T-Bill Futures contracts?

A. 6 months
B. 3 months
C. 9 months
D. 12 months
E. None of these

Q.21 Recently, Sai Praneeth has entered top 20 in the World Badminton Rankings. Who among the following topped the list in Men's Singles Rankings?

A. Kento Momota
B. Shi Yu Qi
C. Anders Antonsen
D. Chou Tien Chen
E. Chen Long

Q.22 In May, 2019 who among the following has become India's first woman pilot to qualify to undertake Combat Missions?

A. Akshaya Patra
B. Aparna Kumar
C. Apurvi Chandela
D. Bhawana Kanth
E. Ashalata Devi

Q.23 Which of the following states will host the 10th National Science Film Festival of India in 2020?

A. Assam
B. Uttarakhand
C. Tripura
D. Kerala
E. Odisha

Q.24 World Youth Skills Day 2020 was observed on July 15. What was the 2020 theme of the same Day ?

A. Youth skills for work and life
B. Skills for the Future of Work
C. Skills Development to Improve Youth Employment
D. Skills for a Resilient Youth
E. Improving the image of Technical and Vocational Education and Training

Q.25 Kaleshwaram Lift Irrigation Project is located in________.

A. Telangana
B. Odisha
C. Karnataka
D. Andhra Pradesh
E. None of these

Q.26 BSNL has partnered with __________ to increase access to its WiFi footprint in the country.

A. Google
B. Facebook
C. Microsoft
D. IBM
E. None of the above

Q.27 Recently, which state has become the first state to have own water policy for addressing water issues and protection of sources?

A. Meghalaya
B. Mizoram
C. Manipur
D. Assam
E. Uttarakhand

Q.28 Which of the following Financial Institutions in June, 2019 made its 1st ever investment in Nepal?

A. ADB
B. AIIB
C. NDB
D. World Bank
E. EBRD

Q.29 Bank rate policy and ________ are complementary measures in the area of monetary management.

A. Moral Suasion
B. Credit Authorization
C. Open Market Operations
D. Credit Planning
E. Selective Credit Control

Q.30 The government has set a target to raise the expenditure on health services to _________ percentage of the country's GDP by 2025.

A. 3.5%
B. 3%
C. 2.5%
D. 1.5%
E. 4.2%

Q.31 A company may raise capital from the primary market through __________.

A. Public issue
B. Rights issue
C. Bought out deals
D. (A) and (B) both
E. All of the above

Q.32 Which exchange member is assigned to a specific trading post?

A. Commission broker
B. Floor trader
C. Specialist
D. Dealer
E. All of these

Q.33 A fixed rate of ________ is payable on debentures.

A. dividend
B. Commission
C. Interest
D. Brokerage
E. None of these

Q.34 According to traditional approach, the average cost of capital ___________.

A. Remains constant up to a degree of leverage and rises sharply thereafter with every increase in leverage
B. Rises constantly with increase in leverage
C. Decrease up to certain point, remains unchanged for moderate increase in leverage and rises beyond a certain point
D. Decrease at an increasing rate with increase in leverage
E. increase at an increasing rate with increase in leverage

Q.35 A computerized trading network that matches buy and sell orders electronically entered by customers is a________.

A. national markets system
B. electronic communications networks
C. internet investment service

D. global investment network

E. None of these

Q.36 Ownership securities are represented by ______.

A. stock

B. loan

C. debt

D. debentures

E. None of these

Q.37 The cost of capital of a firm is ___________.

A. The dividend paid on the equity capital

B. The weighted average of the cost of various long-term and short-term sources of finance

C. The average rate of return it must earn on its investments to satisfy the various investors

D. The minimum rate of return it must earn on its investments to keep its investors satisfied

E. None of these

Q.38 If an investor is attempting to buy a stock that is very volatile, it would be best to use________.

A. market order

B. limit order

C. stop-loss order

D. contingency order

E. All of these

Q.39 Net working capital refers to?

A. total assets minus fixed assets

B. current assets minus current liabilities

C. current assets minus inventories

D. current assets.

E. None of these

Q.40 The constant growth model of equity valuation assumes that __________.

A. The dividends paid by the company remain constant

B. The dividends paid by the company grow at a constant rate of growth

C. The cost of equity may be less than or equal to the growth rate

D. The growth rate is less than the cost of equity.

E. The growth rate is greater than the cost of equity.

Q.41 Which of the following has helped to eliminate the use of stock certificates by placing stock transactions on computers?

A. Demat account

B. Securities Exchange Commission

C. Depository Trust Company

D. Federal Depository Insurance Corporation.

E. None of these

Q.42 The expansion of EAR is?

A. equivalent annual rate

B. equivalent annuity rate

C. equally applied rate

D. equal advance rate

E. None of these

Q.43 The formula for cost of debt is ________.

A. I × (1 - t)

B. I+p

C. ×I-P

D. Ip

E. I/p

Q.44 Total return is equal to______

A. capital gain and yield

B. yield and interest

C. capital gain

D. yield

E. None of these

Q.45 Traditional theorists believe that?

A. there exists an optimal capital structure

B. no optimal capital structure

C. equal optimal capital structure

D. 100% debt financial organizations

E. All of these

Q.46 Which of the following is / are assumption(s) underlying the Miller and Modigliani analysis?

A. Capital markets are perfect

B. Investors are assumed to be rational and behave accordingly

C. There is no corporate or personal income tax

D. (A) and (B) both

E. All of the above.

Q.47 The return component that gives periodic cash flows to the investor is known as the__________.

A. capital gain

B. interest rate

C. yield

D. unrealized gain.

E. All of these

Q.48 The dividend-payout ratio is equal to ________.

A. the dividend yield plus the capital gains yield

B. dividends per share divided by earnings per share

C. dividends per share divided by par value per share

D. dividends per share divided by current price per share.

E. None of these

Q.49 Altering the leverage ratio does not influence the market value of the firm. This is the basic premise of ______.

A. net income approach

B. traditional approach

C. modern approach

D. net operating income approach

E. None of these

Q.50 While calculating the weighted average cost of capital, market value weights are preferred because __________.

A. Book value weights are historical in nature

B. This is in conformity with the definition of cost of capital as the investors minimum required rate of return

C. Book value weights fluctuate violently

D. Market value weights are fairly consistent over a period of time

E. None of these

Q.51 If market interest rates are expected to rise, you would expect________.

A. bond prices to fall more than stock prices

B. bond prices to rise more than stock prices

C. stock prices to fall more than bond prices

D. stock prices to rise and bond prices to fall.
E. None of these

Q.52 Which of the following is an argument for the relevance of dividends?
A. Informational content
B. Reduction of uncertainty
C. Some investors' preference for current income
D. (A) and (B) both
E. All of the above.

Q.53 Which of the following is/are false regarding capital structure theory as stated by Miller and Modigliani?
1) If agency costs are considered, the expected agency costs increases as the debt-equity ratio decreases.
2) With the given assumptions, there is no optimal capital structure.
3) In the presence of taxes, the market value of the firm decreases by the tax shield of debt
A. Only 1st statement
B. Only 2nd statement
C. Both 1st and 3rd statements
D. All the three statements
E. Both 1st and 2nd statements

Q.54 Financial risk is most associated with______________.
A. the use of equity financing by corporations
B. the use of debt financing by corporations
C. Equity investments held by corporations
D. Debt investments held by corporations.
E. None of these

Q.55 Retained earnings are ?
A. an indication of a company's liquidity
B. the same as cash in the bank
C. not important when determining dividends
D. the cumulative earnings of the company after dividends
E. None of these

Q.56 Which of the following factors does not affect the capital structure of a company?
A. Cost of capital
B. Composition of the current assets
C. Size of the company
D. Expected nature of cash flows
E. None of these

Q.57 Political stability is the major factor concerning______________.
A. Exchange risk
B. Systematic risk
C. Non-systematic risk
D. Country risk
E. Non exchange risk

Q.58 Arbitrage is the level processing technique introduced in ________.
A. Net income approach
B. MM approach
C. Operating approach
D. Traditional approach

E. None of these

Q.59 The rational expectations model of dividend policy says that ______________.
A. Since the expectations of the investors are always rational, there will be no effect of dividend policy on the valuation of the firm
B. If the investors have rational expectations, they will value a dividend paying firm higher than a non-dividend paying firm
C. If the declared dividend is in line with expectations of the investors, there will be no effect on the valuation of the firm
D. If the declared dividend is in accordance with the expectations, the change in the firms value will be minimal
E. None of these

Q.60 Liquidity risk______________.
A. is the risk that investment bankers normally face
B. is lower for small OTCEI stocks than for large NSE stocks
C. is the risk associated with secondary market transactions
D. increases whenever interest rates increase.
E. decreases whenever interest rates increase.

Q.61 In finance, "working capital" means the same thing as
A. total assets
B. fixed assets
C. current assets
D. current assets minus current liabilities.
E. None of these

Q.62 The Debt-Equity ratio of a Company______________.
A. Measure its financial leverage
B. Does not affect the Earnings per share
C. Affects the dividend decision of the company
D. Affect the Earnings per share
E. None of the above.

Q.63 Which of the following is not related to overall market variability?
A. Financial risk
B. Interest rate risk
C. Purchasing power risk
D. Market risk
E. None of these

Q.64 In proper capital budgeting analysis we evaluate incremental?
A. accounting income
B. cash flow
C. earnings
D. operating profit
E. None of these

Q.65 Which of the following statement are true in respect of working capital?
A. Gross Working Capital is the sum of the total current assets
B. Net working capital represents current assets - current liablities
C. Net working capital can be negative
D. (A) and (B) both

E. All the above

// Smart Answer Sheet //

Correct Indicates percentage of students who answered questions correctly.

Skipped Indicates percentage of students who skipped questions.

Q.	Ans.	Correct / Skipped	Q.	Ans.	Correct / Skipped	Q.	Ans.	Correct / Skipped	Q.	Ans.	Correct / Skipped	Q.	Ans.	Correct / Skipped
1	D	83.67 % / 10.1 %	14	D	88.66 % / 10.03 %	27	A	77.76 % / 17.25 %	40	B	90.0 % / 10.0 %	53	D	85.19 % / 14.12 %
2	A	80.66 % / 16.39 %	15	B	76.06 % / 11.33 %	28	B	85.46 % / 13.86 %	41	A	78.36 % / 18.45 %	54	B	78.32 % / 19.12 %
3	B	77.52 % / 12.13 %	16	B	86.92 % / 12.28 %	29	C	80.01 % / 17.48 %	42	A	76.35 % / 16.74 %	55	D	79.67 % / 11.74 %
4	B	82.75 % / 11.52 %	17	A	82.36 % / 16.64 %	30	C	82.28 % / 15.64 %	43	A	85.12 % / 13.93 %	56	B	78.5 % / 16.62 %
5	D	83.76 % / 13.24 %	18	C	87.35 % / 10.47 %	31	E	86.59 % / 10.28 %	44	A	79.96 % / 17.99 %	57	D	84.3 % / 11.38 %
6	E	86.29 % / 10.36 %	19	D	78.23 % / 15.19 %	32	C	86.27 % / 10.28 %	45	A	86.07 % / 10.15 %	58	B	86.73 % / 11.11 %
7	C	89.33 % / 10.37 %	20	D	76.35 % / 23.56 %	33	C	84.28 % / 13.86 %	46	E	76.97 % / 15.89 %	59	D	77.39 % / 18.79 %
8	A	89.95 % / 10.02 %	21	A	79.22 % / 14.3 %	34	C	87.81 % / 10.04 %	47	C	88.69 % / 10.68 %	60	D	83.66 % / 10.83 %
9	C	86.78 % / 10.26 %	22	D	76.77 % / 20.5 %	35	B	84.05 % / 12.78 %	48	B	83.27 % / 13.79 %	61	D	81.31 % / 11.14 %
10	E	78.26 % / 20.7 %	23	C	76.34 % / 11.15 %	36	A	77.84 % / 12.25 %	49	D	89.39 % / 10.07 %	62	A	80.43 % / 13.42 %
11	B	81.59 % / 17.0 %	24	D	83.72 % / 11.41 %	37	D	83.73 % / 11.69 %	50	A	82.53 % / 12.83 %	63	A	83.48 % / 16.13 %
12	A	77.16 % / 21.24 %	25	A	76.29 % / 23.36 %	38	B	79.76 % / 15.51 %	51	A	86.38 % / 10.46 %	64	B	88.99 % / 10.33 %
13	B	76.71 % / 22.07 %	26	A	86.41 % / 11.44 %	39	B	76.88 % / 17.69 %	52	E	77.0 % / 22.28 %	65	D	80.14 % / 12.91 %

Performance Analysis

Avg. Score (%)	30.0%
Toppers Score (%)	55.0%
Your Score	

//Hints and Solutions//

1. Tata group Chairman N Chandrasekaran and Lockheed Martin CEO Jim Taiclet will receive the USIBC Global Leadership Award this year, business advocacy group USIBC said on Tuesday. "Every year, the USIBC Global Leadership Awards are conferred upon executives in recognition of outstanding leadership and for promoting Indo-US trade and business," Washington-based US-India Business Council (USIBC) said.

Hence the correct answer is option (d).

2. Amazon India head Amit Agarwal has been named as the new chairman of the Internet and Mobile Association of India (IAMAI). According to recently launched Mary Meeker report, India accounts for 12% of the world's internet users, behind only to China (21%).

Hence the correct answer is option (a).

3. However, the Government of India has revised the interest rate on GPF again for the period between 1 April 2020 and 30 June 2020 in the financial year 2020-21 (April-March). In this period, it will fetch an interest rate of 7.1% for all the subscribers to the General Provident Fund and other similar funds.

Hence the correct answer is option (b).

4. India's **seventh Economic Census** (a three-month-long fieldwork) began from **Tripura.**

The fieldwork in other States and Union Territories would be undertaken in August and September. The IT-enabled economic census would be done by the Common Service Centres (CSC) in each gram panchayat. The enumerators and supervisors engaged by the CSCs have been trained to collect data on a mobile application developed for data capture, validation, report generation and dissemination.

Hence the correct answer is option (b).

5. HDFC Limited has partnered with India Mortgage Guarantee Corporation (IMGC) to offer a mortgage-guaranteed home loan product. The partnership aims to make it possible for HDFC to further penetrate home loan market and access an enlarged customer base, helping them to own a home of their choice.

Hence the correct answer is option (d).

6. An asset is said to be liquid if it is easy to sell or convert into cash without any loss in its value. By definition, bank notes and checking accounts are the most liquid assets.

Cash is a highly liquid asset followed by the banking accounts, checkable account, short-term promissory notes, treasury bills and other government bonds.

Hence the correct answer is option (e).

7. The 2020 edition of the Global Innovation Index (GII) presents the latest global innovation trends and the annual innovation ranking of 131 economies. The theme of this year's GII - **Who Will Finance Innovation?** - is timely given the human and global economic damage wreaked by the COVID-19 global pandemic.

Hence the correct answer is option (c).

8. BSE, formerly known as the Bombay Stock Exchange, has appointed its first independent woman director Jayshree Vyas. BSE has two non-executive women directors namely Usha Sangwan and Rajreshree Sabnavis on its Board.

The Companies Act of 2013 mandates a certain class of companies to have at least one woman director on board.

Hence the correct answer is option (a).

9. Kyriakos Mitsotakis has been sworn in as Greece's new prime minister.

The election result gave New Democracy an outright majority with 158 seats in the 300-member Greek parliament. The election came as Greece struggles to emerge from a nearly decade-long financial crisis that saw its economy plunge by a quarter and hundreds of thousands of mostly young people head abroad seeking better economic opportunities.

Hence the correct answer is option (c).

10. Small Industries Development Bank of India (SIDBI) is the implementing agency for FFS with a corpus of **Rs 10,000 crore** on behalf of the Government of India. SIDBI introduced a web-based application system for contribution from the Fund of Funds for Start-ups (FFS) to improve the turnaround time and increase transparency.

Hence the correct answer is option (e).

11. BharatPe has launched India's first UPI ,which allows merchants to record their cash/credit sales customer wise, request accounts receivable from customers via SMS payment links, and keep track of accounts payable to suppliers. It serves as a networking platform for merchants.

Hence the correct answer is option (b).

12. Subir Gokarn was appointed by the Narendra Modi government as Executive Director on the board of the **International Monetary Fund** (IMF) in November 2015.

Noted economist and former RBI Deputy Governor Subir Vithal Gokarn passed away after a brief illness. He was the Reserve Bank of India Deputy Governor from 2009-12 and oversaw Monetary Policy, Research, Financial Markets, Communications and Deposit Insurance.

He was also Chief Economist of Standard & Poor's Asia-Pacific and before that the Executive Director and Chief Economist of CRISIL.

Hence the correct answer is option (a).

13. The government has set up a working group under NITI Aayog member **Ramesh Chand** to revise the current series of Wholesale Price Index with base 2011-12 and devise a new Producer Price Index.The group would review the commodity basket of the current series of WPI, suggest changes in commodities.

PPI measures the average change in the price a producer receives for his goods and services sold in the domestic market and exports.

Hence the correct answer is option (b).

14. The number of Indians moving to London for higher studies rose by **20%** in 2017-18, marking an increase from 4,545 in 2016-17 to 5,455 in 2017-18.

London has been named the world's best city for students for the second consecutive year. Tokyo and Melbourne place at second and third place respectively.

The QS Best Student Cities Ranking compiled by global education consultancy QS Quacquarelli Symonds highlights each city's performance across different categories.

Hence the correct answer is option (d).

15. Real Economic Growth Rate is the rate at which a nation's **Gross Domestic product** (GDP) changes/grows from one year to another. GDP is the market value of all the goods and services produced in a country in a particular time period.

Hence the correct answer is option (b).

16. Under Section **22 of the Reserve Bank of India Act**, the bank has the sole sight to issue bank notes of all denominations. The system of note issue as it exists today is known as the minimum reserve system. All affairs of the Bank relating to note issue are conducted through its Issue Department.

Hence the correct answer is option (b).

17. Mangaluru City Police has launched an all-women police patrol unit named 'Rani Abbakka Force' in the city.The force will handle issues related to eve-teasing and chain-snatching, among others.At present, 50 women policewomen have been deployed in 'Rani Abbakka Force' in the city.

Hence the correct answer is option (a).

18. India's largest export destination country continues to be the **United States of America** (USA). USA accounted for 16% of India's exports, followed by the United Arab Emirates (UAE), China and Hong Kong. China continues to be the largest source of imports in India. The other important sources from which India imports are the USA, UAE and Saudi Arabia. China continues to be the largest exporter to India. India's imports from China fell in 2018-19 registering negative growth.

Hence the correct answer is option (c).

19. The 23rd National Conference on e-Governance, a platform for policy makers, practitioners, industry, academia for actionable strategy in public service delivery, held at NSCI Dome, Mumbai on February 7-8, 2020.

Hence the correct answer is option (d).

20. The maximum maturity of the contract is for **12 months.**

Treasury Bills are short term borrowing instruments of the Government of India which enable investors to park their short-term surplus funds while reducing their market risk.

Hence the correct answer is option (d).

21. Kento Momota has topped the World Badminton Rankings in Men's Singles category.

Indian shuttler B. Sai Praneeth has jumped four places to enter in the top 20 players in the latest World Badminton Rankings.

Praneeth is now World No.19 in Men's Singles badminton ranking.Among other Indian Men's singles shuttlers, Kidambi Srikanth has maintained his tenth position while Sameer Verma retains his 13th position. In Women's Singles, P.V.Sindhu has retained her 5th position and Saina Nehwal 8th position.

Hence the correct answer is option (a).

22. Bhawana Kanth has become the first woman to qualify for combat missions on a fighter jet.

She has successfully completed the operational syllabus for carrying out combat missions on MiG-21 Bison aircraft. She was commissioned into the Indian Air Force as one of the first women fighter pilots in 2016.

The MiG-21 is the oldest frontline combat jet in service with the Indian Air Force, having first entered service in 1964.

Hence the correct answer is option (d).

23. To raise awareness about science and environment through films, the 10th National Science Film Festival of India (NSFFI) will be organised in **Tripura, in 2020**. The film festival would include films from UNICEF, UNESCO & filmmakers from different countries.

Hence the correct answer is option (c).

24. Virtual Event, 15 July 2020

The importance of developing skilled youth is at the core of this year's message for World Youth Skills Day. Several virtual events focused on the theme of "Skills for a Resilient Youth" will take place.

Hence the correct answer is option (d).

25. Kaleshwaram Lift Irrigation Project is located in **Telangana**. It is world's largest lift irrigation project being built at about Rs 80,000 crore, aimed at meeting over two-thirds of state's agriculture, drinking and industrial water needs.

Hence the correct answer is option (a).

26. BSNL has partnered with **Google** to increase access to its WiFi footprint in the country. With the launch of this service, people across the country will be able to enjoy BSNL's free WiFi services. This initiative will allow customers use BSNL's high speed internet services on WiFi.

BSNL is also taking steps to increase the rural WiFi footprint, promoting the government's 'Digital India' initiative.

Hence the correct answer is option (a).

27. Meghalaya cabinet became the first state to approve a draft water policy to address water issues, conservation, and protection of water sources in the state.The policy intends to achieve sustainable development, management and use of water resources with community participation. This will improve health and livelihood and reduce vulnerability among the people.

Hence the correct answer is option (a).

28. AIIB has made its 1st investment in Nepal with the provision of up to $90m loan to help fund a $650m hydropower project. It has approved the loan for the Upper Trishuli-1 Hydropower

Project expected to increase Nepal's power generation by almost 20%.

Hence the correct answer is option (b).

29. Bank rate policy and **open market operations** are complementary measures in the area of monetary management. Open market operation is mainly related to the sale of government securities and during the busy season, they sell the securities. When commercial banks sell the securities and when RBI purchases them, the reserve position of the banks is improved and they can expand their credit to meet growing demands.

Hence the correct answer is option (c).

30. The government has set a target to raise its expenditure on health services **to 2.5% of the country's GDP** by 2025. The National Health Policy 2017 recommends that State governments should spend more than 8% of their budget on the health sector by 2020.

The government proposes to set up 1.5 lakh health and wellness centres by 2022 under the Aayushman Bharat programme.

Hence the correct answer is option (c).

31. A company may raise capital from the primary market through Public issue, Rights issue and Bought out deals.

32. Specialist exchange member is assigned to a specific trading post. A specialist is a person who is a member of a stock exchange, such as the New York Stock Exchange, whose role is to facilitate trading in certain stocks.

33. A fixed rate of Interest is payable on debentures. Debentures are a debt instrument used by companies and government to issue the loan. The loan is issued to corporates based on their reputation at a fixed rate of interest.

34. According to traditional approach, the average cost of capital decrease up to certain point, remains unchanged for moderate increase in leverage and rises beyond a certain point.

35. A computerized trading network that matches buy and sell orders electronically entered by customers is an electronic communications networks. An electronic communication network (ECN) is a computerized system that automatically matches buy and sell orders for securities in the market.

36. Ownership securities consist of equity stock and preferred stock. The term 'ownership securities,' also known as 'capital stock' represents shares. Shares are the most universal form of raising long-term funds from the market. Every company, except a company limited by guarantee, has a statutory right to issue shares.

37. The cost of capital of a firm is the minimum rate of return it must earn on its investments to keep its investors satisfied.

38. If an investor is attempting to buy a stock that is very volatile, it would be best to use limit order.

39. Net working capital refers to current assets minus current liabilities. Working capital, also known as net working capital (NWC), is the difference between a company's current assets, such as cash, accounts receivable (customers' unpaid bills) and inventories of raw materials and finished goods, and its currentliabilities, such as accounts payable.

40. The constant growth model of equity valuation assumes that the dividends paid by the company grow at a constant rate of growth.

41. Demat account has helped to eliminate the use of stock certificates by placing stock transactions on computers. Demat Account is an account that is used to hold shares and securities in electronic format. The full form of Demat account is a dematerialised account.

42. The expansion of EAR is equivalent annual rate. The Effective Annual Rate (EAR) is the interest rate that is adjusted for compounding over a given period. Simply put, the effective annual interest rate is the rate of interest that an investor can earn (or pay) in a year after taking into consideration compounding.

43. The formula for cost of debt is$= I \times (1 - t)$.

44. Total return is equal to capital gain and yield. Total return is the amount of value an investor earns from a security over a specific period, typically one year, when all distributions are reinvested.

45. Traditional theorists believe that there exists an optimal capital structure. An optimal capital structure is the objectively best mix of debt, preferred stock, and common stock that maximizes a company's market value while minimizing its cost of capital.

46. Capital markets are perfect, Investors are assumed to be rational and behave accordingly and there is no corporate or personal income tax are the assumptions underlying the Miller and Modigliani analysis.

47. The return component that gives periodic cash flows to the investor is known as the yield. Yield is the periodic cash flow (or return on investment in the form of interest or dividends).

48. The dividend-payout ratio is equal to dividends per share divided by earnings per share.

49. Net Operating Income Approach was also suggested by Durand. This approach is of the opposite view of Net Income approach. This approach suggests that the capital structure decision of a firm is irrelevant and that any change in the leverage or debt will not result in a change in the total value of the firm as well as the market price of its shares. This approach also says that the overall cost of capital is independent of the degree of leverage.

50. While calculating the weighted average cost of capital, market value weights are preferred because Book value weights are historical in nature.

51. If market interest rates are expected to rise, you would expect bond prices to fall more than stock prices. The prevailing rate of interest offered on cash deposits, determined by demand and supply of deposits and based on the duration (the longer the duration, the higher the rate) and amount (the higher the amount, the higher the rate) of deposits.

52. Informational content, Reduction of uncertainty and Some investors' preference for current income is an argument for the relevance of dividends.

53. The Modigliani-Miller theorem (M&M) states that the market value of a company is calculated using its earning power and the risk of its underlying assets and is independent of the way it finances investments or distributes dividends. There are three methods a firm can choose to finance: borrowing, spending profits (versus handing them out to shareholders in the form of dividends), and straight issuance of shares. While complicated, the theorem in its simplest form is based on the idea that with certain assumptions in place, there is no difference between a firm financing itself with debt or equity.

54. Financial risk is most associated with the use of debt financing by corporations. Financial risk is the risk that a company won't be able to meet its obligations to pay back its debts. Which in turn could mean that potential investors will lose the money invested in the company. The more debt a company has, the higher the potential financial risk.

55. Retained earnings are the cumulative earnings of the company after dividends. Retained earnings are the profits that a company has earned to date, less any dividends or other distributions paid to investors. This amount is adjusted whenever there is an entry to the accounting records that impacts a revenue or expense account.

56. Composition of the current assets does not affect the capital structure of a company. Current assets include cash, cash equivalents, accounts receivable, stock inventory, marketable securities, pre-paid liabilities, and other liquid assets.

57. Political stability is the major factor concerning country risk. Political stability in this case refers to the lack of real competition for the governing elite. The 'politically stable' system enforces stringent barriers to personal freedoms.

58. Arbitrage is the level processing technique introduced in MM approach. Arbitrage is the simultaneous purchase and sale of an asset to profit from an imbalance in the price.

59. The rational expectations model of dividend policy says that If the declared dividend is in accordance with the expectations, the change in the firms value will be minimal.

60. Liquidity risk increases whenever interest rates increase. Liquidity risk is the risk that a company or bank may be unable to meet short term financial demands.

61. In finance, "working capital" means the same thing as current assets minus current liabilities. Working capital is the amount of cash a business can safely spend. It's commonly defined as current assets minus current liabilities.

62. The Debt-Equity ratio of a Company measure its financial leverage. The debt-to-equity (D/E) ratio is calculated by dividing a company's total liabilities by its shareholder equity.

63. Financial risk is not related to overall market variability. Financial risk is the risk that a company won't be able to meet its obligations to pay back its debts.

64. In proper capital budgeting analysis we evaluate incremental cash flow. Capital budgeting, and investment appraisal, is the planning process used to determine whether an organization's long term investments such as new machinery, replacement of machinery, new plants, new products, and research development projects are worth the funding of cash through the firm's capitalization structure.

65. Gross Working Capital is the sum of the total current assets, Net working capital represents current assets - current liablities and Net working capital can be negative of the following statement are true in respect of working capital.

Q.1 Who is the Managing Director and Chief Executive Officer (CEO) of National Stock Exchange?

A. Ashish Chauhan
B. Rajiv Lall
C. V Vaidyanathan
D. Vikram Limaye
E. None of these

Q.2 _________ Nirmala Sitharaman has unveiled two new IT Initiatives ICEDASH and ATITHI for improved monitoring and pace of customs clearance of imported goods and facilitating arriving international passengers.

A. Minister of Railways of India
B. Minister of Electronics and Information Technology
C. Minister for Road Transport & Highways of India
D. Finance Minister
E. Defence Minister

Q.3 The National Council of Applied Economic Research (NCAER) has pegged India's gross domestic product (GDP) growth for 2019-20 at _________ as against 6.8 % in 2018 (or FY-19).

A. 4.50%
B. 4.70%
C. 4.90%
D. 4.30%
E. 4.40%

Q.4 The Asian Development Bank has approved the 2nd tranche of USD 150 million (about Rs 1,065 crore) for _____________ to boost capital investment and infrastructure in the state.

A. Odisha
B. West Bengal
C. Kerala
D. Maharashtra
E. Tamil Nadu

Q.5 Global rating agency Moody's expects the Centre's fiscal deficit to touch 3.7% of the GDP recently. Where is the headquarters of Moody's?

A. New York
B. Geneva
C. Vienna
D. London
E. Switzerland

Q.6 The Asian Development Bank (ADB) and the Government of India has signed a $490 million loan to upgrade about 1,600 km of state highways and major district roads in the state of-?

A. Sikkim
B. Madhya Pradesh
C. West Bengal
D. Kerala
E. Maharashtra

Q.7 Union Government informed that loans worth over _________ crore rupees have been sanctioned till 1st November this year under the Pradhan Mantri Mudra Yojana.

A. Rs 25 lakh
B. Rs 20 lakh
C. Rs 50 lakh
D. Rs 10 lakh
E. Rs 30 lakh

Q.8 The Reserve Bank of India (RBI) has waived NEFT, RTGS transfer charges for savings account holders. The new rule will be effective from-?

A. 1st January, 2020
B. 1st April, 2020
C. 1st July, 2020
D. 1st October, 2020
E. 1st February, 2020

Q.9 Which of the following bank has signed a loan agreement worth of $277 million (about Rs 1,958 crore) with Kreditanstalt für Wiederaufbau (KfW) development bank for establishing an energy-efficient housing programme in India?

A. Indian Bank
B. United Bank of India
C. Bank of Baroda
D. State Bank of India
E. Punjab National Bank

Q.10 The Indian Council of Agricultural Research (ICAR) and ______________ signed a Memorandum of Understanding (MoU) to promote sustainable agriculture and climate-resilient farming systems recently.

A. IRDAI
B. SEBI
C. NABARD
D. TRAI
E. IDBI

Q.11 Which of the following issues LC?

A. Sellers bank
B. Buyers Bank
C. Negotiating Bank
D. Advising Bank
E. None of these

Q.12 Which of the following is a real time settlement system in Europe?

A. Target
B. Fedwire
C. Chips
D. Chaps
E. All the above

Q.13 The counter party to every cleared futures or futures option trade is ....

A. The customer's futures commission merchant.
B. The exchange's clearinghouse.
C. The customer who took the opposite side of the trade.
D. ASBA applicant has got secured allotment of shares
E. all the above

Q.14 A futures option that gives the buyer the right to buy the underlying futures contract is called a ......

A. Straddle
B. Put
C. Call
D. Take
E. all the above

Q.15 Futures contracts can be settled ......

A. Only by delivery.
B. Only by cash-settlement.
C. Either by delivery or cash settlement
D. Neither by delivery nor cash settlement
E. None of the above

Q.16 When price of underlying asset increases then best option is ......

A. buy call option
B. sell call option
C. buy put option
D. sell put option
E. None of these

Q.17 When price of underlying asset increases then good option is buy call option. Buying a call option entitles the buyer of the option the right to purchase the underlying futures contract at the strike price any time before the contract expires.

A. Increase in stock price
B. Decrease in stock price
C. Increase in maturity duration
D. Decrease in maturity duration
E. None of these

Q.18 The Asian Development Bank is committed to achieving a prosperous, inclusive, resilient, and sustainable Asia and the Pacific, while sustaining its efforts to eradicate extreme poverty. In which of the following year Asian Development Bank was established?

A. 1956 **B.** 1966 **C.** 1982 **D.** 1992
E. 1972

Q.19 Vreedhi Financial Services (VFS) has secured a non-banking finance company licence from the Reserve Bank of India recently. Vreedhi Financial Services based in-

A. Thiruvananthapuram
B. Chennai
C. Mumbai
D. Hyderabad
E. Goa

Q.20 The Reserve Bank has imposed a penalty of _____________ on Tamilnad Mercantile Bank for violating norms on fraud classification and notification.

A. Rs 35 lakh
B. Rs 20 lakh
C. Rs 65 lakh
D. Rs 10 lakh
E. Rs 15 lakh

Q.21 Bajaj Allianz General Insurance has launched a new mobile app called __________ for the ease of farmers.

A. Farbetter
B. Farsakhi
C. Farmitra
D. Farsahyog
E. None of these

Q.22 Who is the Managing Director and Chief Executive Officer of Ujjivan Small Finance Bank Limited?

A. Rajiv Lall
B. Ittira Davis
C. Aditya Puri
D. Shyam Srinivasan
E. Praful Patel

Q.23 Bajaj Allianz General Insurance is a private general insurance company in India. Where is the headquarters of Bajaj Allianz General Insurance?

A. Varanasi
B. Jaipur
C. Kochi
D. Gurugram
E. Pune

Q.24 From January 2020, banks can no longer charge savings bank account holders for online transactions in the __________ system.

A. NEFT
B. IMPS
C. SWIFT
D. CBS
E. None of these

Q.25 The Karnataka Gramin Bank (KGB) has launched 'mobile ATMs' in Kalaburagi, among several other districts in the Karnataka. Karnataka Gramin Bank based in-

A. Bengaluru
B. Mysuru
C. Belgaum
D. Dharwad
E. Haveri

Q.26 The economic research team from the State Bank of India (SBI) has revised India's Gross Domestic Product (GDP) to _____________ from its earlier estimate of 6.1% for the Fiscal Year 2020 (FY20).

A. 6.50% **B.** 5.90% **C.** 5.00% **D.** 5.20%
E. 5.40%

Q.27 Option that can be exercised only at date of expiration is classified as ......

A. European option
B. Canadian option
C. Australian option
D. American option
E. Indian Option

Q.28 Consider buying of put option, probability that a buyer would have negative payoff increases with the ......

A. Increase in stock price
B. Decrease in stock price
C. Increase in maturity duration
D. Decrease in maturity duration
E. None of these

Q.29 In UCPDC-600 what does 600 mean?

A. It has total 600 rules
B. It is group of 600 countries
C. Publication no 600 is the latest version
D. It is amended 600 times since implemented
E. None of these

Q.30 The difference between spot rate and forward rate (interest rate differential) is ____ the ____ rate for low-interest yielding currency and this is known as forward ......

A. added to, spot, premium
B. added to, forward, premium
C. subtracted from, spot, discount
D. subtracted from, forward. discount
E. None of these

Q.31 Which one of the following factor relates to family that influences consumer behavior?

A. Cultural
B. Social
C. Personal
D. Business
E. None of these

Q.32 Unique psychological characteristics that lead to relatively consistent and lasting responses to one's own environment refers to which one of the following?

A. Belief   **B.** Culture
C. Personality   **D.** Self-awareness
E. All of these

Q.33 Which one of the following statements by a company chairman BEST reflects the marketing concept?

A. We have organized our business to satisfy the customer needs

B. We believe that marketing department must organize to sell what we produce

C. We try to produce only high quality, technically efficient products

D. We try to encourage company growth in the market

E. All of the above

Q.34 The factors such as the buyer's age, life-cycle stage, occupation, economic situation, lifestyle, personality and self-concept that influences buyer's decisions refers to which one of the following characteristic?

A. Personal characteristics
B. Psychological characteristics
C. Behavioral characteristics
D. Demographical characteristics
E. None of these

Q.35 Which one of the following is a key to build lasting relationships with consumers?

A. Price of the product
B. Need recognition
C. Customer satisfaction
D. Quality of product
E. None of these

Q.36 Which of the following is NOT one of the four philosophies of marketing?

A. Production orientation
B. Societal marketing orientation
C. Sales orientation
D. Promotion orientation
E. None of these

Q.37 Of the four competing philosophies, the Furniture Industry is an example of what kind of orientation:

A. Sales Orientation
B. Societal Marketing Orientation
C. Marketing Orientation
D. Production Orientation
E. None of these

Q.38 Which of the following firms emphasizes on product's benefits to the customers rather product attributes?

A. Product oriented   **B.** Market oriented
C. Sales oriented   **D.** Production oriented
E. All of these

Q.39 Which product is MOST likely to be purchased through routine decision making?

A. Television set   **B.** Soft drink
C. Shirt   **D.** Car

E. Bike

Q.40 Products that are usually purchased due to adversity and high promotional back up rather than desire are called:

A. Sought goods   **B.** Unique goods
C. Unsought goods   **D.** Preferred goods
E. None of these

Q.41 Document in a corporation which consists of amount of stock, name and addresses of directors is classified as

A. liability plan
B. stock planning
C. corporation paperwork
D. charter
E. All of these

Q.42 A price for equity is called

A. Interest rate   **B.** Cost of equity
C. Debt rate   **D.** Investment return
E. None off these

Q.43 Risk in which value of investment depends on what happens to foreign exchange rates is classified as

A. Preferred risk   **B.** Exchange rate risk
C. Country risk   **D.** Foreign risk
E. None of these

Q.44 Ability to trade at net price very quickly is classified as

A. Original trading   **B.** Liquidity
C. Offline trading   **D.** Fixed price trading
E. None of these

Q.45 Members and employees of credit unions are loaned for

A. Mortgages
B. Home improvement loans
C. Auto purchases
D. Investment return
E. All of above

Q.46 Bonds which are more risky than corporate bonds and are issued by major corporations are classified as

A. Common stocks   **B.** Corporate stocks
C. Leases   **D.** Preferred stocks
E. Innominate

Q.47 In financial markets, period of maturity within one to five years of financial instruments is classified as

A. short-term   **B.** long-term
C. intermediate term   **D.** capital term
E. None of these

Q.48 Collection of money from investors and spending money in other investment activities is classified as

A. future funds   **B.** hedge funds
C. retirement funds   **D.** pension funds
E. None of these

Q.49 Markets for products such as wheat, rice, cotton, real estate and autos dealing is classified as

A. physical asset markets

B. intangible assets
C. competitive markets
D. easy markets
E. None of these

Q.50 Price of stock that companies observe in financial markets is called

A. Market price
B. Intrinsic price
C. Extrinsic price
D. Fundamental price
E. Sell price

Q.51 Professionals such as doctors, accountants and lawyers often make corporations are classified as

A. general professionals
B. Professional Corporation
C. professional association
D. Both B and C
E. Both A and C

Q.52 Markets which deals with high liquid and short term debt securities are classified as

A. Capital markets
B. Money markets
C. Liquid markets
D. Short-term markets
E. None of these

Q.53 Low default-risk security issued by financially secure firms is classified as

A. U.S treasury bills
B. Commercial paper
C. Certificate of deposit
D. Mutual funds
E. None of these

Q.54 Firm's promise to pay and is backed or guaranteed by bank is classified as

A. Customer's acceptance
B. Banker's acceptance
C. Federal acceptance
D. Treasury acceptance
E. None of these

Q.55 Financial markets include

A. Primary markets
B. Capital markets
C. Physical asset markets
D. Derivatives markets
E. All of above

Q.56 Funds which are used as an interest-bearing checking accounts are classified as

A. Money market funds
B. Capital market funds
C. Money mutual funds
D. Insurance money funds
E. All of these

Q.57 Physical location exchange or telephone networks are types of

A. Long-term markets
B. Secondary markets

C. Money markets
D. Capital markets
E. None of these

Q.58 Method of matching orders by posting orders of buying and selling is classified as

A. Electronic communication network
B. Electronic dealer network
C. Electronic stock network
D. Electronic order network
E. None of these

Q.59 Business owned by a single person in unincorporated way is called

A. Proprietorship
B. Personal business
C. Private Corporation
D. Personal ownership
E. All of these

Q.60 An earning of business which is available for free distribution to all stockholders and creditors is classified as

A. Free cash flows
B. Free distribution
C. Available income
D. Cash income
E. None of these

Q.61 Loans by finance companies, banks and credit unions is classified as

A. Consumer credit loans
B. Dollar bonds
C. Eurodollar market deposits
D. Euro bonds
E. None of these

Q.62 Bonds issue by corporations which are more risky than preferred stocks are classified as

A. Leases
B. Preferred stocks
C. Common stocks
D. Corporate stocks
E. All of these

Q.63 Federal Reserve policy and federal surplus or deficit of budget affect the

A. Cost of production
B. Cost of money
C. Opportunity cost
D. Inflation risk
E. All of these

Q.64 Market where market makers keep record of stock of financial instruments is classified as

A. Stock market
B. Dealer market
C. Outcry auction system
D. Face to face communication
E. All of these

Q.65 An unlimited liability for business debts and less capital for growth are limitations of

A. Proprietorship
B. Personal business
C. Private Corporation
D. Personal ownership
E. None of these

// Smart Answer Sheet //

Correct Indicates percentage of students who answered questions correctly.

Skipped Indicates percentage of students who skipped questions.

Q.	Ans.	Correct / Skipped
1	D	79.48 % / 18.28 %
2	D	83.27 % / 10.24 %
3	C	77.27 % / 13.26 %
4	B	83.44 % / 15.32 %
5	A	79.32 % / 15.41 %
6	B	80.62 % / 19.25 %
7	D	80.85 % / 17.35 %
8	A	83.45 % / 11.38 %
9	D	83.06 % / 15.2 %
10	C	78.75 % / 12.41 %
11	B	81.87 % / 16.92 %
12	A	82.55 % / 13.32 %
13	B	86.88 % / 11.07 %

Q.	Ans.	Correct / Skipped
14	C	88.26 % / 11.38 %
15	C	83.41 % / 13.52 %
16	A	78.07 % / 11.84 %
17	B	83.86 % / 11.5 %
18	B	78.46 % / 10.07 %
19	D	85.52 % / 11.01 %
20	A	84.78 % / 13.11 %
21	C	88.85 % / 10.61 %
22	B	88.72 % / 10.96 %
23	E	87.91 % / 10.68 %
24	A	86.17 % / 11.46 %
25	D	82.0 % / 10.11 %
26	C	81.9 % / 15.36 %

Q.	Ans.	Correct / Skipped
27	A	85.89 % / 10.96 %
28	A	84.15 % / 11.75 %
29	C	84.82 % / 10.86 %
30	A	87.36 % / 10.94 %
31	B	76.42 % / 20.49 %
32	A	86.86 % / 10.85 %
33	A	89.64 % / 10.03 %
34	D	82.82 % / 15.2 %
35	C	78.05 % / 18.84 %
36	D	76.66 % / 16.25 %
37	D	83.09 % / 13.71 %
38	B	86.47 % / 12.78 %
39	B	79.02 % / 16.48 %

Q.	Ans.	Correct / Skipped
40	C	81.01 % / 16.36 %
41	D	87.84 % / 11.46 %
42	B	77.75 % / 16.31 %
43	B	84.73 % / 11.59 %
44	B	89.21 % / 10.71 %
45	D	79.23 % / 20.47 %
46	D	86.28 % / 13.5 %
47	C	78.5 % / 20.85 %
48	B	89.61 % / 10.17 %
49	A	84.86 % / 12.74 %
50	A	78.91 % / 13.72 %
51	D	76.45 % / 15.98 %
52	B	82.86 % / 16.1 %

Q.	Ans.	Correct / Skipped
53	B	88.66 % / 10.43 %
54	B	80.32 % / 10.09 %
55	E	89.11 % / 10.42 %
56	A	79.19 % / 18.41 %
57	B	88.11 % / 11.36 %
58	A	86.51 % / 12.7 %
59	A	83.5 % / 16.05 %
60	A	83.07 % / 13.09 %
61	A	82.55 % / 14.97 %
62	C	81.97 % / 13.37 %
63	B	85.09 % / 12.57 %
64	B	87.58 % / 10.93 %
65	A	78.74 % / 18.5 %

Performance Analysis

Avg. Score (%)	51.0%
Toppers Score (%)	66.0%
Your Score	

//Hints and Solutions//

1. Vikram Limaye is the Managing Director and CEO of the National Stock Exchange of India Limited.

2. Finance Minister Nirmala Sitharaman unveiled two new IT Initiatives – ICEDASH and ATITHI for improved monitoring and pace of customs clearance of imported goods and facilitating arriving international passengers.

3. The National Council of Applied Economic Research (NCAER) has pegged India's gross domestic product (GDP) growth for 2019-20 at 4.9% as against 6.8 % in 2018 (or FY-19). It lowers its outlook due to the slowdown in almost all sectors & it is primarily driven by a simultaneous deceleration of all the drivers of aggregate demand.

4. The Asian Development Bank has approved the 2nd tranche of USD 150 million (about Rs 1,065 crore) for West Bengal to boost capital investment and infrastructure in the state. The board of ADB approved a loan of $ 300 million (about Rs 2,130 crore) to continue a comprehensive series of fiscal reforms in West Bengal to revive financial health of public sector enterprises, the introduction of medium-term expenditure frameworks in two departments, and implementation of an integrated tax monitoring system, among others.

5. Global rating agency Moody's expects the Centre's fiscal deficit to touch 3.7% of the GDP. The Centre has targeted to keep the deficit at 3.3 per cent for the current fiscal (2019-20), but it has already reached 92.6 per cent of the Budget estimate in first six months of the current fiscal. For all the state governments, the fiscal deficit estimated to be around 3%. Headquarters: New York City, United States; Moody's founded: 1909.

6. The Asian Development Bank (ADB) and the Government of India has signed a $490 million loan. The loan is signed for public-private partnership (PPP) project through the hybrid-annuity model (HAM) to upgrade about 1,600 km of state highways and major district roads in the state of Madhya Pradesh. An additional $286 million investment will be mobilised through private sector participation under the PPP modality. The upgradation of these roads under the project will improve rural and peri-urban connectivity in the state and improve access to markets and better services.

7. Union Government informed that loans worth over 10 lakh crore rupees have been sanctioned till 1st November this year under the Pradhan Mantri Mudra Yojana, PMMY. As per the findings of the PMMY survey, around five crore persons were working in the establishments for which MUDRA loans were availed between April 2015 to March 2018.

8. The Reserve Bank of India (RBI) has waived NEFT, RTGS transfer charges for savings account holders. In an order, RBI instructed banks to make all online payments done through RTGS and NEFT free of cost for savings account holders. The new rule will be effective from 1st January, 2020.

9. State Bank of India (SBI) has signed a loan agreement worth of $277 million (about Rs 1,958 crore) with Kreditanstalt für Wiederaufbau (KfW) German development bank for establishing an energy-efficient housing programme in India. The programme shall be part of the Indo-German Development Co-operation, guided by the 2030 Agenda for Sustainable Development.

10. The Indian Council of Agricultural Research (ICAR) and the National Bank for Agriculture and Rural Development (NABARD) signed a Memorandum of Understanding (MoU) to promote sustainable agriculture and climate-resilient farming systems. The research will be of active participation in climate-resilient practices, models and integrated and hi-tech farming practices in a participatory model. The aim of this MoU was to promote sustainable agriculture and climate-resilient farming systems.

11. Among the following issues is the Buyers Bank LC.

12. TARGET2 (Trans-European Automated Real-time Gross Settlement Express Transfer System) is the real-time gross settlement (RTGS) system for the Eurozone, and is available to non-Eurozone countries. It was developed by and is owned by the Eurosystem.

13. The counter party to every cleared futures or futures option trade is The exchange's clearinghouse.
Clearing houses provide clearing and settlement services for futures traded at an exchange. They act as the neutral counterparty between every buyer and seller, ensuring the soundness and integrity of every trade.

14. A futures option that gives the buyer the right to buy the underlying futures contract is called a call.

15. Futures contracts can be settled Either by delivery or cash settlement.

All futures and options contracts are cash settled, i.e. through exchange of cash. The underlying for index futures/options of the Nifty index cannot be delivered. These contracts, therefore, have to be settled in cash. Futures and options on individual securities can be delivered as in the spot market.

16. When price of underlying asset increases then good option is buy call option. Buying a call option entitles the buyer of the option the right to purchase the underlying futures contract at the strike price any time before the contract expires.

17. Consider call option writing, probability that a buyer would have positive payoff increases with the decrease in stock price.

18. ADB is committed to achieving a prosperous, inclusive, resilient, and sustainable Asia and the Pacific, while sustaining its efforts to eradicate extreme poverty. Established in 1966, it is owned by 68 members.

19. Vridhi Financial Services (VFS) has obtained a non-banking finance company license from the Reserve Bank of India. It aims to provide loans and other services to micro enterprises operating in tier two-three cities and small towns. Vridhi Financial Services is located in Hyderabad.

20. The Reserve Bank has imposed a penalty of ₹35 lakh on Tamilnad Mercantile Bank for violating norms on frauds classification and notification.

21. Bajaj Allianz General Insurance has launched a new mobile app called 'Farmitra' for the ease of farmers. This app intends to help the farmers needs and address their worries. It also resolves with relevant information, which they can use in optimizing their farming practices.

22. Ittira Davis is the Managing Director and Chief Executive Officer of Ujjivan Small Finance Bank Limited.

23. Bajaj Allianz General Insurance is a private general insurance company in India. Pune is the headquarters of Bajaj Allianz General Insurance.

24. From January 2020, banks can no longer charge savings bank account holders for online transactions in the **NEFT** system. The Reserve Bank of India (RBI) has now mandated banks to do this through a press release on Friday.

25. The Karnataka Gramin Bank (KGB) has launched 'mobile ATMs' in Kalaburagi, among several other districts in the Karnataka. Karnataka Gramin Bank based in Dharwad, Karnataka.

26. The economic research team from the State Bank of India (SBI) has revised India's Gross Domestic Product(GDP) to **5.0%** from its earlier estimate of 6.1% for the Fiscal Year 2020 (FY20). This downgrade was due to global slowdown in the index of industrial production (IIP). The SBI economic research team group has projected the second quarter (July-September) GDP growth at 4.2% in their report titled "EcoWrap". It expects the growth rate to pick up in FY2021 to 6.2%.

27. Type of option that can be exercised only at date of expiration is classified as European option. A European option is a version of an options contract that limits execution to its expiration date.

28. Consider buying of put option, probability that a buyer would have negative payoff increases with the increase in stock price.

29. The UCP 600 ("Uniform Customs & Practice for Documentary Credits") is the official publication which is issued by the International Chamber of Commerce (ICC). It is a set of 39 articles on issuing and using Letters of Credit, which applies to 175 countries around the world, constituting some $1tn USD of trade per year.

30. The difference between spot rate and forward rate (interest rate differential) is added to, the spot, rate for low-interest yielding currency and this is known as forward premium.

31. Social factor relates to family that influences consumer behavior. Social factors play an essential role in influencing the buying decisions of consumers. Human beings are social animals. We need people around to talk to and discuss various issues to reach to better solutions and ideas. We all live in a society and it is really important for individuals to adhere to the laws and regulations of society.

32. Unique psychological characteristics that lead to relatively consistent and lasting responses to one's own environment refers to belief. A Belief is a descriptive thought that a person holds about something.

33. We have organized our business to satisfy the customer needs statements by a company chairman BEST reflects the marketing concept.

34. The factors such as the buyer's age, life-cycle stage, occupation, economic situation, lifestyle, personality and self-

concept that influences buyer's decisions refers to Demographical characteristics. Demographic segmentation is one of the ways to target a specific group of consumers.

35. Customer satisfaction is a key to build lasting relationships with consumers. Customer satisfaction indicates the fulfillment that customers derive from doing business with a firm. In other words, it's how happy the customers are with their transaction and overall experience with the company.

36. Promotion orientation is NOT one of the four philosophies of marketing. Four competing philosophies strongly influence an organization's marketing activities. These philosophies are commonly referred to as production, sales, marketing, and societal orientations.

37. Of the four competing philosophies, the Furniture Industry is an example of Production Orientation. Production Orientation is the general approach of any business that is primarily concerned with manufacturing and production processes. In a product oriented approach, business focuses and develops products based on what it is good at making or doing, rather than what the customer wants.

38. Market oriented firms emphasizes on product's benefits to the customers rather product attributes. Market orientation often includes improvements in customer service and product support geared to solving concerns raised by consumers. This helps ensure customer satisfaction remains high with the company as a whole and promotes brand loyalty and positive word-of-mouth advertising.

39. Soft drink product is MOST likely to be purchased through routine decision making. People usually make hundreds of decisions everyday. Rather than thinking a lot for each, people instead rely on routines. These are decisions which need an introduction and identification then it becomes your regular activity.

40. Products that are usually purchased due to adversity and high promotional back up rather than desire are called Unsought goods. Unsought products typically are products that the consumers are not aware and don't have any knowledge about it. It is difficult to sell because it has no demand.

41. Document in a corporation which consists of amount of stock, name and addresses of directors is classified as charter. A charter plane or boat is one which is hired for use by a particular person or group and which is not part of a regular service.

42. A price for equity is called cost of equity. The cost of equity is the return a company requires to decide if an investment meets capital return requirements.

43. Risk in which value of investment depends on what happens to foreign exchange rates is classified as exchange rate risk. Exchange rate risk, also known as currency risk, is the financial risk arising from fluctuations in the value of a base currency against a foreign.

44. Ability to trade at net price very quickly is classified as liquidity. Liquidity describes the degree to which an asset or security can be quickly bought or sold in the market at a price reflecting its intrinsic value. In other words: the ease of converting it to cash.

45. Members and employees of credit unions are loaned for mortgages, home improvement loans and auto purchases.

46. Bonds which are more risky than corporate bonds and are issued by major corporations are classified as preferred stocks. Preferred stockholders have a higher claim to dividends or asset distribution than common stockholders.

47. In financial markets, period of maturity within one to five years of financial instruments is classified as intermediate term. A term is an intermediate (or innominate) term if the remedy for its breach depends on the effect of the breach at the time it happens.

48. Collection of money from investors and spending money in other investment activities is classified as hedge funds. A hedge fund is basically a fancy name for an investment partnership. It's the marriage of a professional fund manager, who can often be known as the general partner, and the investors, sometimes known as the limited partners, who pool their money together into the fund.

49. Markets for products such as wheat, rice, cotton, real estate and autos dealing is classified as physical asset markets. Physical asset markets are for physical products such as wheat, autos, real estate, computers, and machinery.

50. Price of stock that companies observe in financial markets is called market price. The market price for goods and services is the current price it can be bought or sold for.

51. Professionals such as doctors, accountants and lawyers often make corporations are classified as Professional Corporation and professional association.

52. Markets which deals with high liquid and short term debt securities are classified as money markets. The money market is the trade in short-term debt investments.

53. Low default-risk security issued by financially secure firms is classified as commercial paper. Commercial paper is an unsecured, short-term debt instrument issued by a corporation, typically for the financing of accounts payable and inventories and meeting short-term liabilities.

54. Firm's promise to pay and is backed or guaranteed by bank is classified as banker's acceptance. A banker's acceptance (BA) is a short-term debt instrument issued by a company that is guaranteed by a commercial bank. Banker's acceptances are issued as part of a commercial transaction.

55. Financial markets include primary markets, capital markets, physical asset markets and derivatives markets.

56. Funds which are used as an interest-bearing checking accounts are classified as money market funds. A money market fund is a kind of mutual fund that invests only in highly liquid instruments such as cash, cash equivalent securities, and high credit rating debt-based securities with a short-term, maturity—less than 13 months.

57. Physical location exchange or telephone networks are types of secondary markets. The secondary market is where investors buy and sell securities they already own. It is what most people typically think of as the "stock market," though stocks are also sold on the primary market when they are first issued.

58. Method of matching orders by posting orders of buying and selling is classified as electronic communication network. An electronic communication network (ECN) is a computerized system that automatically matches buy and sell orders for securities in the market.

59. Business owned by a single person in unincorporated way is called proprietorship. A sole proprietorship, also known as the sole trader, individual entrepreneurship or proprietorship, is a type of enterprise that is owned and run by one person and in which there is no legal distinction between the owner and the business entity.

60. An earning of business which is available for free distribution to all stockholders and creditors is classified as free cash flows. Free cash flow represents the cash a company generates after cash outflows to support operations and maintain its capital assets.

61. Loans by finance companies, banks and credit unions is classified as consumer credit loans. Consumer credit is personal debt taken on to purchase goods and services. A credit card is one form of consumer credit.

62. Common stock is a form of corporate equity ownership, a type of security.

63. Federal Reserve policy and federal surplus or deficit of budget affect the cost of money. The Federal Reserve System is the central banking system of the United States of America. The Federal Open Market Committee (FOMC) sets monetary policy.

64. Market where market makers keep record of stock of financial instruments is classified as dealer market. A dealer market is a financial market mechanism wherein multiple dealers post prices at which they will buy or sell a specific security of instrument.

65. An unlimited liability for business debts and less capital for growth are limitations of proprietorship. Since the owner takes all the profits, he must also accept full personal responsibility for all the losses, even to the extent of his personal possessions.

Q.1 Which of the following Organizations are not Insured by DICGC (Deposit Insurance Credit Guarantee Corporation) which is a wholly owned subsidary of Reserve Bank of India?

A. Local Area Banks
B. Public Sector Banks
C. Primary Cooperative Societies
D. Regional Rural Banks
E. Cooperative Banks

Q.2 If the Interest rates remain unchanged during the pendency of the bond, the rate of return will be equal to which of the following ?

A. Discount rate
B. Coupon rate
C. Current Yield rate
D. Yield to maturity
E. Bank rate

Q.3 Which of the following is the currency of Albania?

A. Franc Pesta
B. Dram
C. Ruble
D. Euro
E. Lek

Q.4 If an Infrastructure Debt Fund is established as a company, it will be regulated by which of the following organizations?

A. Ministry of Finance
B. Securities and Exchange Board of India
C. Insurance Regulatory Development Authority of India
D. Reserve Bank of India
E. Small Industries Development Bank of India

Q.5 According to the traditional approach cost of capital affected by?

A. debt-equity mix
B. debt-capital mix
C. equity expenses mix
D. debt-interest mix
E. None of these

Q.6 For which of the following factors are the debentures more attractive to the investors?

A. The principal is redeemable at maturity
B. A debenture-holder enjoys prior claim on the assets of the company over its shareholders in the event of liquidation
C. trustee is appointed to preserve the interest of the debenture holders
D. Both (A) and (B)
E. All the above.

Q.7 Financial securities that can be converted into cash at closing to their book value price are classified as

A. inventories
B. short-term investments
C. cash equivalents
D. long-term investments
E. None of these

Q.8 Who among the following has been appointed as the director of the Institute of Banking Personal Selection (IBPS)?

A. Anup Sankar Bhattacharya
B. B Harideesh Kumar
C. Malvika Sinha
D. Sankara Narayanan
E. Rajkiran Rai G

Q.9 Discounted cash flow analysis is also classified as

A. time value of stock
B. time value of money
C. time value of bonds
D. time value of treasury bonds
E. None of these

Q.10 Prices of bonds will be decreased if an interest rates

A. rises
B. declines
C. equals
D. Both (A) and (B)
E. none of above

Q.11 Right side of balance sheet states the

A. appreciated earnings
B. liabilities
C. assets
D. stocks earnings
E. None of these

Q.12 The Women Start-up Summit 2019 was held recently in ____________.

A. Thiruvananthapuram
B. Kochi
C. Palakad
D. Kottayam
E. Kannur

Q.13 Wages and salaries of employees which company owns in this accounts are called

A. accrued expenses
B. accruals accounts
C. Both A and B
D. zero liabilities
E. None of these

Q.14 According to a report by RBI, ____________ is the most affordable city for homebuyers.

A. Mumbai
B. Bhubaneswar
C. Bengaluru
D. Chennai
E. Hyderabad

Q.15 Legendary Lee Iacocca recently passed away. He was the famous CEO of which of the following company?

A. Chevrolet
B. Nissan
C. JEEP
D. Chrysler
E. Mercedes Benz

Q.16 India in August, 2019 (till now) contributed __________ to the UN Special Purpose Trust Fund for the Resident Coordinator System.
A. $5 million
B. $4 million
C. $3 million
D. $2 million
E. $1 million

Q.17 Securities future value is Rs 1,000,000 and present value of securities is Rs 500,000 with an interest rate of 4.5%, 'N' will be
A. 16.7473 years
B. 0.0304 months
C. 15.7473 years
D. 0.7575 years
E. None of these

Q.18 If payment of security is paid as Rs 100 at end of year for three years, it is an example of
A. fixed payment investment
B. lump sum amount
C. fixed interval investment
D. annuity
E. None of these

Q.19 Which company will implement RBI's centralized information and management system (CIMS)?
A. Wipro
B. TCS
C. Infosys
D. HCL technologies
E. Mindtree

Q.20 G-20 ministerial meet on Trade & digital economy was recently held in which of the following country?
A. Saudi Arabia
B. USA
C. Germany
D. Japan
E. Australia

Q.21 Payment of security if it is made at end of each period such as beginning of year is classified as
A. annuity due
B. payment fixed series
C. ordinary annuit
D. deferred annuity
E. None of these

Q.22 Recently, __________ has introduced a web-based application system for contribution from Fund of Funds for Start-ups.
A. RBI
B. SEBI
C. NHB
D. SIDBI
E. Ministry of MSME

Q.23 What is the tenure of(years) the Central Board of Trustees in EPFO?
A. 5
B. 4
C. 3
D. 2
E. 1

Q.24 IAF has inked a Rs 300 crore deal to procure SPICE 2000 bombs from which country?
A. Afghanistan
B. Argentina
C. France
D. US
E. Israel

Q.25 Net worth is also called
A. asset net of liabilities
B. liabilities net of assets
C. earnings net on assets
D. liabilities net of earnings
E. None of these

Q.26 An annual rate of 16% if quoted by credit card issuer usually a bank is classified as
A. loan rate of return
B. local rate of return
C. annual percentage rate
D. annual rate of return
E. None of these

Q.27 Value of payment is Rs 25 and an interest rate is 2%, then present value will be
A. Rs 12.54
B. Rs 12,500.00
C. Rs 12,504.00
D. Rs 8,400.00
E. None of these

Q.28 Collection of net income, amortization and depreciation is divided by common shares outstanding to calculate
A. cash flow of financing activities
B. cash flow per share
C. cash flow of investment
D. cash flow of operations
E. None of these

Q.29 Which company recently partnered with National Skill Development Corporation's Logistics Sector Skill Council (LSC) to train 20,000 of its delivery executives across the country?
A. Amazon India
B. Paytm
C. Flipkart
D. Google India
E. Twitter India

Q.30 India has handed over 250 pre-fabricated houses to __________.
A. China
B. Inonesia
C. Vietnam
D. Myanmar
E. Bhutan

Q.31 According to the text, a product is
A. Everything the customer receives in an exchange.
B. The physical object the customer receives in an exchange.
C. The service that is rendered to a customer
D. The idea that the customer receives in an exchange
E. All of these

Q.32 An example of a convenience consumer product is
A. Stereo equipment
B. Petrol
C. A motorcycle
D. A bicycle
E. Athletic shoes

Q.33 Which one of the following is NOT an industrial product?
A. Oil to be refined into fuel for homes
B. Transistors used as components for portable radios
C. Paper, pens, and glue used in bank branch offices
D. Computer software to help people complete personal tax

forms

E. None of these

Q.34 Sai Nath called several airlines to compare rates and chose a flight on British Midland as it had a better reputation for service and competitive prices. The airline ticket is an example of which type of product?

A. Convenience
B. Shopping
C. Specialty
D. Unsought
E. All of these

Q.35 Large tools and machines used in a production process for a considerable length of time are classified as

A. Major equipment
B. Accessory equipment
C. Component parts
D. Raw materials
E. Consumable supplies

Q.36 Items that are purchased routinely, do not become part of the final physical product, and are treated like expense items rather than capital goods are called

A. Raw materials
B. Major equipment
C. Accessory equipment
D. Component parts
E. Process materials

Q.37 Products that are used directly in the production of a final product but are not easily identifiable are categorised as

A. Accessory products
B. Component parts
C. Consumable supplies.
D. Assembly components
E. Process materials

Q.38 Industrial products are

A. Purchased for personal consumption
B. Frequently purchased for both their functional aspects and their psychological rewards
C. Traditionally classified according to their characteristics and intended uses.
D. Not purchased by non-business organisations.
E. All of these

Q.39 A company designs the product with little or no input from customers, the company is practicing which of the following concept?

A. Product concept
B. Marketing concept
C. Selling concept
D. Production concept
E. None of these

Q.40 Which of the following 4Ps of marketing mix involves decisions regarding channels coverage, assortments, locations, inventories or transports?

A. Product
B. Price
C. Place
D. Promotion
E. All of these

Q.41 Which of the following is NOT a part of marketing communication mix?

A. Telemarketing
B. Public relations
C. Sales promotion
D. Advertising
E. All of these

Q.42 A fundamental part of the distribution function is to get the product:

A. To the right place at the right time
B. Launched into new markets
C. To intermediaries
D. To market to avoid channel conflict
E. All of these

Q.43 Which of the following are products and services bought by final consumers for personal consumption? These include convenience products, shopping products, specialty products, and unsought products.

A. Material and parts
B. Consumer products
C. Industrial products
D. Capital items
E. None of these

Q.44 Low Consumer involvement in purchase and little significant brand difference comes in which types of buying behaviors.

A. Complex buying behavior
B. Dissonance-reducing buying behavior
C. Habitual buying behaviors
D. Variety-seeking buying behaviors
E. All of the above

Q.45 Distribution of product to get it in the marks refers to which of the following activities?

A. Selling Activities
B. Advertising activities
C. Promotion Activities
D. Place or distribution activities
E. None of these

Q.46 How many stages are involved in the consumer buying / adoption process?

A. Six
B. Seven
C. Three
D. Five
E. Four

Q.47 "Buy it now" refers to which one of the following options?

A. Personal selling
B. Advertising
C. Sales promotion
D. Publicity
E. All of the above

Q.48 At least how many parties should be included in "Exchange"?

A. Two
B. Three
C. Four
D. Five
E. Seven

Q.49 The buyer decision process consists of five stages. Which of the following is NOT one of these stages?

A. Evaluation of Alternatives
B. Information search
C. Variety-seeking buying behavior

D. Post purchase behavior
E. None of these

Q.50 You are planning to install a steel manufacturing plant in your city. For that purpose you want to have a supplier who supplies you the steel in raw form for manufacturing. Here supplier supplies you which of the following form of industrial product?
A. Material and parts
B. Capital items
C. Supplies and services
D. Suppliers
E. None of the given options

Q.51 Section 9 of the Banking Regulation Act prohibits the banking Companies from holding any immovable property except for its own use for a period of not more property. The RBI may extend this period for a further period of _____:
A. 2 years   **B.** 4 years   **C.** 5 years   **D.** 6 years
E. 7 years

Q.52 Which of the following stock exchange is derecognized by SEBI on 19.11.2014 on the allegations of serious irregularities in its functioning?
A. Bombay Stock Exchange
B. Delhi Stock Exchange
C. Calcutta Stock Exchange
D. Bangalore Stock Exchange
E. None of these

Q.53 Which of the following is not a function of General Insurance?
A. Cattle Insurance   **B.** Crop Insurance
C. Fire Insurance   **D.** Medical Insurance
E. All of the above

Q.54 Liability- side of the balance-sheet comprises:
A. Capital and reserve
B. Long-term liabilities
C. Current liabilities
D. Balance-sheet
E. All of the above

Q.55 Minimum cash reserves fixed by law constitute ___
A. A percentage of aggregate deposits of the bank
B. A percentage of aggregate loans and advances of the bank
C. A percentage of capital & reserves of the bank
D. A percentage of minimum cash
E. None of these

Q.56 Which of the following organizations/ agencies has sought an emergency fund of Rs.1000 crore from banks to tackle acute liquidity crisis, which is coming in the way to give loans to micro borrowers?
A. Regional Rural & Cooperative Banks
B. RBI
C. Micro Finance Institutions
D. NABARD
E. All of the above

Q.57 Which of the following types of accounts are known as "Demat Accounts"?
A. Zero Balance Accounts
B. Accounts which are opened to facilitate repayment of a loan taken from the bank. No other business can be conducted from there
C. Accounts in which shares of various companies are traded in electronic form
D. Accounts which are operated through internet banking facility
E. None of these

Q.58 Mortgage is a:
A. Security on movable property for a loan
B. Security on immovable property for a loan
C. Concession on immovable property
D. Facility on immovable property
E. Security on loan sanctioned against fixed deposits

Q.59 ___ assumed charge as the Minister of State for Micro, Small & Medium Enterprises (MSME) on 11th November 2014.
A. Gopal Singh   **B.** Veerabhadra Singh
C. Manoj Tiwari   **D.** Giriraj Singh
E. All of these

Q.60 Identify the well known person related to Banking field in India from the following?
A. Mrs. Meira Kumar   **B.** Mrs. Kiran Shaw
C. Mr. Arun Jaitley   **D.** Dr. D Subbarao
E. All of the above

Q.61 Currency notes deposited in the currency chest are the property of ___?
A. Respective bank
B. RBI
C. SBI
D. Government of India
E. None of these

Q.62 A fixed deposit receipt is kept with the bank for its safety, is known as ___?
A. Safe custody   **B.** Safe deposit
C. Locker   **D.** Valid safe deposit
E. None of the above

Q.63 Who among the following is the primary regulator of Banking business?
A. Reserve Bank of India
B. Central Government
C. State Government
D. Parliament
E. All of the above

Q.64 Banks are required to monitor transactions of suspicious nature for reporting to the authorities under anti- money laundering measures. The purpose of reporting is:
A. Combating finance of terrorism
B. To check hawala transactions
C. To check the inflow of crime money

D. To check inflow of the money earned out of sale of narcotics

E. All the above

Q.65 Cryptocurrency is a _______ .

A. Plastic Money.

B. Digital Medium of Exchange

C. Digital payment

D. Both A & B

E. None of these

// Smart Answer Sheet //

Correct   Indicates percentage of students who answered questions correctly.

Skipped   Indicates percentage of students who skipped questions.

Q.	Ans.	Correct / Skipped	Q.	Ans.	Correct / Skipped	Q.	Ans.	Correct / Skipped	Q.	Ans.	Correct / Skipped	Q.	Ans.	Correct / Skipped
1	C	77.88 % / 13.96 %	14	B	86.41 % / 10.85 %	27	C	86.72 % / 11.77 %	40	C	77.43 % / 17.53 %	53	D	82.01 % / 14.62 %
2	D	84.98 % / 10.77 %	15	D	82.16 % / 11.24 %	28	B	87.86 % / 10.83 %	41	A	81.33 % / 15.42 %	54	E	83.79 % / 15.05 %
3	E	78.07 % / 19.93 %	16	E	79.29 % / 17.91 %	29	C	76.75 % / 17.05 %	42	A	76.51 % / 20.36 %	55	A	86.3 % / 10.98 %
4	D	83.33 % / 13.66 %	17	C	80.49 % / 12.24 %	30	D	79.3 % / 10.95 %	43	B	83.87 % / 14.82 %	56	D	80.42 % / 17.69 %
5	A	83.23 % / 10.68 %	18	D	88.26 % / 10.86 %	31	A	80.84 % / 13.51 %	44	D	81.83 % / 16.75 %	57	C	82.53 % / 16.3 %
6	D	77.5 % / 22.21 %	19	B	86.31 % / 10.26 %	32	B	80.24 % / 15.23 %	45	D	86.28 % / 11.78 %	58	B	89.66 % / 10.33 %
7	C	81.87 % / 17.36 %	20	D	88.5 % / 10.63 %	33	D	78.53 % / 13.15 %	46	D	83.59 % / 12.61 %	59	D	80.36 % / 14.83 %
8	B	79.09 % / 13.3 %	21	A	79.61 % / 17.47 %	34	B	83.85 % / 10.27 %	47	A	77.87 % / 14.53 %	60	D	87.9 % / 10.83 %
9	B	80.57 % / 10.47 %	22	D	88.6 % / 10.76 %	35	A	88.05 % / 10.79 %	48	A	88.61 % / 10.84 %	61	B	87.94 % / 10.45 %
10	A	78.08 % / 15.35 %	23	A	79.42 % / 19.31 %	36	C	88.44 % / 11.0 %	49	C	79.18 % / 14.27 %	62	A	81.95 % / 10.53 %
11	C	80.66 % / 13.46 %	24	E	79.74 % / 19.21 %	37	E	83.32 % / 12.48 %	50	A	84.63 % / 10.04 %	63	A	85.37 % / 10.79 %
12	B	80.56 % / 12.68 %	25	A	78.74 % / 18.46 %	38	C	81.64 % / 12.58 %	51	C	81.87 % / 12.53 %	64	E	85.02 % / 13.54 %
13	C	88.55 % / 10.95 %	26	C	79.89 % / 15.27 %	39	A	78.95 % / 18.61 %	52	B	82.8 % / 10.6 %	65	B	88.39 % / 10.17 %

Performance Analysis

Avg. Score (%)	37.0%
Toppers Score (%)	66.0%
Your Score	

//Hints and Solutions//

1. Primary Cooperative Societies not Insured by DICGC (Deposit Insurance Credit Guarantee Corporation) which is a wholly owned subsidiary of Reserve Bank of India.

Hence the correct answer is option (C).

2. If the Interest rates remain unchanged during the pendency of the bond, the rate of return will be equal to Yield to maturity.

Hence the correct answer is option (D).

3.

- Albenia capital - Tirana.
- Albenian Lek- Currency of Albania.
- Dram- Currency of Armenia.
- Belarisian Ruble- Currency of Belarus.
- Euro- Currency of Austria, Greece and other EU nations.

Hence the correct answer is option (e).

4. If an Infrastructure Debt Fund is established as a company, it will be regulated by Reserve Bank of India.

Hence the correct answer is option (D).

5. The traditional approach to capital structure advocates that there is a right combination of equity and debt in the capital structure, at which the market value of a firm is maximum. As per this approach, debt should exist in the capital structure only up to a specific point, beyond which, any increase in leverage would result in the reduction in value of the firm.

Hence the correct answer is option (A).

6. The principal is redeemable at maturity, A debenture-holder enjoys prior claim on the assets of the company over its shareholders in the event of liquidation and trustee is appointed to preserve the interest of the debenture holders are the factors why the debentures more attractive to the investors.

7. Financial securities that can be converted into cash at closing to their book value price are classified as cash equivalents. Cash equivalents are investments securities that are meant for short-term investing; they have high credit quality and are highly liquid.

Hence the correct answer is option (C).

8. B Harideesh Kumar has been appointed as director of Institute of Banking Personnel Selection (IBPS) for a period of three years. Earlier, he was Executive Director of Canara Bank. He started his banking career with e Vijaya Bank in the year 1978.

Hence the correct answer is option (b).

9. Discounted cash flow analysis is also classified as time value of money. The time value of money (TVM) is the concept that money available at the present time is worth more than the identical sum in the future due to its potential earning capacity.

Hence the correct answer is option (B).

10. Prices of bonds will be decreased if an interest rates rises. An existing bond's price or present value moves in the opposite direction of the change in market interest rates: Bond prices will go up when interest rates go down, and Bond prices will go down when interest rates go up.

Hence the correct answer is option (A).

11. Right side of balance sheet states the assets. An asset is a resource with economic value that an individual, corporation or country owns or controls with the expectation that it will provide a future benefit.

Hence the correct answer is option (C).

12. Kerala Startup Mission hosted Women Startup Summit in Kochi.

The Women Startup Summit 2019 aims at encouraging aspiring women professionals to take up their entrepreneurial journey & develop an inclusive entrepreneurship ecosystem in the State. The theme is, Developing an Inclusive Entrepreneurship Ecosystem.

Hence the correct answer is option (b).

13. Wages and salaries of employees which company owns in this accounts are called accrued expenses and accruals accounts.

Hence the correct answer is option (C).

14. According to a report by the Reserve Bank India, Bhubaneswar remains the most affordable city for homebuyers, while Mumbai remains the least affordable one in India. RBI has been conducting a quarterly residential asset price monitoring survey (RAPMS) since July 2010.

Hence the correct answer is option (b).

15. Lee Iacocca, the auto executive and master pitchman who put the Mustang in Ford lineup in the 1960s and became a corporate folk hero when he resurrected Chrysler 20 years later, passed away in Bel Air, California. He was 94.

Hence the correct answer is option (d).

16. India has contributed USD **one million** to the UN Special Purpose Trust Fund for the Resident Coordinator System.

The Special Purpose Trust Fund (SPTF) is a specific fund housed within the UN Secretariat established to receive, consolidate, manage and account for all contributions and financial transactions of the new Resident Coordinator system in a transparent and effective way.

The SPTF web portal, displays in real time all commitments, contributions and expenditures recorded for the fund.

Hence the correct answer is option (e).

17. Securities future value is Rs 1,000,000 and present value of securities is Rs 500,000 with an interest rate of 4.5%, 'N' will be 15.7473 years.

Hence the correct answer is option (C).

18. If payment of security is paid as Rs 100 at end of year for three years, it is an example of annuity. An annuity is a contract between you and an insurance company in which you make a lump sum payment or series of payments and, in return, obtain regular disbursements beginning either immediately or at some point in the future.

Hence the correct answer is option (D).

19. IT major TCS will implement RBI's centralized information and management system (CIMS) for seamless data collection and validations at a cost of 310.52 crore. The project has to be completed within a year of the commencement of the contract with the RBI.

Hence the correct answer is option (b).

20. Commerce and Industry Minister Piyush Goyal attended the G-20 ministerial meeting on Trade and digital economy in Japan. They agreed to find a common method to tax technology giants whose digital business models have grown faster than systems to tax them. The host of G20 Summit 2020 - Saudi Arabia.

Hence the correct answer is option (d).

21. Payment of security if it is made at end of each period such as beginning of year is classified as annuity due. An annuity due is a repeating payment that is made at the beginning of each period, such as a rent payment.

22. SIDBI has introduced a web-based application system for contribution from Fund of Funds for Start-ups to improve the turnaround time and increase transparency. SIDBI is the implementing agency for FFS with a corpus of Rs 10,000 crore.

Hence the correct answer is option (D).

23. The Central Board of Trustees, EPF is a statutory body constituted by the Central Government under the provisions of section 5A of the Employees' Provident Funds and Miscellaneous Provisions Act,1952 (Act 19 of 1952).

The tenure of the Board is five years. The constitution of the Board as per section 5A of the Act.

Hence the correct answer is option (A).

24. The IAF has signed a Rs 300 crore deal with a Israeli defence firm to procure a batch of SPICE 2000 guided bombs. The deal was signed with Israel's Rafael Advanced Defense Systems and the bombs are expected to be supplied in the next three months.

Hence the correct answer is option (E).

25. Net worth is also called asset net of liabilities. Net worth is the value of all the non-financial and financial assets owned by an institutional unit or sector minus the value of all its outstanding liabilities.

Hence the correct answer is option (A).

26. An annual rate of 16% if quoted by credit card issuer usually a bank is classified as annual percentage rate. An annual percentage rate (APR) is the annual rate charged for borrowing or earned through an investment. APR is expressed as a percentage that represents the actual yearly cost of funds over the term of a loan.

Hence the correct answer is option (C).

27. Value of payment is Rs 25 and an interest rate is 2%, then present value will be Rs 12,504.00.

Hence the correct answer is option (C).

28. Collection of net income, amortization and depreciation is divided by common shares outstanding to calculate cash flow per share. Cash flow per share can be calculated by dividing cash flow earned in a given reporting period (usually quarterly or annually) by the total number of shares outstanding during the same term. Because the number of shares outstanding can fluctuate, a weighted average is typically used.

Hence the correct answer is option (B).

29. Walmart-owned **Flipkart** has partnered with National Skill Development Corporation's Logistics Sector Skill Council (LSC) to train 20,000 of its delivery executives across the country.

As part of the partnership, the trained supply chain workforce will be certified in all aspects of product delivery and customer experience.

Upon successful completion of the training, the executives will be awarded with 'Recognition of Prior Learning' certification as per National Skill Qualification Framework (NSFQ).

Hence the correct answer is option (C).

30. India had taken up the project under its Rakhine State Development Programme in Myanmar, under which 25 mn $ are allocated for a period of 5 years. 22 other proposals which include solar power related projects are under consideration.

Hence the correct answer is option (D).

31. According to the text, a product is everything the customer receives in an exchange.

32. An example of a convenience consumer product is Petrol. A convenience product is a consumer product or service that customers normally buy frequently, immediately and without great comparison or buying effort.

33. Computer software to help people complete personal tax forms is NOT an industrial product. An industrial product is a good used by a company for business consumption.

34. The airline ticket is an example of which type of product Shopping. Shopping products refer to items that the consumers purchase less frequently and compare with available alternatives in the market. Consumers need time, planning and efforts to take the final decision whether to buy the product or not.

35. Large tools and machines used in a production process for a considerable length of time are classified as Major equipment. Process equipment can be used for tasks a varied as storage, controlling flow, and containing chemical reactions.

36. Items that are purchased routinely, do not become part of the final physical product, and are treated like expense items rather than capital goods are called Accessory equipment. Accessory equipment needs to be used in the production process in any business firm.

37. Products that are used directly in the production of a final product but are not easily identifiable are categorised as Process materials. Materials processing is the series of operations that transforms industrial materials from a raw-material state into finished parts or products.

38. Industrial products are traditionally classified according to their characteristics and intended uses. An industrial product is a good used by a company for business consumption.

39. A company designs the product with little or no input from customers, the company is practicing Product concept. The idea of production concept – "Consumers will favor products that are available and highly affordable". This concept is one of the oldest Marketing management orientations that guide sellers.

40. Place of the 4Ps of marketing mix involves decisions regarding channels coverage, assortments, locations, inventories or transports. Place decisions outline where a company sells a product and how it delivers the product to the market. The goal of business executives is to get their products in front of the consumers most likely to buy them.

41. Telemarketing is NOT a part of marketing communication mix. Telemarketing is a marketing strategy that involves connecting with customers over the telephone or, more recently, through web-based video conferencing.

42. A fundamental part of the distribution function is to get the product to the right place at the right time. Distribution channels are a key element in all the marketing strategies that revolve around the product. They help you reach the customer in a way to maximise your revenue and brand awareness.

43. Consumer products are products and services bought by final consumers for personal consumption. Consumer products, also referred to as final goods, are products that are bought by individuals or households for personal use. In other words, consumer products are goods that are bought for consumption by the average consumer.

44. Low Consumer involvement in purchase and little significant brand difference comes in Variety-seeking buying behaviors. Variety-seeking buyer behavior is the buying tendency of those consumers that do not have a high involvement with a product when there is a significant difference between brands.

45. Distribution of product to get it in the marks refers to place or distribution activities. Placement, or distribution, is the way a company ensures its target market or markets have access to its products or services. The goal is to ensure that the customer has access to the products or services a company sells in the location he or she would be most likely to look for that product or service.

46. Five stages are involved in the consumer buying / adoption process. Philip Kotler considers five steps in consumer adoption process, such as awareness, interest, evaluation, trial, and adoption.

47. "Buy it now" refers to Personal selling. The Buy It Now price is available until someone bids on the item or the reserve price is met.

48. At least Two parties should be included in "Exchange". An exchange process is simply when an individual or an organisation decides to satisfy a need or want by offering some money or goods or services in exchange.

49. Variety-seeking buying behavior is NOT one of these stages. There are 5 steps in a consumer decision making process a need or a want is recognized, search process, comparison, product or service selection, and evaluation of decision.

50. Here material and parts are the form of industrial product.

51. Section 9 of the Banking Regulation Act prohibits the banking Companies from holding any immovable property except for its own use for a period of not more property. The RBI may extend this period for a further period of 5 years.

52. Delhi stock exchange is derecognized by SEBI on 19.11.2014 on the allegations of serious irregularities in its functioning?

53. Medical is not a function of General Insurance.

54. Liability- side of the balance-sheet comprises capital and reserve long-term liabilities and current liabilities.

55. Minimum cash reserves fixed by law constitute a percentage of aggregate deposits of the bank.

56. NABARD organizations/ agencies has sought an emergency fund of Rs.1000 crore from banks to tackle acute liquidity crisis, which is coming in the way to give loans to micro borrowers.

57. Accounts in which shares of various companies are traded in electronic form known as "Demat Accounts".

58. Mortgage is a security on immovable property for a loan.

59. Giriraj Singh assumed charge as the Minister of State for Micro, Small & Medium Enterprises (MSME) on 11th November 2014.

60. Dr. D Subbarao well known person related to Banking field in India.

61. Currency notes deposited in the currency chest are the property of RBI.

62. A fixed deposit receipt is kept with the bank for its safety, is known as safe custody.

63. Reserve Bank of India is the primary regulator of Banking business.

64. The purpose of reporting is combating finance of terrorismt and to check hawala transactions.

65. Cryptocurrency is a digital medium of exchange.

Q.1 Working capital turn over ratio is 4 and current ratio is 3:1. If current liabilities are Rs. 15 lac and net profit to sales percent 7%, what is the amount of net profit?

A. Rs. 10.2 lac
B. Rs. 12.6 lac
C. Rs. 11.4 lac
D. Rs. 13.8 lac
E. None of these

Q.2 By Parallel economy is meant an economy ......
A. Which runs side by side of the existing economy?
B. Which has the same characteristics as the main economy?
C. Which has variety of parallel businesses?
D. Which has plentiful of black money?
E. None of these

Q.3 Calculate Inflation, if Price index in current year is 15 and price index in base year is 12.
A. 20
B. 25
C. 30
D. 35
E. None of these

Q.4 Given,
Currency with public - Rs. 250000 Crores
Demand deposit with banking system - Rs. 400000 Crores
Time deposits with banking system - Rs. 500000 Crores
Other deposit with RBI - Rs. 600000 Crores
Savings deposit of post office savings banks - Rs. 200000 Crores
All deposit with post office savings bank excluding NSCs - Rs. 100000 Crores
Calculate broad money M3.
A. Rs. 1250000 Crores
B. Rs. 1500000 Crores
C. Rs. 1750000 Crores
D. Rs. 2000000 Crores
E. None of these

Q.5 Go through the following data and answer the question.
1. Consumptions - Rs. 100000 Cr
2. Gross investment - Rs. 75000 Cr
3. Govt spending - Rs. 25000 Cr
4. Export - Rs. 100000 Cr
5. Import - Rs. 75000 Cr
6. Indirect Taxes - Rs. 15000 Cr
7. Subsidies(on production and import) - RS. 10000 Cr
8. Compensation of employee - Rs. 500 Cr
9. Property Income - Rs. 500 Cr
7,8,9 - Net receivable from aboard
10.Total capital gains from overseas investment - Rs. 20000 Cr
11.Income earned by foreign national domestically - Rs. 10000 Cr
Calculate GNP
A. Rs. 220000 Cr
B. Rs. 225000 Cr
C. Rs. 230000 Cr
D. Rs. 235000 Cr
E. None of these

Q.6 Which ONE of the following methods is generally used in qualitative sampling?

A. Random digit dialling
B. Quota
C. Stratified random
D. Simple random
E. None of these

Q.7 XYZ Pvt Ltd has the following assets and liabilities as on 31st March 2016 (in Lakhs) :
Non Current Assets
Goodwill 75
Fixed Assets 75
Current Assets
Cash in hand 25
Cash in bank 50
Short term investments 45
Inventory 25
Receivable 100
Current Liabilities
Trade payables 100
Income tax payables 60
Non Current Liabilities
Bank Loan 50
Deferred tax payable 25
Find the Quick Ratio
A. 1.38
B. 1.42
C. 1.46
D. 1.52
E. None of these

Q.8 XYZ Pvt Ltd has the following assets and liabilities as on 31st March 2016 (in Lakhs) :
Non Current Assets
Goodwill 75
Fixed Assets 75
Current Assets
Cash in hand 25
Cash in bank 50
Short term investments 45
Inventory 25
Receivable 100
Current Liabilities
Trade payables 100
Income tax payables 60
Non Current Liabilities
Bank Loan 50
Deferred tax payable 25
XYZ shoes sells shoes. It is applying for loans to help fund to increase the inventory. The bank asks for its balance sheet so they can analysis the current debt levels. According to XYZ shoes's balance sheet it reported 10,00,000 of current liabilities and only 2,50,000 of current assets. Will the loan get approved?
A. 0.25
B. 0.5
C. 0.75
D. 1
E. None of these

Q.9 ABC Agency has several loans from banks for equipment they purchased in the last five years. All of these loans are

coming due which is decreasing their working capital. At the end of the year, they had 1,00,000 of current assets and 1,25,000 of current liabilities. Find out its Working Capital Ratio.

A. 0.6

B. 0.8

C. 1

D. 1.2

E. None of these

Q.10 Suppose you purchased a bond Rs.1000 for Rs.920. The interest is 10 percent, and it will mature in 10 years. Calculate Yield to maturity

A. 10.75 %

B. 11.00 %

C. 11.25 %

D. 11.50 %

E. None of these

Q.11 A company has 1,00,000 of bank lines of credit and a 5,00,000 mortgage on its property. The shareholders of the company have invested 12,00,000. Calculate the debt to equity ratio.

A. 0.25

B. 0.5

C. 0.75

D. 1

E. None of these

Q.12 A company has total assets at 1,50,000 and its total liabilities are 50,000. Based on the accounting equation, we can assume the total equity is 1,00,000. Find the Equity Ratio.

A. 0.33

B. 0.5

C. 0.67

D. 0.75

E. None of these

Q.13 Mechanistic (or Behaviorist) theories, Cognitive theories and Organismic (humanistic. theories are three theories of learning. Which one of these theories equates man with his brain?

A. Behaviorist or mechanistic theories

B. Cognitive theories

C. Organismic or humanistic theories

D. Both (A) and (B)

E. All of the above

Q.14 In balance sheet amount of total assets is Rs 10 lac , current liabilities Rs 5 lac and capital and reserves Rs 2 lac. What is the debt-equity ratio?

A. 1:1

B. 1.5:1

C. 1.75:1

D. 2:1

E. None of these

Q.15 Working capital turn over ratio is 6 and current ratio is 2:1. If current liabilities are Rs 10 lac and net profit to sales percent 5% . What is the amount of net profit?

A. Rs 10 lac

B. Rs 8 lac

C. Rs 7 lac

D. Rs 6 lac

E. None of these

Q.16 DER is 3:1, the amount of total assets Rs 20 lac , current ratio is 1.5:1 and owned funds Rs 3 lac. What is amount of current assets?

A. 3 lac

B. 5 lac

C. 12 lac

D. 15 lac

E. None of these

Q.17 Which of the follwing cannot be included in capital as factor of production?

A. Factory building

B. river

C. machinery

D. car used for factory work

E. None of these

Q.18 A bond has been issued with a face value of Rs. 20000 at 12% Coupon for 3 years. The required rate of return is 10%. What is the value of the bond?

A. 20595

B. 29095

C. 25095

D. 20995

E. None of these

Q.19 Calculate Inflation, if Price index in current year is 13 and price index in base year is 10.

A. 20

B. 25

C. 30

D. 35

E. None of these

Q.20 ...... is the rate at which banks park their short term excess liquidity with the RBI.

A. Reverse Repo rate

B. Repo Rate

C. OMO

D. Bank rate

E. None of these

Q.21 Find the present value of quarterly payment of Rs. 250 for 5 years @ 12% compounded quarterly.

A. 3179

B. 3019

C. 3109

D. 3719

E. None of these

Q.22 What is the discount factor for Re. 1 to be received at the end of 2 yr with prevalent rate of 8% ?

A. 0.890

B. 0.873

C. 0.857

D. 0.842

E. None of these

Q.23 Which of the following factor/s affect elasticity of demand? (i) Share in the total expenditure, (ii) Multiple uses of the commodity, (iii) Availability of close substitutes

A. Only (i) and (ii)

B. Only (i) and (iii)

C. Only (ii) and (iii)

D. (i), (ii) and (iii)

E. Cannot be determined

Q.24 According to personality job fit theory of John Holland, there are 6 types of personality. Which of the following are among such personality? (i) realistic, (ii) conventional, (iii) artistic

A. Only (i) and (ii)

B. Only (i) and (iii)

C. Only (ii) and (iii)

D. (i), (ii) and (iii)

E. Cannot be determined

Q.25 The people component is becoming the key factor to success of strategy ......

A. For survival
B. For growth
C. For achieving excellence.
D. For social status
E. None of these

Q.26 As per Union Budget, 2018-19, Tax rate has been reduced to 25% for companies with annual turnover up to Rs. _____ crore.
A. 100   **B.** 200
C. 400   **D.** 800
E. None of these

Q.27 Frequency of review should vary depending on the magnitude of risk for the average risk account.
A. 01 month   **B.** 03 months
C. 06 months   **D.** 12 months
E. None of these

Q.28 A bond has been issued with a face value of Rs. 1000 at 10% Coupon for 3 years. The required rate of return is 8%. What is the value of the bond if the Coupon amount is payable on half-yearly basis?
A. 1520   **B.** 1052
C. 1205   **D.** 1025
E. None of these

Q.29 The target given for advances to weaker sections in percentage of ANBC
A. 10% for domestic banks
B. 12% for foreign banks
C. No target for domestic banks
D. 10% for foreign banks
E. None of these

Q.30 Base Rate is determined in each bank by ......
A. ALCO   **B.** BPLR
C. ALM   **D.** DSCR
E. None of these

Q.31 ...... is/are not prominent features of Type B personalities. (i) Doing several things at one time, (ii) Feeling guilty when relaxing, (iii) Being aggressive
A. Only (i) and (ii)   **B.** Only (i) and (iii)
C. Only (ii) and (iii)   **D.** (i), (ii) and (iii)
E. None of these

Q.32 In April 2013, A Bill has been introduced in the Lok Sabha to raise the authorised capital of the Regional Rural Banks to Rs _____ .
A. 1000 Crore   **B.** 500 Crore
C. 2500 Crore   **D.** 5 Crore
E. None of these

Q.33 In Take Out Financing there is/are how many parties involve ?
A. One   **B.** Two
C. Three   **D.** Four
E. None of these

Q.34 In India, main Products of Retail Banking are _______.
A. Loan products   **B.** Card Products
C. Deposit Products   **D.** All of these
E. None of these

Q.35 Microcredit is defined as ____.
A. It is the small credit given to poor.
B. It is the instalment given by Farmers against Loan.
C. It is the amount given by Govt. for Small Industries Development.
D. All of above
E. None of these

Q.36 Priority Sector does not includes the ____.
A. Agricultural Finance
B. Education Loans
C. Housing loans
D. Life Insurance Policy
E. None of these

Q.37 Kelkar Committee Gave recommendations on _________.
A. Tax Structure Reforms
B. Delisting in Share market
C. Broad Frame work of Insurance Sector
D. Company Law Reforms
E. None of these

Q.38 Which one is not the Government Securities ?
A. T- Bill.
B. Floating rate Bonds
C. Dated Securities
D. Call/Put Option Bonds.
E. None of these

Q.39 Your Perfect banking Partner is the punch line of _____ Bank.
A. Bank of Maharastra   **B.** UTI Bank
C. BOB   **D.** Federal Bank
E. None of these

Q.40 Head office of Bank of Maharashtra is located at _______.
A. New Delhi   **B.** Bhopal
C. Pune   **D.** Mumbai
E. None of these

Q.41 In which year, Credit Guarantee Corporation created ?
A. 1975   **B.** 1971
C. 1975   **D.** 2001
E. None of these

Q.42 A draft issued by the bank has been lost by the payee. He sends a letter to the issuing bank to stop payment. Bank will:
A. Note caution and will advice the payee to contact purchaser of the draft
B. Not act on the request
C. Stop payment
D. Performs no action
E. None of these

Q.43 Mutual funds are required to be registered with:

A. AMFI   **B.** SEBI

C. IBA   **D.** RBI

E. None of these

Q.44 What is Yield Curve Risk?

A. It is a line of graph plotting the yield of all maturities of a particular instrument.

B. Yield curve changes its slope and shape from time to time.

C. Yield curve can be twisted to the desired direction through the intervention of RBI.

D. All of the above

E. None of these

Q.45 The biggest international financial centre in the world:

A. Frankfurt   **B.** Geneva

C. London   **D.** New York

E. None of these

Q.46 Degree of total leverage can be applied in measuring change in ________.

A. EBIT to a percentage change in quantity

B. EPS to a percentage change in EBIT

C. EPS to a percentage change in quantity

D. Quantity to a percentage change in EBIT

E. None of these

Q.47 Investors can normally afford to assume larger risks in the ___ phase of the life- cycle.

A. accumulation   **B.** consolidation

C. spending   **D.** gifting

E. None of these

Q.48 The measure of business risk is ________.

A. operating leverage

B. financial leverage

C. total leverage

D. working capital leverage

E. None of these

Q.49 ________ is the most important investment decision because it determines the risk-return characteristics of the portfolio.

A. Hedging

B. Market timing

C. Performance measurement

D. Asset allocation

E. None of these

Q.50 The value of EBIT at which EPS is equal to zero is known as ________.

A. Break-even point

B. Financial break-even point

C. Operating break-even point

D. Overall break-even point

E. None of these

Q.51 A model for optimizing the selection of securities is the ______ model.

A. Miller-Orr   **B.** Black-Sholes

C. Markowitz   **D.** Gordon

E. None of these

Q.52 Degree of financial leverage is a measure of relationship between ________.

A. EPS and EBIT

B. EBIT and quantity produced

C. EPS and quantity produced

D. EPS and sales

E. None of these

Q.53 The Markowitz model identifies the efficient set of portfolios, which offers the ________.

A. highest return for any given level of risk or the lowest risk for any given level of return

B. least-risk portfolio for a conservative, middle-aged investor

C. long-run approach to wealth accumulation for a young investor

D. risk-free alternative for risk-averse investors

E. None of these

Q.54 Operating leverage examines.

A. The effect of the change in the quantity on EBIT

B. The effect of the change in EBIT on the EPS of the company

C. The effect of the change in output to the EPS of the company

D. The effect of change in EPS on the output of the company

E. None of these

Q.55 Which of the following is not normally one of the reasons for a change in an investor's circumstances?

A. Change in market conditions

B. Change in legal considerations

C. Change in time horizon

D. Change in tax circumstances

E. None of these

Q.56 Which of the following is the expression for operating leverage?

A. Contribution/EBIT

B. EBT/Contribution

C. Contribution/EAT

D. Contribution/Quantity

E. None of these

Q.57 The material wealth of a society is equal to the sum of ________.

A. all financial assets

B. all real assets

C. all financial and real assets

D. all physical assets

E. None of these

Q.58 Operating Leverage is the response of changes in ________.

A. EBIT to the changes in sales

B. EPS to the changes in EBIT

C. Production to the changes in sales

D. All of above

E. None of these

Q.59 _______ is example of financial intermediaries.

A. Commercial banks

B. Investment bank

C. Insurance companies

D. All of the above

E. None of these

Q.60 Walters model on dividend policy assumes that.

A. the firm offers an increasing amount of dividend per share at a given level of price per share

B. the firm has a finite life

C. the cost of capital of the firm is variable

D. equal to current assets plus current liabilities including bank borrowings

E. None of these

Q.61 Financial intermediaries exist because small investors cannot efficiently _______.

A. diversify their portfolios

B. gather all relevant information

C. assess credit risk of borrowers

D. advertise for needed investments

E. all of above

Q.62 The use of preference share capital as against debt finance.

A. Reduces DFL

B. Increases DFL

C. Increases financial risk

D. Both a and b

E. None of these

Q.63 Firms that specialize in helping companies raise capital by selling securities are called _______.

A. commercial banks

B. investment banks

C. savings banks

D. credit unions

E. None of these

Q.64 The Degree of Financial Leverage (DFL)

A. Measures financial risk of the firm

B. Is zero at financial break-even point

C. Increases as EBIT increases

D. Both a and b

E. None of these

Q.65 Financial assets _______.

A. directly contribute to the country's productive capacity

B. indirectly to the country's productive capacity

C. contribute to the country's productive capacity both directly and indirectly

D. do not contribute to the country's productive capacity either directly or indirectly

E. None of these

// Smart Answer Sheet //

Correct   Indicates percentage of students who answered questions correctly.

Skipped   Indicates percentage of students who skipped questions.

Q.	Ans.	Correct / Skipped	Q.	Ans.	Correct / Skipped	Q.	Ans.	Correct / Skipped	Q.	Ans.	Correct / Skipped	Q.	Ans.	Correct / Skipped
1	C	76.78 % / 11.04 %	14	B	81.73 % / 11.18 %	27	C	87.92 % / 11.46 %	40	C	84.15 % / 10.33 %	53	A	84.87 % / 12.83 %
2	D	87.44 % / 12.06 %	15	D	79.73 % / 19.46 %	28	B	77.43 % / 19.67 %	41	B	85.27 % / 14.66 %	54	A	85.13 % / 10.31 %
3	B	79.98 % / 18.65 %	16	C	88.29 % / 10.54 %	29	A	88.32 % / 10.56 %	42	A	82.61 % / 14.4 %	55	B	89.09 % / 10.87 %
4	C	78.01 % / 12.78 %	17	B	87.17 % / 10.22 %	30	A	89.48 % / 10.0 %	43	B	76.34 % / 18.19 %	56	A	79.62 % / 18.24 %
5	D	78.24 % / 12.97 %	18	D	85.48 % / 10.29 %	31	D	84.89 % / 13.99 %	44	D	82.2 % / 10.54 %	57	C	89.75 % / 10.14 %
6	B	88.56 % / 10.23 %	19	C	78.12 % / 19.75 %	32	B	77.65 % / 22.11 %	45	C	81.39 % / 12.23 %	58	A	80.09 % / 11.93 %
7	A	80.22 % / 19.45 %	20	A	85.95 % / 10.71 %	33	C	82.77 % / 16.37 %	46	C	78.95 % / 13.88 %	59	D	82.02 % / 16.56 %
8	A	86.2 % / 12.98 %	21	D	89.07 % / 10.26 %	34	D	89.43 % / 10.47 %	47	B	88.14 % / 11.39 %	60	D	77.72 % / 16.31 %
9	B	85.79 % / 13.11 %	22	C	85.43 % / 11.51 %	35	A	76.28 % / 11.87 %	48	B	76.57 % / 23.12 %	61	E	76.55 % / 22.51 %
10	C	85.15 % / 12.12 %	23	D	88.96 % / 10.6 %	36	D	87.92 % / 11.02 %	49	D	86.87 % / 12.48 %	62	A	88.9 % / 10.84 %
11	B	89.21 % / 10.36 %	24	D	77.36 % / 17.98 %	37	A	78.4 % / 16.7 %	50	B	86.93 % / 11.6 %	63	B	84.65 % / 14.5 %
12	C	88.23 % / 11.68 %	25	D	77.28 % / 20.49 %	38	A	85.76 % / 10.65 %	51	C	87.31 % / 10.81 %	64	A	76.03 % / 13.59 %
13	B	88.9 % / 10.06 %	26	C	77.88 % / 10.9 %	39	D	86.14 % / 13.68 %	52	A	83.77 % / 10.73 %	65	A	88.68 % / 11.3 %

Performance Analysis

Avg. Score (%)	43.0%
Toppers Score (%)	69.0%
Your Score	

//Hints and Solutions//

1. Since CR=3:1 and current liabilities are Rs. 15 lac

Current assets will be Rs. 45 lac

Now since wc turn over ratio is 4 that means the total turn over will be 45 × 4 = 180 lac

Then profit should be 180 × 7% = 12.6 lac

Hence the correct answer is option (B).

2. Parallel economy is the functioning of an unsanctioned sector in the economy whose objectives run in opposite to the objectives of official, sanctioned or legitimate sector. The parallel economy has political, commercial, legal, industrial, social and ethical aspects.

Prevalence of black money gives rise to parallel economy. The term parallel economy is also referred as black economy, unaccounted economy, illegal economy, subterranean economy or unsanctioned economy.

Hence the correct answer is option (D).

3. Inflation = (price index in current year-price index in base year)/(price index in base year)*100

= (15-12)/12*100

= 3/12*100

= 25

Hence the correct answer is option (B).

4. M1 = currency with public + demand deposit with the banking system + other deposits with RBI

M1 = 250000+400000+600000

M1 = 1250000

M3 = M1+Time deposit with banking system

So,

M3 = 1250000+500000

M3 = 1750000 Crores

Hence the correct answer is option (C).

5. GDP = Consumption + Gross investment + Government spending + (Exports - Imports)

GDP = C+I+G+(X-M)

= 100000+75000+25000+(100000-75000)

= 225000

GNP=GDP+NR(total capital gains from Overseas investment-income earned by foreign national

domestically)

= 225000 + (20000-10000)

= 235000

Hence the correct answer is option (D).

6. In qualitative research, there are various sampling techniques that you can use when recruiting participants. The two most popular sampling techniques are purposeful and convenience sampling because they align the best across nearly all qualitative research designs. Sampling techniques can be used in conjunction with one another very easily or can be used alone within a qualitative dissertation. Here we will describe the two most popular techniques in a bit more detail.

Hence the correct answer is option (B).

7. Quick Ratio = (Cash in hand + Cash at Bank + Receivables + Marketable Securities) / Current Liabilities

= (25+50+45+100) / 160

= 220 / 160

= 1.38

Hence the correct answer is option (A).

8. Current Ratio = Current Assets / Current Liabilities

= 250000 / 1000000

= 0.25

XYZ shoes only has enough current assets to pay off 25 percent of his current liabilities. This shows that XYZ shoes is highly leveraged and highly risky. Banks would prefer a current ratio of at least 1 or 2, so that all the current liabilities would be covered by the current assets. Since XYZ shoes's ratio is so low, it is unlikely that it will get approved for his loan.

Hence the correct answer is option (A).

9. The working capital ratio is calculated by dividing current assets by current liabilities.

WC Ratio = CA/CL

= 100000 / 125000

= 0.80

Hence the correct answer is option (B).

10. C=Coupon payment

F=Face value

P=Price

n=Years to maturity

Yield To Maturity=C+(F-P/n)/(F+P/2)

=100+(1000-920/10)/(1000+920/2)

=100+(80/10)/(1920/2)

=100+8/960

=108/960

=0.1125

=11.25%

Hence the correct answer is option (C).

11. DER = TL / Total Equity

= (100000+500000) / 1200000

= 600000 / 1200000

= 0.5

Hence the correct answer is option (B).

12. ER = Total Equity / TA

= 100000 / 150000

= 0.67

Hence the correct answer is option (C).

13. Is all behavior learned from the environment? Should psychology, as science, focus on observable behavior—the result of stimulus-response, as opposed to internal events like thinking and emotion? Is there little difference between the learning that takes place in humans and that in other animals? These are types of questions considered by behaviorists, which we'll learn more about in this section. We'll also consider cognitive theories, which examine the construction of thought processes, including remembering, problem-solving, and decision-making, from childhood through adolescence to adulthood.

Hence the correct answer is option (B).

14. As per Balance sheet rule Total assets = Total liabilities

Since total assets here is Rs 10 lac hence total liabilities must be 10 lac.

Now Long term debt = 10-(5+2)=3 lac and capital + reserve(TNW i.e tangible net worth) = 2 lac

Since DER = TL/TNW or debt/ equity or TL/ equity hence 3/2 = 1.5 lac

Hence the correct answer is option (B).

15. Since CR=2:1 and liabilities are 10 lac

Hence current asset will be 20 lac

Now since wc turn over is 6 that means the total turn over will be 20×6= 120 lac

Then profit should be 120×5%=6 lac

Hence the correct answer is option (D).

16. Owned fund= equity= 3 lac

Since DER = 3:1

i.e Debt: equity = 3:1

Hence Debt = 9 lac

(if we consider debt and equity as long term liabilities then term liability works out to 12(9+3 lac)

Here total assets is 20 lac

Now as per balance sheet equation total Assets= total liabilities

Hence here total liabilities will be 20 lac also

Now term liabilities of Rs 12 lac and remaining 8 lac as current liabilities (12+8=20)

Hence CL=8 lac

Since here CR=1.5:1 then

1.5:1=CA:8

i.e CA= 1.5×8=12 lac

Hence the correct answer is option (C).

17. Capital as a Factor of Production. When economists refer to capital, they are referring to the assets–physical tools, plants, and equipment–that allow for increased work productivity. Capital comprises one of the four major factors of production, the others being land, labor, and entrepreneurship.

Hence the correct answer is option (B).

18. FV = 20000

Coupon Rate (CR) = 0.12

t = 3 yr

R (YTM) = 0.10

Coupon = FV × CR = 2400

Bond Price = $(1/(1+R)^t)((coupon*((1+R)^t-1)/R)+Face Value)$

So, Value of bond = 20995

(Since Coupon rate > YTM, so FV < Bond's Value)

Hence the correct answer is option (D).

19. Inflation = (price index in current year-price index in base year)/(price index in base year)*100

= (13-10)/10*100

= 3/10*100

= 30

Hence the correct answer is option (C).

20. Banks can park their money with the RBI at a lower interest rate than the Repo Rate or Repurchase Rate. The Reverse Repo Rate is lower than the Repo Rate. The spread between the two is the RBI's income.

Hence the correct answer is option (A).

21. P = Rs. 250

T = 5 years = 5 × 4 = 20 quarters

R = 12% = 12% ÷ 4 = 0.03% quarterly

PV = P / R * $[(1+R)^T - 1]/(1+R)^T$

PV = 250 × (1.0320 − 1) ÷ (0.03 × 1.0320)

= 3719

Hence the correct answer is option (D).

22. = 1/(1+r)n

= $1/(1.08)^2$ = 0.857

Hence the correct answer is option (C).

23. There are several factors that affect how elastic (or inelastic) the price elasticity of demand is, such as the availability of substitutes, the timeframe, the share of income, whether a good is a luxury vs. a necessity, and how narrowly the market is defined. We explore each of these in this video.

Hence the correct answer is option (D).

24. According to John Holland's theory, most people are one of 6 personality types;

Realistic,

Investigative,

Artistic,

Social,

Enterprising, and.

Conventional.

Hence the correct answer is option (D).

25.

- People (Personnel, Staff, Learning, Development)
- Operations (Processes, Work)
- Marketing (Customer Relations, Sales, Responsiveness)
- Finances (Assets, Facilities, Equipment)

Hence the correct answer is option (D).

26. As per, Union Budget 2019-2020, Tax rate has been reduced to 25% for companies with annual turnover up to Rs. **400 crore.** Surcharge has been increased on individuals having taxable income from Rs. 2 crore to Rs. 5 crore and Rs. 5 crore and above. Direct tax revenue increased by over 78% in past 5 years to Rs. 11.37 lakh crore.

Hence the correct answer is option (c).

27. The frequency of review should vary depending on the magnitude of risk (say, for the high risk accounts – 3 months, for the average risk accounts- 6 months , for the low risk accounts- 1 year). Feedback on general regulatory compliance.

Hence the correct answer is option (C).

28. FV = 1000

CR = 10% half-yearly = 5% p.a.

Coupon = FV × CR = 50

R = 8% yearly = 4% p.a.

t = 3 years

Bond Price = $(1/(1+R)^t)((coupon*((1+R)^{t-1})/R)+Face Value)$

= 1052

(Since Coupon rate > YTM, so FV < Bond's Value)

Hence the correct answer is option (B).

29. The additional priority sector lending target of 2 percent of ANBC each year from 2016-17 to 2019- 20 has to be achieved by lending to sectors other than exports. The sub targets for these banks, if to be made applicable post 2020, would be decided in due course.

Hence the correct answer is option (A).

30. Asset Liability Management Committee (ALCO)

Each bank can determine their base rate in accordance with the norms given by the RBI. According to the RBI, Base Rate shall include all those elements of the lending rates that are common across all categories of borrowers. The base rate may differ from one bank to the other.

Hence the correct answer is option (A).

31. Type A and Type B are two types of trait classification. Type A individuals are aggressive, ambitious, controlling, highly competitive, preoccupied with status, workaholics, hostile, and lack patience. Type B people are relaxed, less stressed, flexible, emotional and expressive, and have a laid-back attitude.

Hence, the correct option is (D).

32. In April 2013, A Bill has been introduced in the Lok Sabha to raise the authorised capital of the Regional Rural Banks to Rs 500 Crore .

33. In Take Out Financing there is/are Three parties involve .

34. In India, main Products of Retail Banking are Loan products ,Card Product, ,Deposit Products.

35. Microcredit is defined as It is the small credit given to poor.

36. Priority Sector does not includes the Life Insurance Policy.

37. Kelkar Committee Gave recommendations on Tax Structure Reforms.

38. T- Bill is not the Government Securities.

39. Your Perfect banking Partner is the punch line of Federal Bank.

40. Head office of Bank of Maharashtra is located at Pune.

41. In 1971, Credit Guarantee Corporation created .

42. A draft issued by the bank has been lost by the payee. He sends a letter to the issuing bank to stop payment. Bank will Note caution and will advice the payee to contact purchaser of the draft.

43. Mutual funds are required to be registered with SEBI.

44. Yield Curve Risk-
It is a line of graph plotting the yield of all maturities of a particular instrument.
Yield curve changes its slope and shape from time to time.
Yield curve can be twisted to the desired direction through the intervention of RBI.

45. The biggest international financial centre in the world London.

46. Degree of total leverage can be applied in measuring change in EPS to a percentage change in EBIT.

47. Investors can normally afford to assume larger risks in the consolidation phase of the life- cycle.

48. The measure of business risk is operating leverage. Operating leverage is a cost-accounting formula that measures the degree to which a firm or project can increase operating income by increasing revenue.

49. Asset allocation is the most important investment decision because it determines the risk-return characteristics of the portfolio. Asset allocation is an investment strategy that aims to balance risk and reward by apportioning a portfolio's assets according to an individual's goals, risk tolerance and investment horizon.

50. The value of EBIT at which EPS is equal to zero is known as Financial break-even point. Financial break-even point is the level of earnings before interest and taxes that will result in zero net income or zero earnings per share. It equals the company's interest expense plus dividends paid to preferred stock-holders and associated taxes.

51. A model for optimizing the selection of securities is the Markowitz model. Harry Markowitz model (HM model), also known as Mean-Variance Model because it is based on the expected returns (mean) and the standard deviation (variance) of different portfolios, helps to make the most efficient selection by analyzing various portfolios of the given assets.

52. Degree of financial leverage is a measure of relationship between EPS and EBIT. The degree of financial leverage (DFL) measures the percentage change in EPS for a unit change in operating income, also known as earnings before interest and taxes (EBIT). This ratio indicates that the higher the degree of financial leverage, the more volatile earnings will be.

53. The Markowitz model identifies the efficient set of portfolios, which offers the highest return for any given level of risk or the lowest risk for any given level of return. Harry Markowitz model (HM model), also known as Mean-Variance Model because it is based on the expected returns (mean) and the standard deviation (variance) of different portfolios, helps to make the most efficient selection by analyzing various portfolios of the given assets.

54. Operating leverage examines the effect of the change in the quantity on EBIT. Operating leverage is a cost-accounting formula that measures the degree to which a firm or project can increase operating income by increasing revenue. A business that generates sales with a high gross margin and low variable costs has high operating leverage.

55. Change in legal considerations is not normally one of the reasons for a change in an investor's circumstances.

56. Contribution/EBIT is the expression for operating leverage. Operating leverage is a cost-accounting formula that measures the degree to which a firm or project can increase operating income by increasing revenue.

57. The material wealth of a society is equal to the sum of all financial and real assets. The material wealth of a society is determined ultimately by the productive capacity of its economy— the goods and services that can be provided to its members.

58. Operating Leverage is the response of changes in EBIT to the changes in sales. Operating leverage is a cost-accounting formula that measures the degree to which a firm or project can increase operating income by increasing revenue.

59. Commercial banks, Investment bank and Insurance companies are example of financial intermediaries.

60. Walters model on dividend policy assumes that equal to current assets plus current liabilities including bank borrowings. Walter's model shows the relevance of dividend policy and its bearing on the value of the share.

61. Financial intermediaries exist because small investors cannot efficiently diversify their portfolios, gather all relevant information, assess credit risk of borrowers and advertise for needed investments.

62. The use of preference share capital as against debt finance reduces DFL. A degree of financial leverage (DFL) is a leverage ratio that measures the sensitivity of a company's earnings per share (EPS) to fluctuations in its operating income, as a result of changes in its capital structure.

63. Firms that specialize in helping companies raise capital by selling securities are called investment banks. An investment bank (IB) is a financial intermediary that performs a variety of services.

64. The Degree of Financial Leverage (DFL) measures financial risk of the firm. The degree of financial leverage (DFL) measures the percentage change in EPS for a unit change in operating income, also known as earnings before interest and taxes (EBIT).

65. Financial assets directly contribute to the country's productive capacity. A financial asset is a liquid asset that gets its value from a contractual right or ownership claim.

Q.1 What was the theme of the 4th Edition of Women Transforming India (WTI) Awards?
A. Women First, Prosperity for All
B. Women and Entrepreneurship
C. Equal Opportunities
D. Working Together
E. None of the above

Q.2 Recently, ISRO has announced its _______ Journalism Award in Space Science, Technology and Research.
A. Homi J. Bhabha
B. A. P. J. Abdul Kalam
C. Satish Dhawan
D. Vikram Sarabhai
E. Jagadish Chandra Bose

Q.3 The Government of India has instituted an annual award titled Aapda Prabandhan Puraskar. This award will be given in honour of whom?
A. Subhash Chandra Bose
B. Mahatma Gandhi
C. Sardar Vallabhai Patel
D. Bal Gangadhar Tilak
E. Swami Vivekanand

Q.4 10th National Science Film Festival of India will be held at which of the following states in January-February 2020?
A. Assam
B. Sikkim
C. Tripura
D. West Bengal
E. Bihar

Q.5 Who clinched the German Grand Prix at Hockenheim in July 2019?
A. Sebastian Vettel
B. Max Verstappen
C. Daniil Kvyat
D. Lewis Hamilton
E. Daniel Ricciardo

Q.6 In Boxing, who won silver medal in 51 kg category in the Thailand Open International Tournament in Bangkok in July 2019?
A. Sarjubala Devi
B. Nikhat Zareen
C. Pinki Jangra
D. Simranjit Kaur
E. Swapna Barman

Q.7 Who won the Indonesia Open title in Jakarta in July 2019?
A. PV Sindhu
B. Akane Yamaguchi
C. Carolina Marin
D. Wang Yihan
E. Saina Nehwal

Q.8 The 'Titanwala Museum' in Rajasthan showcases the hand-block printing of which community?
A. Meena
B. Chhipa
C. Bhils
D. Khatri
E. Gonds

Q.9 In this technique, managers prepare lists of statements of very effective and very ineffective behavior of an employee.
A. Management by Objective
B. Essay Evaluation
C. Forced Choice
D. Critical Incident Technique
E. None of these

Q.10 Which city has been announced as the World Capital of Architecture for 2020 by UNESCO?
A. Paris
B. Rio de Janeiro
C. Amsterdam
D. Rome
E. Madrid

Q.11 United Nations honoured 150 Indian peacekeepers serving with the UNMISS with medals of honour. UNMISS is committed to helping build durable peace in _______.
A. South Sudan
B. Nigeria
C. South Africa
D. Sudan
E. Chad

Q.12 The President Ram Nath Kovind was recently honoured with the Grand Order of Tomislav in March 2019. To which Country does this belong?
A. Russia
B. Croatia
C. Bolivia
D. Chile
E. Slovakia

Q.13 Which of the following award was won by Amartya Sen in March 2019?
A. Fisher Black Prize
B. Fields Medal
C. Bodley Medal
D. Adams Smith Prize
E. None of the above

Q.14 Which of the following state had won the prestigious World Summit on the Information Society awards of the United Nations?
A. Assam
B. Odisha
C. Punjab
D. West Bengal
E. Rajasthan

Q.15 Bagurumba is the dance form of which among the following Indian state?
A. Gujarat
B. Uttarakhand
C. Assam
D. Andhra Pradesh
E. Uttar Pradesh

Q.16 Which Act provides the definition of banking?
A. Negotiable Instruments Act, 1881
B. Banking Regulation Act, 1949
C. Reserve Bank of India Act, 1935
D. Nowhere, it is defined
E. a) and b)

Q.17 What does L in World Economic Forum's GLN stand for?
A. Liquid
B. Liquor

C. Lighthouse   D. Lab
E. Location

Q.18 The book titled "Exam Warrior" was authored by _______.
A. Arvind Chaturvedi
B. Narendra Modi
C. Atal Bihari Vajpayee
D. Prakash Javdekar
E. Manish Sisodia

Q.19 When is the 'International Chess Day' observed?
A. 18 July   B. 19 July   C. 20 July   D. 21 July
E. 22 July

Q.20 Which state will host a 3-day Global Investors Summit in October 2019?
A. Karnataka
B. Maharashtra
C. Punjab
D. Jammu and Kashmir
E. Gujarat

Q.21 Madhya Pradesh Cabinet recently passed resolution to increase reservation for OBCs to _____ %
A. 34   B. 27   C. 18   D. 20
E. 25

Q.22 Nayib Bukele has been sworn in as the president of which country?
A. Italy   B. France
C. Germany   D. El Salvador
E. Netherlands

Q.23 Admiral __________ took charge as the 24th Chief of the Naval Staff.
A. Karambir Singh   B. Amitesh Dhanoa
C. Suresh Thakur   D. A K Bharadwaj
E. None of the above

Q.24 Which country has recently awarded Ex-President Pratibha Patil its highest civilian's award?
A. Ethiopia   B. Canada   C. Australia   D. France
E. Mexico

Q.25 __________ is the amount of money that households have available for spending after all types of tax deductions.
A. Factor Income   B. Net Domestic value
C. Net Citizen value   D. Disposable Income
E. Gross Salary

Q.26 Who has been sworn in as the new Australian Prime Minister recently?
A. Scott Morrison
B. Peter Cosgrove
C. Billy Hughes
D. Michael McCormack
E. Edmund Barton

Q.27 Government has constituted a High Powered Committee of CMs for "Transformation for Indian Agriculture" with which of the following state's CM as convenor?
A. Uttar Pradesh   B. Bihar
C. Telangana   D. Odisha
E. Maharashtra

Q.28 FICCI survey forecasts India's GDP growth at _______ for FY20.
A. 7.1%   B. 8.7%   C. 9.2%   D. 8.1%
E. 7.8%

Q.29 Mr. Modi approved the increase from Rs2,250 to __________ a month for girls in National Defence Fund.
A. Rs 3000   B. Rs5000   C. Rs7000   D. Rs8000
E. Rs4000

Q.30 What do we call an organisation which holds securities of investors in electronic form at the request of the investors?
A. Stock Exchange   B. Demat organisation
C. Security Bank   D. Investment bank
E. Depository

Q.31 The expansion of BIFR, in the context of the Indian Industry is:
A. Board for Industrial and Financial Reconstruction
B. Bureau for Industrial and Financial Reconstruction
C. Board for Investment and Financial Reconstruction
D. Bureau for Investment and Financial Reconstruction
E. None of these

Q.32 The largest financial conglomerate of India is?
A. HDFC Bank   B. ICICI Bank
C. IFCI   D. SBI
E. ADB

Q.33 Under which of the following methods of depreciation, amount of depreciation varies every year?
A. Written Down Value Method
B. Straight Line Method
C. Amount of depreciation does not vary on year to year basis
D. Either a or b
E. Either a or c

Q.34 Usually, the validity period of an Income Tax Refund Order is:
A. 1 month   B. 2 months
C. 3 months   D. 6 months
E. 7 months

Q.35 Which of the following is true about "White Card"?
A. It is related to companies producing milk products
B. It does not carry on its face, the brand of the issuer
C. It is meant to covert blank money into the economy
D. It is a card that provides white money
E. It is not a card that provides white money

Q.36 First bank in India to launch its interactive banking service through Dish TV:

A. HSBC   **B.** ICICI Bank
C. HDFC Bank   **D.** Axis Bank
E. ADB

Q.37 First Indian Governor of the RBI:
A. C.D. Deshmukh   **B.** Sachindra Ray
C. S. Mukherjee   **D.** D.I.G. Patel
E. None of these

Q.38 CGTMSE (Credit Guarantee Fund Trust for Micro and Small Enterprises) has been set up on the recommendations of?
A. Narashimham Committee
B. Ghosh Committee
C. Chore Committee
D. Kapoor Committee
E. None of these

Q.39 The primary relationship between the banker and the customer is that of:
A. Trustee and beneficiary
B. Debtor and Creditor
C. Principal and agent
D. Lesser and lessee
E. None of these

Q.40 A debt becomes time-barred after:
A. One year   **B.** Two and a half year
C. Three years   **D.** Five years
E. Six years

Q.41 In the matter of handling bills of exchange for collection, the relationship between customer and the bank is:
A. Trustee and the beneficiary
B. Principal and agent
C. Bailor and Bailee
D. Both (A) and (B)
E. None of these

Q.42 Hypothecation is:
A. A transaction of conditional sale
B. A legal transaction whereby goods may be made available as security for a debt
C. Transfer of ownership by the borrower to the lender
D. None of the above
E. A transaction of non conditional sale

Q.43 Payment of a cheque may be countermanded by the ___
A. Payee   **B.** True owner
C. Drawee   **D.** Drawer
E. None

Q.44 J.S. Verma Committee Report relates to:
A. Strengthening of weak banks
B. Corporate Governance
C. Bank Mechanization
D. Both (a) and (b)
E. None of the above

Q.45 A Usance Bill when presented for acceptance has to be accepted/ dishonoured within:
A. 24 hours   **B.** 36 hours   **C.** 48 hours   **D.** 60 hours
E. 68 hours

Q.46 Dividend changes are perceived important than the absolute level of dividends because.
A. management change dividends to protect their seats
B. dividend changes are thought to signal future expectations
C. MM state that absolute level of dividends is irrelevant
D. changes determine the level of borrowing
E. None of these

Q.47 Investment bankers perform the following role _________.
A. market new stock and bond issues for firms
B. provide advice to the firms as to market conditions, price, etc
C. design securities with desirable properties
D. Both (a) and (b)
E. all of the above

Q.48 Which of the following is the assumption of the MM model on dividend policy?
A. The firm is an all-equity firm
B. The investments of the firm are financed solely by retained earnings
C. The firm has an infinite life
D. Both (A) and (B)
E. All of above

Q.49 Investors seeking to avoid actively managing their portfolios will prefer which of the following assets?
A. Common stock
B. Commercial bank deposits
C. Financial futures
D. Real estate
E. None

Q.50 Which of the following short term securities is inappropriate for an individual, desiring funds for financial emergencies?
A. treasury bills
B. certificates of deposit
C. financial futures
D. savings accounts
E. None of these

Q.51 Which of the following methods does a firm resort to avoid dividend payments?
A. Share splitting
B. Declaring bonus shares
C. Rights issue
D. New issue
E. wrong issue

Q.52 Asset allocation affects the investor's return by___________.
A. altering the returns on individual assets
B. weighting the portfolio return by the allocation

C. assuring diversification

D. increasing the investor's use of mutual funds

E. None

Q.53 Which of the following characteristics are true, with reference to preference capital?

A. Preference dividend is not tax deductible

B. The claim of preference shareholders is prior to the claim of equity shareholders

C. Preference shareholders are not the owners of the concern

D. Both (A) and (B)

E. None

Q.54 Diversification reduces ________.

A. Interest rate risk

B. Market risk

C. Unique risk

D. Inflation risk

E. None

Q.55 What are the factors which make debentures attractive to investors?

A. They enjoy a high order of priority in the event of liquidation

B. Stable rate of return

C. No risk

D. All of the above

E. No issue

Q.56 Unsystematic risk is _____.

A. the risk associated with movements in security prices

B. reduced through diversification

C. higher when interest rates rise

D. the risk of loss of purchasing power

E. increased through diversification

Q.57 The method of raising equity capital from existing members by offering securities on pro rata basis is referred to as ________.

A. Public issue

B. Right Issue

C. Private placement

D. Bought-Out-Deal

E. Wrong issue

Q.58 The expected return on an investment in stock is________.

A. the expected dividend payments

B. the anticipated capital gains

C. the sum of expected dividends and capital gains

D. less than the realized return

E. greater than the realized return

Q.59 Which of the following is not a source of long-term finance?

A. Equity shares

B. Preference shares

C. Commercial papers

D. Reserves and surplus

E. None

Q.60 If the dispersion around a security's return is larger __________.

A. the expected return is smaller

B. the standard deviation is smaller

C. the stock's price is higher

D. the security's risk is higher

E. None

Q.61 EBIT means __________.

A. Operating Income

B. Operating Profit

C. Earnings before interest and tax

D. All of the above

E. none of these

Q.62 Another name for stock brokers is__________.

A. specialists

B. registered representatives

C. security analysts

D. portfolio manager

E. None

Q.63 Which of the following factors influence(s) the capital structure of a business entity?

A. Bargaining power with the suppliers

B. Demand for the product of the company

C. Technology adopted

D. Adequate of the assets to meet any sudden spurt in demand

E. None of these

Q.64 Investment professionals whose jobs may depend on their performance relative to the market are the__________.

A. registered representatives

B. security analysts

C. investment bankers

D. portfolio managers

E. None of these

Q.65 Which of the following ratios is not affected by the financial structure and the tax rate of a company?

A. Net profit margin

B. Earning power

C. Earnings per share

D. Capitalization rate

E. None of these

// Smart Answer Sheet //

Correct   Indicates percentage of students who answered questions correctly.

Skipped   Indicates percentage of students who skipped questions.

Q.	Ans.	Correct / Skipped	Q.	Ans.	Correct / Skipped	Q.	Ans.	Correct / Skipped	Q.	Ans.	Correct / Skipped	Q.	Ans.	Correct / Skipped
1	B	89.9 % / 10.08 %	14	D	83.97 % / 15.52 %	27	E	88.49 % / 11.29 %	40	C	81.22 % / 16.35 %	53	D	81.22 % / 12.28 %
2	D	79.99 % / 12.19 %	15	C	76.88 % / 18.31 %	28	A	89.87 % / 10.06 %	41	B	86.42 % / 12.05 %	54	C	87.17 % / 12.19 %
3	A	85.2 % / 10.57 %	16	B	79.01 % / 16.82 %	29	A	85.2 % / 13.53 %	42	B	79.11 % / 14.92 %	55	D	81.76 % / 13.0 %
4	C	76.14 % / 18.94 %	17	C	83.49 % / 12.95 %	30	E	79.92 % / 10.36 %	43	D	82.35 % / 12.42 %	56	B	86.1 % / 12.91 %
5	B	87.1 % / 11.58 %	18	B	84.19 % / 14.85 %	31	A	83.19 % / 11.26 %	44	A	86.12 % / 12.95 %	57	B	76.35 % / 13.91 %
6	B	83.04 % / 13.76 %	19	C	88.54 % / 10.52 %	32	D	88.17 % / 11.52 %	45	C	83.73 % / 10.61 %	58	C	77.99 % / 11.12 %
7	B	83.88 % / 12.42 %	20	D	85.84 % / 13.45 %	33	A	89.61 % / 10.12 %	46	B	84.13 % / 14.31 %	59	C	82.64 % / 12.7 %
8	B	85.31 % / 13.39 %	21	B	78.38 % / 18.93 %	34	C	87.78 % / 11.09 %	47	E	88.96 % / 10.87 %	60	D	79.62 % / 14.38 %
9	D	76.91 % / 12.85 %	22	D	79.34 % / 15.37 %	35	B	79.33 % / 16.88 %	48	C	88.81 % / 10.12 %	61	D	86.56 % / 13.05 %
10	B	89.59 % / 10.35 %	23	A	83.04 % / 11.07 %	36	C	89.51 % / 10.42 %	49	B	84.39 % / 14.62 %	62	B	83.5 % / 15.74 %
11	A	84.57 % / 13.32 %	24	E	80.21 % / 17.82 %	37	A	82.49 % / 15.52 %	50	C	89.93 % / 10.06 %	63	C	79.26 % / 19.72 %
12	B	81.16 % / 13.55 %	25	D	77.73 % / 10.64 %	38	D	81.54 % / 13.62 %	51	B	89.07 % / 10.32 %	64	A	79.46 % / 15.66 %
13	C	78.81 % / 19.34 %	26	A	79.85 % / 10.85 %	39	B	87.87 % / 10.66 %	52	B	79.63 % / 15.65 %	65	C	79.12 % / 19.1 %

Performance Analysis

Avg. Score (%)	42.0%
Toppers Score (%)	58.0%
Your Score	

//Hints and Solutions//

1.

- The NITI Aayog launched the 4th Edition of Women Transforming India (WTI) Awards on 9 August 2019.
- The theme for 2019 is '**Women and Entrepreneurship**'.
- WhatsApp has collaborated with NITI Aayog for WTI Awards 2019 and will be providing support amounting to US$100,000 to the award winners.

Hence the correct answer is option (B).

2.

- ISRO has announced its **Vikram Sarabhai** Journalism Award in Space Science, Technology and Research.
- It recognizes and rewards journalists who have actively contributed towards the field of space science, applications, and research.
- The articles published from 2019 to 2020 will be considered.
- The nominations are open to all Indians who have a good experience in journalism.

Hence the correct answer is option (D).

3.

- **Government of India** has instituted an **annual award titled** Subhash Chandra Bose **Aapda Prabandhan Puraskar.** The award is to be announced every year on **23rd January** on the **birth anniversary** of **Netaji Subhash Chandra Bose.**
- All Indian **Citizens and organizations,** who have excelled in areas of **Disaster Management; like Prevention, Mitigation, Preparedness, Rescue, Response, Relief, Rehabilitation, Research/ Innovations or Early Warning** are eligible for the award.
- The Award recipient will receive a certificate and a cash prize of Rs. 51 lakhs.
- For the year 2019, 8th Battalion of National Disaster Response Force (NDRF) located at Ghaziabad has been selected for the award for its commendable work in Disaster Management.
- The battalion came for rescue operations in in **Leh Cloud Burst (2011), Kedarnath Floods (2013), Cyclone Hudhud (2014), Chennai Floods (2015) and Tripura Floods (2018).** The battalion had worked efficiently to neutralise the threat during Radiation Incident at **Mayapuri, Delhi during the year 2010**. They have also done commendable Disaster Management related work internationally. In the aftermath of **Nepal Earthquake in 2015,** six teams of the battalion were among the first responders to land at Kathmandu. Their teams were also sent to **Japan during Fukushima Daiichi nuclear disaster (2011) and recent Tsunami in Indonesia (2108).**

Hence the correct answer is option (A).

4.

- 10th National Science Film Festival of India will be in Agartala, Tripura in January-February 2020.
- This is for the second time the event will be held in a North-Eastern city. It will be jointly hosted by Vigyan Prasar of the Central Government, State Government, and Tripura Central University.
- Chief Minister of Tripura is Biplab Kumar Deb.

Hence the correct answer is option (C).

5.

- Red Bull's driver **Max Verstappen** clinched the rain-hit German Grand Prix at Hockenheim on 28 July 2019.
- Verstappen now has the second title of the Formula One season.
- Four-time former champion Ferrari driver Sebastian Vettel claimed the second spot after starting from the rear of the grind.
- Russian Daniil Kvyat achieved the third spot for Toro Rosso.

Hence the correct answer is option (B).

6.

- In Boxing, former junior world champion **Nikhat Zareen** in 51 kg and Asian silver-winner Deepak Singh in 49 kg category won silver medals in the Thailand Open International Tournament in Bangkok on 27 July 2019.
- Deepak Singh lost to Mirzakhmedov Nodirjon of Uzbekistan and Nikhat bowed out to Chang Yuan of China.

Hence the correct answer is option (B).

7.

- Fourth seed **Akane Yamaguchi** defeated PV Sindhu in straight games 21-15, 21-16 to lift her maiden Indonesia Open title at Istora Senayan Stadium in Jakarta.
- Sindhu had to settle for just a silver medal in her first final of 2019.
- The last time the Indian lost to the Japanese was at the semifinals of the All England Championship in 2018.

Hence the correct answer is option (B).

8.

- Union Textiles Minister Smriti Irani inaugurated the 'Titanwala Museum' in Bagru, Rajasthan on 25 February 2019.
- The museum showcases the Chhipa community's hand-block printing.
- It will be open from Monday to Sunday between 9 a.m. and 6 p.m.

Hence the correct answer is option (B).

9. The critical incident method of performance appraisal involved identifying and describing specific events (or incidents) where the employee did something really well or something that needs improvement. It's a technique based on the description of the event, and does not rely on the assignment of ratings or rankings, although it is occasionally coupled with a ratings type system.

10.

- The UNESCO has announced that the Brazilian city of Rio de Janeiro will be the World Capital of Architecture for 2020.
- Rio will be the first city to receive the title under a program launched together by UNESCO and the International Union of Architects (UIA) in November last year.
- The city will host the World Congress of UIA, in July 2020, an event that occurs every three years.

Hence the correct answer is option (B).

11.

- United Nations honoured 150 Indian peacekeepers serving with the **UN Mission in South Sudan** (UNMISS) with medals of honour for their dedicated service and sacrifice.
- UNMISS is working to deter violence against civilians by providing a safe and secure environment for South Sudanese people.
- UNMISS is committed to helping build durable peace in South Sudan.

Hence the correct answer is option (A).

12.

- President Ram Nath Kovind was honoured with Croatia's highest civilian award, the Grand Order of the King of Tomislav on 26 March 2019.
- He was on an 8-day visit to Croatia, Bolivia, and Chile to further strengthen bilateral ties between India and the three countries.
- It is awarded to heads of state for their important contribution towards the development of relations with Croatia.

Hence the correct answer is option (B).

13.

- Nobel Prize-winning economist Amartya Sen was awarded the prestigious Bodley Medal.
- It is the highest honour granted by the University of Oxford's world-famous Bodleian Libraries.
- The medal is awarded to individuals who have made outstanding contributions to the fields in which the Bodleian is awarded are, including literature, culture, science, and communication.

Hence the correct answer is option (C).

14.

- Two schemes of the West Bengal government for skill development and distribution of bicycles to students had won the prestigious World Summit on the Information Society awards of the United Nations.
- The 2 schemes are the Utkarsh Bangla and Sabooj Sathi projects for youngsters.

Hence the correct answer is option (D).

15.

- **Bagurumba** is the dance form of **Assam.**
- It is a **tribal dance** performed by **females**.
- Bihu dance is another dance form of Assam.
- The capital of Assam is **Dispur** & Chief minister is **Sarbananda Sonowal.**
- Gujarat - Garba, Dandiya, Tippani, Padhar, Bhavai
- Uttarakhand - Dhurang, LangvirNritya, BaradaNati, etc.
- Andhra Pradesh - Kuchipudi, Bhamakalpam, Burrakatha, Lambadi, etc.

Hence the correct answer is option (C).

16. As per Section 5(b) of the Banking Regulation Act, 1949, "banking" means the accepting, for the purpose of lending or investment, of deposits of money from the public, repayable on demand or otherwise, and withdrawable by cheque, draft, order or otherwise.

Hence the correct answer is option (B).

17.

- Tata Steel Kalinganagar (TSK) has been included in the **World Economic Forum's (WEF) Global Lighthouse Network (GLN).**
- GLN is a community of manufacturers showing leadership in applying Fourth Industrial Revolution technologies to drive financial and operational impact.
- TSK in Odisha's Jajpur district is the first and the only Indian manufacturing plant to be included in the GLN.

Hence the correct answer is option (C).

18.

- The book "Exam Warrior" is authored by **Prime Minister Narendra Modi.**
- It was released by (Late) Sushma Swaraj.
- The book aims to inspire the youth of the country to face the difficult moments of examinations and life with fresh and new energy.
- The book has emphasised on the importance of play, sleep and even travel for the students.

Hence the correct answer is option (B).

19.

- The 'International Chess Day' is observed every year on **20 July**.
- It's a special day for India as Chess is one of the precious gifts of India to the world.

- Just two days ago, Indian chess got its 64th Grandmaster Prithu Gupta, a very symbolic day as the chess board is made up of 64 squares.
- The origin of chess is found in 'Chaturanga' – a strategy game played in India in the medieval era.

Hence the correct answer is option (C).

20.

- **Jammu and Kashmir** government will host a 3-day Global Investors Summit from 12th October 2019 in Srinagar.
- The first ever summit in the state will provide J&K an opportunity to showcase its strengths, strategies and potential.
- The summit will also provide an opportunity to allay fears and apprehensions in the minds of outside trade and business community.

Hence the correct answer is option (D).

21. The Madhya Pradesh Cabinet passed a resolution to increase reservation quota for Other Backward Classes (OBC) from existing 14 per cent to 27 per cent.The Cabinet has also increased by three per cent the dearness allowance for employees and pensioners.

Hence the correct answer is option (B).

22. In the Central American country of El Salvador, Nayib Bukele has been sworn-in as the nation's President. Delegations from 83 countries attended the ceremony. Bukele was elected to succeed Salvador Sanchez Ceren.

Hence the correct answer is option (D).

23. Admiral Karambir Singh took charge as the 24th Chief of the Naval Staff. He is the 1st helicopter pilot from the Indian Navy to lead the naval armed forces. He has commanded missile corvette INS Vijaydurg, guided-missile destroyers INS Rana & INS Delhi.

Hence the correct answer is option (A).

24. The ambassador of Mexico to India, Melba Pria, presented "Orden Mexicana del Aguila Azteca" (Order of the Aztec Eagle) to Ms Patil, who had served as the first woman president of the country during 2007-12, at a special ceremony held in MCCIA Bhavan.

Hence the correct answer is option (E).

25. The money that a person has left over from your salary after they have paid all kinds of state and local taxes is the **disposable personal income** (DPI), also referred to as your net pay.

Disposable income is an important measure of household financial resources.

Disposable income minus all payments for necessities, such as mortgage, health insurance, food and transportation, equals discretionary income.

Hence the correct answer is option (D).

26. Mr. Morrison became Australia's 30th Prime Minister. Along with Deputy Prime Minister Michael McCormack, Mr. Morrison was sworn in by Queen Elizabeth's official representative in Australia, Governor-General Sir Peter Cosgrove.

Hence the correct answer is option (A).

27. PM has set up a High Powered Committee of Chief Ministers for Transformation of Indian Agriculture with Maharashtra CM as Convenor of committee to suggest modalities for adoption and time bound implementation of agriculture sector reforms.

Hence the correct answer is option (E).

28. According to a survey by FICCI, the country's median GDP is forecast at 7.1% for FY20 and 7.2% for FY 21.Inflation is expected to remain moderate and the WPI based inflation rate is projected at 3.1% in FY19-20.

Hence the correct answer is option (A).

29. PM Modi has approved changes to the PM Scholarship Scheme for wards of deceased defence personnel under the National Defence Fund. Mr. Modi approved the increase from 2,000 to 2,500 a month for boys and from 2,250 to 3,000 a month for girls.

Hence the correct answer is option (A).

30. A **depository** is an organisation which holds securities (like shares, debentures, bonds, government securities, mutual fund units etc.) of investors in electronic form at the request of the investors through a registered depository participant.

It also provides services related to transactions in securities.

Hence the correct answer is option (E).

31. Board for Industrial and Financial Reconstruction

32. The largest financial conglomerate of India is SBI.

33. Written Down Value Method

34. Usually, the validity period of an Income Tax Refund Order is 3 months.

35. It does not carry on its face, the brand of the issuer

36. First bank in India to launch its interactive banking service through Dish TV is HDFC Bank.

37. First Indian Governor of the RBI is C.D. Deshmukh.

38. CGTMSE (Credit Guarantee Fund Trust for Micro and Small Enterprises) has been set up on the recommendations of Kapoor Committee.

39. The primary relationship between the banker and the customer is that of Debtor and Creditor.

40. A debt becomes time-barred after Three years.

41. In the matter of handling bills of exchange for collection, the relationship between customer and the bank is Principal and agent.

42. Hypothecation is a legal transaction whereby goods may be made available as security for a debt.

43. Payment of a cheque may be countermanded by the Drawer.

44. J.S. Verma Committee Report relates to Strengthening of weak banks.

45. A Usance Bill when presented for acceptance has to be accepted/ dishonoured within 48 hours.

46. Dividend changes are perceived important than the absolute level of dividends because dividend changes are thought to signal future expectations.

47. Investment bankers perform the following role market new stock and bond issues for firms B. provide advice to the firms as to market conditions, price, etc C. design securities with desirable properties. An investment banker is an individual who often works as part of a financial institution and is primarily concerned with raising capital for corporations, governments, or other entities.

48. The firm has an infinite life is the assumption of the MM model on dividend policy. According to Miller and Modigliani Hypothesis or MM Approach, dividend policy has no effect on the price of the shares of the firm and believes that it is the investment policy that increases the firm's share value.

49. Investors seeking to avoid actively managing their portfolios will prefer Commercial bank deposits. A commercial bank accepts deposits in the form of current, savings and fixed deposits.

50. Financial futures short term securities is inappropriate for an individual, desiring funds for financial emergencies. Futures contract to buy or sell a specific financial instrument (such as treasury bills, certificates of deposit, or foreign currencies) at a specific future date and at a specified price. The market value of these contracts generally moves in a direction opposite to that of the interest rates.

51. Declaring bonus shares methods does a firm resort to avoid dividend payments. Bonus shares are shares distributed by a company to its current shareholders as fully paid shares free of charge. to capitalise a part of the company's retained earnings.

52. Asset allocation affects the investor's return by weighting the portfolio return by the allocation. Asset allocation is an investment strategy that aims to balance risk and reward by apportioning a portfolio's assets according to an individual's goals, risk tolerance and investment horizon.

53. Preference dividend is not tax deductible, The claim of preference shareholders is prior to the claim of equity shareholders and Preference shareholders are not the owners of the concern characteristics are true, with reference to preference capital.

54. Diversification reduces Unique risk. Diversification is a technique that reduces risk by allocating investments among various financial instruments, industries, and other categories.

55. They enjoy a high order of priority in the event of liquidation, Stable rate of return and No risk are the factors which make debentures attractive to investors.

56. Unsystematic risk is reduced through diversification. Unsystematic risk is the risk that is inherent in a specific company or industry. By investing in a range of companies and industries, unsystematic risk can be drastically reduced through diversification.

57. The method of raising equity capital from existing members by offering securities on pro rata basis is referred to as Right Issue. A rights issue is an invitation to existing shareholders to purchase additional new shares in the company.

58. The expected return on an investment in stock is the sum of expected dividends and capital gains. The expected return on an investment is the expected value of the probability distribution of possible returns it can provide to investors.

59. Commercial papers is not a source of long-term finance. Commercial paper is an unsecured, short-term debt instrument issued by a corporation, typically for the financing of accounts payable and inventories and meeting short-term liabilities.

60. If the dispersion around a security's return is larger the security's risk is higher. A security risk assessment identifies, assesses, and implements key security controls in applications.

61. EBIT means Operating Income, Operating Profit and Earnings before interest and tax. It is a calculation commonly used to measure the profitability of a company.

62. Another name for stock brokers is registered representatives. A stockbroker is a professional who executes buy and sell orders for stocks and other securities on behalf of clients.

63. Technology adopted factors influence the capital structure of a business entity. The capital structure is how a firm finances its overall operations and growth by using different sources of funds.

64. Investment professionals whose jobs may depend on their performance relative to the market are the registered representatives. There are many types of investment professionals including brokers, investment advisers and financial planners.

65. Earnings per share ratios is not affected by the financial structure and the tax rate of a company. It is calculated by dividing the company's net income with its total number of outstanding shares. It is a tool that market participants use frequently to gauge the profitability of a company before buying its shares.

// Notes //

// Notes //